Comments from Readers and Reviewers

"[One of] the 100 best and most influential [nonfiction books] written in English since 1923, the beginning of TIME . . . magazine."

> **—TIME.com**

"I graduated college in 2008, wallowed hopelessly in career frustration, and later received the best career advice of my life . . . which was to read your book *What Color Is Your Parachute?* Today, I am happily employed in a job that is the envy of my peers. I'm living proof of the power of your book and I recommend it to everyone I meet. It will eternally be the gift I give to recent graduates. Thank you for writing your book! I cannot begin to describe how much I have enjoyed it."

> **—Whitney Moore**

"Anyone looking for career direction advice or solid information about how to find the job that's right for them should begin their search with Richard Bolles's classic book, *What Color Is Your Parachute?* It's been named one of the most influential books of all time for a reason—it has probably changed the course of more people's lives than almost any book except the Bible. Richard updates the book every year so it is always relevant."

> **—Eric Wentworth**

"Love your *Parachute* books, I am on my third one in my thirty-year career, with the 2012 version, and can't believe how much better each one gets, plus they stay so timely and relevant through all the changes over time!"

> **—Anthony DeLisi**

"I just wanted to tell you how grateful I am to you and your book, *What Color Is Your Parachute?* I graduated from a four-year university in May, and I had no clue what I wanted to do, or how to look for a job. Like any kid, I thought I knew the best way to do things and that I didn't need anyone's advice, but after a few months of unemployment I realized that this wasn't true. My dad had given me a copy of your book, but after a few months of nothing, not even an interview, I really read it, did the exercises, and trusted in what you were saying. I didn't believe that I would find MY job, the perfect job for me. But I did, at a nonprofit that does cleft lip and palate surgery missions to China and Africa. This job has literally every single attribute that I listed, and I wouldn't have known what attributes I needed in a job unless I had done your exercises. I'm sure you get probably hundreds of e-mails a week saying the same thing, so I'll keep it short—I just wanted to say that I owe my happiness in my job to you and my dad. I recommend your book to EVERYONE, including strangers."

   —Heather Smith

"Richard is a giant both in my life and certainly in the field. When you think about his contributions to . . . understanding the whole notion of three boxes of life, creating the flower exercise, and the three questions that really help drive our job-finding activity it is quite remarkable because it certainly changed my life personally, and it changed most of the work that career counselors and specialists and coaches perform. And I would expect it changed all of our work as we think about how we grow talent in organizations."

   —Rich Feller, 2012–2013 President of the National Career Development Association (NCDA)

"I have the deepest respect for his wonderful writing and promotion that have inspired establishment of the Career Planning profession."

   —Bernard Haldane

"The new edition of the best-selling job-hunting book *What Color Is Your Parachute?*, in addition to the tried-and-true advice for job seekers Dick Bolles has provided for close to forty years, has new information on job-search productivity, job clubs, and how to organize and manage your job-search. *What Color Is Your Parachute?* is deservedly the world's most popular job-hunting book, with over 11 million copies sold in 26 languages.

This . . . edition is as relevant today as when it was first published. Dick Bolles insightfully stays on the cutting edge of job-searching, and the book is full of new and updated suggestions, along with the classic advice that continues to hold true today."

    —Alison Doyle, About.com Guide

"Dick Bolles is effectively the 'inventor' of career management as we know it today."

    —Tom O'Neil

"The people who can educate employees and job seekers on how to really find jobs (and careers) are career counselors and career coaches. Ideally, a good coach should buy copies of *Parachute* at wholesale and give a copy to every one of their paying clients."

    —Richard Knowdell, trainer of career counselors and coaches

"If you go into the bookstore and find the section on jobs, careers, or networking—the reason that section even exists is because of Dick Bolles. His book, *What Color Is Your Parachute?*, has helped many people find their true passion at work. Plus he is a great man."

    —G. L. Hoffman, JobDig

"Dick Bolles is the last person on earth who needs my recommendation. Everyone knows his value to the world of career development. My recommendation/gratitude is for his friendship. He's a wonderful human being, joyful, resilient, and generous."

    —Ellen Jackson

"I want to recommend Dick for the hard work he has put in both as an author and as a coach. The amount of influence Mr. Bolles has had on people in career transition, such as myself when the dot-com bubble burst, is immeasurable. . . . His sage wisdom has forever changed my life, and I insist that all future employees read the *Parachute* book."

—**Devin Hedge**

"[I was] recently laid off from my job of 13 years due to downsizing. I am proud to say that instead of panicking, one of my first actions after the layoff was to seek out *What Color Is Your Parachute? 2013*. . . . I am grateful to you for helping me realize that instead of this layoff being a traumatic experience, it has actually given me the chance to take a deep breath and set out on a wonderful path of self discovery. . . ."

—**Jeff Bess**

"I just bought my first copy of *What Color Is Your Parachute?* This book brought me back to life, caused me to rethink everything about myself and revived my passion for me to be my best self."

—**Simi Kaila**

"Dick Bolles is clever and witty and has some superb ideas. . . ."

—**Karen Elizabeth Davies, United Kingdom**

"I have been using your book . . . to help job-seekers since 2005. It is fantastic. . . . The book enables me to help people from any walk of life and I find myself coaching the unemployed crossing my path everywhere. I recommend the book and the ideas everywhere, even when I sit at the car wash!"

—**Heléne Steyl, Johannesburg, South Africa**

WHAT COLOR IS YOUR PARACHUTE?

"I DON'T HAVE A PARACHUTE OF ANY COLOR."

WHAT COLOR IS YOUR PARACHUTE?
2014 EDITION

A Practical Manual for Job-Hunters
and Career-Changers

RICHARD N. BOLLES

College of the Ouachitas

TEN SPEED PRESS
Berkeley

This is an annual. That is to say, it is revised each year, often substantially, with the new edition appearing in the early fall. Counselors and others wishing to submit additions, corrections, or suggestions for the 2015 edition must submit them prior to February 1, 2014 using the form provided in the back of this book, or by e-mail (dickbolles40@gmail.com). Forms reaching us after that date will, unfortunately, have to wait for the 2016 edition.

PUBLISHER'S NOTE
This publication is designed to provide accurate and authoritative information in regard to the subject matter covered. It is sold with the understanding that the publisher is not engaged in rendering professional career services. If expert assistance is required, the service of the appropriate professional should be sought.

Published in the United States by Ten Speed Press, an imprint of the Crown Publishing Group, a division of Random House, Inc., New York.
www.crownpublishing.com
www.tenspeed.com

Ten Speed Press and the Ten Speed Press colophon are registered trademarks of Random House, Inc.

Jacket illustration copyright © iStockphoto.com/alexm73.
The drawings on pages 141, 143, and 211 are by Steven M. Johnson, author of *What the World Needs Now*.
Illustration on page 20 by Beverly Anderson.

Trade Paperback ISBN: 978-1-60774-362-0
Hardcover ISBN: 978-1-60774-363-7
eBook ISBN: 978-1-60774-364-4
ISSN: 8755-4658

Printed in the United States of America

Cover design by Katy Brown
Back cover design by Colleen Cain
Interior design by Colleen Cain

10 9 8 7 6 5 4 3 2 1

Revised Edition

The wonderful actress
Anne Bancroft (1931–2005) was once
loosely quoted as saying
about her husband, Mel Brooks,
My heart flutters whenever I hear his key
turning in the door, and I think to myself,
Oh goody, the party is about to begin.
That is exactly how I feel
about my wife,
Marci Garcia Mendoza Bolles,
God's angel from the Philippines,
whom I fell deeply in love with, and married
on August 22, 2004.
What an enchanted marriage this has turned out to be!

THE 2014
TABLE OF CONTENTS

THE PINK PAGES

It was the best of times,
It was the worst of times,
It was the age of wisdom,
It was the age of foolishness,
It was the epoch of belief,
It was the epoch of incredulity,
It was the season of light,
It was the season of darkness,
It was the spring of hope,
It was the winter of despair,
We had everything before us,
We had nothing before us,
We were all going direct to heaven,
We were all going direct the other way . . .

        —*Charles Dickens (1812–1870)*

Chapter 1

It's a Whole New World for Job-Hunters

This book is for you if you are out of work.

This book is for you if you've been out of work a long long time, and have been job-hunting in vain.

This book is for you if you're fed up with your job, have decided to "bail out," and wonder what color your parachute is.

This book is for you if you are trying to figure out what you want to do next, with your life.

This book is for you if you're trying to figure out a first career or a new career.

This book is for you if you are trying to understand yourself better.

This book is for you if you are trying to understand how the world of work really works.

This is, as the title says, a *practical* manual for job-hunters and career-changers. *Practical* means wholly realistic, and *realistic* means looking—without flinching—at both the good news and the bad news out there. Let's save the good news for the third chapter. We'll start here with the bad.

The Bad News: **The Job-Hunt Has Changed Dramatically Since 2008**

If we are out of work, these days, that is bad enough. But add to that a relentless barrage of bad news, day after day, about the global economy, the U.S. job market, unemployment statistics, what the future holds, and—no wonder so many of us are feeling depressed.

But let us begin with the bad news anyway, to rehearse what it is we are up against when we go looking for work or looking to choose or change careers.

For I do not want you to think of these things as anything but a series of challenges, since much of the bad news consists of broad generalizations, and there are ways to deal with them, as I'm going to show you.

The Eight Forces We Are Up Against

Okay, with that background, let's look at what are the changes to the job-hunt since at least 2008, and maybe before:

One, a conservative mood is sweeping around the world these days, and the global economy is currently dominated by concern about deficits rather than jobs—with governments opting for austerity rather than growth. It is precisely the right policy at precisely the wrong moment in history. Austerity right after a worldwide recession has unintended consequences. So, government jobs are still disappearing, and hiring by private employers is stalled because of what's happening with banks, with investors, and with uncertain visions of the future. This isn't a problem just in the U.S. It is global. The unemployment rate for the Eurozone is 12%. In all of Europe, 26 million people are currently out of work.[1]

Two, the length of the average job-hunt has increased dramatically. Many of us have been out of work far longer than we ever dreamed we

---

1. According to Eurostat, *News Release Euro Indicators*, February 2013, found at http://tinyurl.com/cac7aco.

would be—one year, two years, three years, or more. We feel like the job-hunt has turned into something of a detective mystery, which we are unable to solve. From 1994 through 2008, roughly half of all unemployed job-seekers found jobs within five weeks. After 2008, a far greater proportion spent and are still spending more than a year looking for work.

Three, the culture is affecting how job-hunters go about the job-hunt. If a particular culture values hard work, long hours, persistence, and determination, this will affect how the job-hunt is conducted. In many places, since 2008, the culture does not value these things. It values quick fixes, fast food, selective inattention, multitasking, TV ads that constantly change their visuals every two and a half seconds, etc. It is difficult to get people to practice their job-hunt in a different way than the culture behaves everywhere else.

Four, the number of the long-term unemployed in the U.S. has increased dramatically. Currently, 30% of all unemployed persons in the U.S. have been out of work a year or more.[2] Before 2008 that figure was just 10%.[3]

Five, many long-term unemployed feel they have become A Lost Generation. Society has written them off. Employers advertise—well, at least, *some* employers advertise—*"people who are out of work need not apply."* The media talk as though this were universal—witness such headlines as *"The Long-Term Unemployed Are Doomed"*[4]—so we need a little realism here: according to surveys, this is the sentiment of only four out of every one hundred U.S. employers, or at least four who will admit it. On the other hand, forty-four out of every one hundred employers feel this way if we have been unemployed for two years, or more.[5] *(Bad news for sure, although to look on the bright side, that means 96% of employers don't feel this way just because we're out of work, and 56% don't feel this way even if we've been unemployed for two years or more.)*

Furthermore, the data doesn't support this prejudice. *"Employers often avoid hiring candidates with a history of job-hopping or those who have been*

---

2. According to the U.S. Labor Department, in a May 2011 report by Randy Ilq, found at http://tinyurl.com/cks3grd.
3. The Business section of the *Boston Globe* for March 31, 2013, article by Megan Woolhouse, found at http://tinyurl.com/bn9lcoj.
4. That's from *Slate*, April 15, 2013, based on an experiment by economist Rand Ghayad.
5. According to a report in *Forbes* by Susan Adams, September 18, 2012, found at http://tinyurl.com/9og7qa9.

unemployed for a while. The past is prologue, companies assume. There's one problem, though: the data show that it isn't so. An applicant's work history is not a good predictor of future results."[6]

Six, many employers are holding out for the dream employee. Knowing that there is the biggest pool of applicants they have seen in a long time, many employers are over-screening. They reject candidates they would have hired eight years ago, because they keep thinking, with all those out there who are out of work today, maybe someone better will come along next week. Not all employers think this way; but way too many do.

Seven, job-hunting is increasingly a repetitive activity in the lives of many if not most of us. This is because the length of time a job lasts, on average, has decreased in a number of industries since 2008. For example, some employers in the IT industry[7] are increasingly hiring someone just until a project is completed, rather than permanently hiring us. Again, 20% to 30% of those employed by the Fortune 100 now have short-term jobs, either as independent contractors or as temp workers,[8] and this figure is predicted to rise to 50% during the next eight years. Even in industries where people are hired allegedly for longer periods, employers are much more ready to cut the size of their workforce just as soon as things start to even begin to look bad. You thought you were being hired for a number of years, they said that, they meant that, but then fortunes change and suddenly you're back out on the street.

Our typical work history now is going to be three careers over our lifetime, and at least eight jobs. So, even when we find a job now, we may be job-hunting again, sooner than we think. We need to become masters of the job-hunt, in its post-2008 incarnation. Speaking of which, we come to:

Eight, job-hunting methods that worked before 2008 no longer do. Now, I'm exaggerating here, a bit, of course. The three traditional job-hunting methods since back when dinosaurs were roaming the

---

6. From a *New York Times* report on new data by Steve Lohr, April 19, 2013, found at http://tinyurl.com/clgg5bu.
7. IT stands for "information technology," which you probably already knew; but, just in case.
8. Contract workers and "temp" workers are not the same category. An employer can prescribe what a temp worker does and how they do it. The very definition of independent contractor means the employer cannot. The two categories are alike only in the relative shortness of their employment.

Earth—resumes, agencies and ads (*sending out resumes, answering ads for vacancies, turning to federal-state and private agencies for help*)—still work sometimes, and work well. But they are no longer dependable, if ever they were. Their track record has gotten terrible. You've got to have a plan B. And maybe C and D.

If we don't know that, if we think we can go about our job-hunt exactly the way we did it the last time, then we are in for a rude awakening. We will try job-hunting the way we "always did it before," but this time *it . . . just . . . won't . . . work*. Things have changed dramatically since 2008.

Maybe you've already found that out. You sent out resumes. Everywhere. To everyone. Week after week. That used to work. Now, nothing, nada, zip.

Employers Change, Job-Hunters Don't

Here's why this happens. Job-hunters tend to hunt in the same way regardless of whether the times are good or bad, but employers don't. Employers often change their hunting behavior dramatically when times are tough. The reason for this is that when times are good, employers often have difficulty filling their vacancies, so *they will typically cater to the job-hunter's preferences* in such a season. We like resumes, so they will take the trouble to solicit, look at, and read our resumes. We like job-postings, so they will post their vacancies where we can find them: on their own site or on job-boards, typically.

What we are not prepared for, is that during tough times, when employers are finding it much easier to fill a vacancy, many of them will stop reading our resumes and stop posting their vacancies. But we do not change our job-hunting behavior, so we go looking for work the same way we did last year, or four years ago, or ten or thirty, and suddenly find that nothing is working.

We can search until we're blue in the face. We can work like a dog, send out resumes week after week, but . . . *nothing*! Everything that used to work, doesn't work anymore. And we are baffled. It is like turning the key in our faithful car, but for the first time in five years the motor won't start.

We decide, of course, that the reason why nothing is working is that there are no jobs. It never occurs to us that there are jobs, but that employers have changed *their* behavior.[9]

And what is particularly depressing is the degree to which some employers are increasingly using the Internet to hide from job-hunters. They ask job-hunters to fill out an online application, then notify them (without ever offering a face-to-face interview), "Sorry, you do not have the qualifications we are looking for." You *think* you've applied for these jobs, but you never had a chance.

Different Languages:
A Foreign Country

What has gotten worse since 2008 is the fact that employers and job-hunters speak two entirely different languages, using the same words. Take the word "skills." When we're job-hunting, you get turned down because—some employers say—"You don't have the skills we're looking for." You think they're referring to such things as *analyzing, researching, communicating,* etc. No, they really mean "experience," though they use the word "skills." Sample employer memo: "We're looking for someone who has had five years' experience marketing software products to a demographic that is between the ages of twenty-four and thirty."

You should assume that the employers' world is like a foreign country; you must learn their language, and their customs, before you visit.

This is an idea from the authors of a book called *No One Is Unemployable.*[10] They suggested that when you approach the world of business for the first time, you should think of it as going to visit a foreign country; you know you're going to have to learn a whole new language, culture, and customs, there. Same with the job-market. When we are

---

9. See the next chapter for more on this.
10. Debra Angel MacDougall and Elisabeth Harney Sanders-Park. The book was published by Worknet Training Services in 1997. A more recent book of theirs is titled *The 6 Reasons You'll Get the Job: What Employers Look for—Whether They Know It or Not*, published in 2010 by Prentice Hall.

out of work we must now start to think like an employer, learn how employers prefer to look for employees, and figure out how to change our own job-hunting strategies so as to conform to *theirs*. In other words, *adapt to the employer's preferences*.

So, let's take a look at that world of the employer. Employers don't have all the power in the hiring game, but they do have an impressive amount. This explains why parts of the whole job-hunting system in this country will drive you nuts. It wasn't built for you or me. It was built by and for *them*. And they live in a world different from yours and mine, in their head. (That's why I said *foreign* country!) This results in the following five contrasts:

1. You want the job-market to be a hiring game. But the employer regards it as an elimination game—until the very last phase. Larger companies or organizations are looking at that huge stack of resumes on their desk, with a view—first of all—to finding out who they can eliminate. Eventually they want to get it down to the "last person standing."

2. You want the employer to be taking lots of initiative toward finding you, and when they are desperate they will (*especially if you have applied math skills!*). Some HR departments will spend hours and days combing the Internet looking for the right person. But generally speaking the employer prefers that it be you who takes the initiative, toward finding them.

3. In being considered for a job, you want your solid past performance—summarized on your written resume—to be all that gets weighed, but the employer weighs your whole behavior as they glimpse it from their first interaction with you.

4. You want the employer to acknowledge receipt of your resume—particularly if you post it right on their website—but the employer generally feels too swamped with other things to have time to do that, so only 45% do. A majority of employers, 55%, do not. Now that you know this, don't take it personally.

MANY IF NOT MOST EMPLOYERS HUNT FOR JOB-HUNTERS IN THE EXACT OPPOSITE WAY FROM HOW MOST JOB-HUNTERS HUNT FOR THEM

The Way a Typical Employer Prefers to Fill a Vacancy

1 — **6** From Within: Promotion of a full-time employee, or promotion of a present part-time employee, or hiring a former consultant for in-house or contract work, or hiring a former "temp" full-time. Employer's thoughts: *"I want to hire someone whose work I have already seen."* (A low-risk strategy for the employer.)

Implication for Job-Hunters: See if you can get hired at an organization you have chosen as a temp, contract worker, or consultant—aiming at a full-time position only later (or not at all).

2 — **5** Using Proof: Hiring an unknown job-hunter who brings proof of what he or she can do, with regards to the skills needed.

Implication for Job-Hunters: If you are a programmer, bring a program you have done—with its code; if you are a photographer, bring photos; if you are a counselor, bring a case study with you; etc.

3 — **4** Using a Best Friend or Business Colleague: Hiring someone whose work a trusted friend of yours has seen (perhaps they worked for him or her).

Implication for Job-Hunters: Find someone who knows the person-who-has-the-power-to-hire at your target organization, who also knows your work and will introduce you two.

4 — **3** Using an Agency They Trust: This may be a recruiter or search firm the employer has hired; or a private employment agency—both of which have checked you out, on behalf of the employer.

5 — **2** Using an Ad They Have Placed (online or in newspapers, etc.).

6 — **1** Using a Resume: Even if the resume was unsolicited (if the employer is desperate).

The Way a Typical Job-Hunter Prefers to Fill a Vacancy

5. You want employers to save your job-hunt by increasing their hiring, and you want the government to give them incentives to do so. Unhappily, employers tend to wait to hire until they see an increased demand for their products or services. In the meantime, most do not much care for government incentives to hire, because they know such incentives always have a time limit, and once they expire, that employer will be on the hook to continue the subsidy out of their own pocket.

Another example of the fact that the employer's world is increasingly a foreign country to job-hunters, lies in the very different core values of each of us. During the job-hunt, we want strategies that will enable us to cover as much of the job-market as possible. So, our value is: *coverage*. Our chosen vehicle is our resume.

The employer's chief value, on the other hand, concerns *risk*. The employer wants to hire with the lowest risk possible. I mean *the risk that this won't work out*.

These very different values explain the chart on page 8.

Job-Hunting Has Moved More and More Online Since 2008

From the earliest days of the Internet there have been employment websites, commonly called "job-boards." The earliest ones were Net-Start Inc. and The Monster Board (TMP), both launching in 1994. Netstart Inc. changed its name to CareerBuilder in 1998, and TMP changed to Monster.com in 1999.[11] So, online job-hunting has been around a long time.

But job-hunting has moved more and more online ever since, and dramatically so, since 2008. As social media and other famous sites have become more and more popular—LinkedIn, Facebook, Twitter, Yelp, Skype, YouTube, etc.—job-hunters and employers alike have

---

11. Today, Monster.com is the largest online job site in the world; the largest online job site in the U.S. is Indeed.com.

figured out how to use them in the job-hunt. Now, ever larger portions of the job-hunt can be done online.

That's a big change since 1994!

If you are out of work for any length of time, and you do *not* have the skills of knowing how to use a computer or how to access the Internet, you will be wise beyond your years if you go take some computer courses at your local community college or adult school or your nearest CareerOneStop center (now called American Job Centers).[12]

Any job-hunter working online these days will want to pay large attention to the social media sites I just mentioned. Here are some extended comments about them, plus a few other web sites or online activities, such as texting, blogging, and online universities, that I think are worth mentioning:

LinkedIn

URL: www.linkedin.com

Background: This is "the Swiss army knife" of job-sites; it is a multi-tool. It is used (at this writing) by at least 200 million people worldwide. Employers from around the world who are searching for prospective employees are among them.

General Description: LinkedIn gives you a "profile" page on which you can write anything about yourself and your history that you want to, using the standardized format or template that LinkedIn provides.

Usefulness to Job-Hunters: If you have contacted a particular employer, most of them now search to see what there is about you on LinkedIn (and on the Internet in general, anywhere and everywhere) before inviting you in, or deciding to hire you.

Ways to Make It More Effective:[13] Remember, this is a *professional* site. If you are looking for work, don't post anything here that isn't related to your professional goal. (Need I say, leave out parties, dating, summer vacations, etc.) Make your profile page really

---

12. To locate the American Job Center nearest you, go to www.servicelocator.org/onestopcenters.asp.
13. I am indebted here to Patrick Schwerdtfeger, Susan Joyce, Alison Doyle, Jason Alba, Dan DeMaioNewton, and other colleagues for their ideas.

stand out from others' profile pages, when employers go browsing. There are ways to do this. Here are some hints:

1. A PHOTO is mandatory. Every survey has revealed that not having your photo posted there is a turnoff for most employers. Make it a shot just of your head and shoulders, in fact, fill the frame with just your head and shoulders. Make it sharply focused and well lit, even if taken with an iPhone. Dress up for this one. And smile.

2. In the section called JOB TITLE, if you aren't searching for a career-change, and you like what you've been doing, but the title they gave you aren't the words that a hiring manager would normally use to search for someone who does what you do, put in a slash mark, then add the title they would use. Alternatively, if you are looking for a change, after you list your current job title in this title section, enter a slash and then add the industry you want to find a job in (so that an employer's search engine will pick you up).

3. In describing your PAST JOBS OR EXPERIENCE, don't just make a list of tasks or achievements. LinkedIn gives you enough space to tell a story, so tell a story. Summarize some major achievement of yours, in that job, and then tell a story of how you did it, and what the measurable results were (time or money saved, or the profit created, etc.).

4. In the SUMMARY be sure to state whatever it is you think gives you a competitive advantage in your field, i.e. what makes you a better hire than nineteen other people who might compete for the kind of job you want. This is a place to highlight what makes you the best (*or, for the modest, what makes you a better*) choice for that kind of job.

5. Under SPECIALTIES list every keyword you can think of, that would lead a search engine to find you for the job you *want*. If you don't know what keywords to list, find someone on LinkedIn who already has a job like the one you want, and see what keywords *they* listed. Copy the ones that seem relevant in your case.

6. LIST any hobbies, interests, education, training, community service, associations you belong to, etc.

7. ADD LINKS TO ANY WEBSITE you feel would help you stand out: *your blog*? (if you have one, and posts there are *solely* devoted to your area of expertise); *your Twitter account*? (if you have one, and if you've only been posting tweets that manifest your expertise in your field); *your Facebook page*? (doubtful, unless it looks very focused and professional—if it's sloppy, real personal, and all over the map in its content, it is unlikely to help you get hired, and may in fact hinder you). Consider filming a video of you discussing some area of your expertise (with numbers if possible), post it on YouTube, and link to it on your profile page here. If you don't know how to shoot and upload the video, there are loads of free instructions (even on YouTube) telling you step by step how to do this.

8. JOIN one or more LinkedIn groups, related to your expertise. Post sparingly but regularly, when they are discussing something you are an expert on. You want to get a name and reputation, in your field. "Groups" are in the bar across the top of your home page. Once you've filled out your profile completely, click on "Groups" and then on the subheading "Groups You May Like." It will make suggestions, based on your profile, with information about each group, as to whether it is *Very Active, Active,* or very neglected. Join ones, related to your expertise, which are at least *Active.* Be aware, if you join a group and then don't ever contribute, LinkedIn has a cute little habit of summarily removing you from that group without any advance warning. Just a nice brief note after the fact, saying "We removed you" due to your inactivity there. (And you thought they weren't paying attention! Oh yes, they do. They are. They will.)

9. You can use LinkedIn to DESCRIBE a project you're proud of, post a photo, or report on a recent professional event. To post this also on Twitter, always begin not with Twitter but with LinkedIn. Write your update here, check the box with the Twitter icon, and then click "Share."

LinkUp

URL: http://linkup.com

Background: This is a job-search engine, not to be confused with LinkedIn.

General Description: This site pulls job openings only from employers' websites (24,378 at current count).

Usefulness to Job-Hunters: If you live in areas covered by LinkUp, you may find a job opening here.

Facebook

URL: www.facebook.com

Background: Hugely popular; more than 1.11 billion users worldwide.

General Description: The world's largest social media site (but you probably already knew that).

Usefulness to Job-Hunters:

1. Facebook lets you sign up on pages devoted to job-hunting and careers. For example, www.facebook.com/jobhunting.
2. Facebook has an app that enables you to hunt for people who work at a particular company or organization, or who share a particular interest of yours: www.facebook.com/profilesearch.
3. Facebook has an app that enables you to see where your friends work, and helps you build a professional network, plus discover job openings: http://apps.facebook.com/careeramp.
4. Facebook has an app that enables you to network, find friends of friends, and search millions of job listings: http://branchout.com.

Twitter

URL: http://twitter.com

Background: A social networking and micro-blogging site; 500 million users; 8% of Internet users are on Twitter.

General Description: Allows you to send micro-messages using 140 characters or fewer.

Usefulness to Job-Hunters:

1. Twitter will take a background. When you are out of work, you can convey your status in that background (tastefully, professionally). For a tutorial on how to do this, go to Social Media Examiner, found at http://tinyurl.com/25apzgo.

2. Twitter will take a bio. Mention what you're looking for, there. You have 140 characters, so practice the art of succinctness. Put a link to an online resume in your bio.

3. Twitter will take an avatar. Make it professional looking.

4. Twitter has a "follow" option. Follow anyone who is helpful to your job-hunt. If you don't have a clue, follow Susan Joyce of job-hunt.org, Internet expert Joel Cheesman of http://cheesman.typepad.com, and/or Guy Kawasaki (you can follow his top ten per day from @guykawasaki10).

5. Tweet about your job search. Make sure you've done your homework first, and can state exactly what kind of work you're looking for. Put "Twitter hashtags for job seekers" into your favorite search engine, and see what turns up.

6. Put a link in some of your tweets to your website, if you have one. If you don't have one, and you are an expert in some area of knowledge or performance, start your own website. See http://bravenet.com for free help, or www.bluehost.com for inexpensive hosting ($6 a month). Establish yourself as an expert in your field on Twitter.

7. Sign up at www.twitjobsearch.com to locate various job opportunities around the world. Choose what they call "channels"

and then receive instant notification of jobs thereafter. Also sign up at http://tweetmyjobs.com.

Texting

URL: None. You choose a phone number on your contacts list, and then select "Send text."

Background: Wildly popular way to communicate.

General Description: Allows you to send brief text messages between mobile phone users (160 English characters or fewer) using the Short Message Service (SMS) or more ambitious messages containing image, video, and sound content (known as MMS messages).

Usefulness to Job-Hunters: For the infinite number of occasions where you need instant help, texting is very useful. For example, you're on your way to an interview and you suddenly think of a question you might be asked, that you don't know how to answer. You can text a more experienced friend and get the answer before you even arrive at the door of the employer. Moreover, it's helpful to have that answer spelled out on your mobile screen, as you go up in the elevator (tall building??) so you can practice.

Yelp

URL: https://yelp.com (https as opposed to http in any site's URL means their information is heavily encrypted [128 bit], which is considered unhackable).

Background: This website has more than 100 million unique visitors per month.

General Description: Community reviews of various businesses.

Usefulness to Job-Hunters: If there is a particular business or organization you are interested in, you may find feedback about it, here.

Stack Exchange

URL: http://stackexchange.com

Background: A network of 101 question-and-answer sites, with a community contributing, answering, evaluating, and voting; same genre as Quora, Aardvark, Answers.com, etc.; 3.3 million users.

General Description: Useful for finding fast answers to puzzling questions.

Usefulness to Job-Hunters: When you're trying to find something, someone, some business, this is a good place to go to, and see if they know the answer, without your having to do detailed research forever. Great time-saver.

Skype

URL: www.skype.com

Background: Over 280 million registered users, bought by eBay in 2005, Microsoft in 2011.

General Description: Telephone calls over the Internet, utilizing both voice and video; free if the hookup is between registered users.

Usefulness to Job-Hunters: You can use video interviewing for informational interviewing with members of your network who live far away. More important, if an employer lives in another country of interest to you, and you or they want to do an interview, this is an inexpensive way to do it. If an employer can only talk to you over the phone, this at least adds video to your phone call, if the employer is also a Skype user. You can find video interview tips on the Web at sites such as Alison Doyle's http://tinyurl.com/nmbt5r.

YouTube

URL: www.youtube.com

Background: Wildly popular; one billion users monthly.

General Description: You can find a video on almost any subject, or post a video of your own, thus saving you from using up bandwidth on your own website (if you have one).

Usefulness to Job-Hunters: You can post a video resume, you can demonstrate your skills in a demonstration video you shoot and post, etc. You can create your own channel through a widget (www.widgetbox.com/widgets). Widgets can be embedded on all your other sites, as well. You might even find some videos devoted to job-hunting techniques, such as: http://tinyurl.com/4ynl42n (*smile*).

Blogs

URL: If it's your blog, you know the URL. If you're looking for someone else's, do a search through Google, or Technorati (below).

Background: There are now over 181 million blogs, averaging one million posts a day according to Technorati (http://technorati.com)—the central headquarters for all things *blog*.

General Description: At their best, blogs offer an expert's advice and wisdom.

Usefulness to Job-Hunters: If you can find a blog on your particular field or industry, you may discover openings through that blog. Also consider starting your own blog related to the field in which you are you looking for work, where—if you keep your blog focused—you can develop a reputation as an expert in your specialty, thus attracting the attention of prospective employers—maybe. (Possible but not likely; still, you never know. It's worth trying!) Remember, the Web is the modern way to attract attention to yourself. A blog, carefully managed, can ideally serve that purpose. Of course, you are only one out of 160 million blogs, so don't put all your eggs in this basket.

Job Shadow

URL: www.jobshadow.com

Background: This site gets 75,000 visitors a month (mostly the young), and growing.

General Description: Traditional job-shadowing requires getting permission from employers. That sometimes was easier said than done. No permission needed here. This website is conducting interviews with hundreds of people in different jobs, asking them the same standard questions, sometimes with names, often anonymously because they are asked to be candid about the financial rewards in such a job.

Usefulness to Job-Hunters: *You* can't ask them any questions, of course, you just eavesdrop, but as a faint shadow of job-shadowing, this is worth looking at.

Ways to Make It More Effective: If you want to use this site effectively, prior to going to it make a list of what you hated about any job you had in the past, so that while you are listening to these interviews, you will be more alert to "Oh no, I don't want a job that does *that*, again."

Note: Aside from this site, if you are looking for some of the old ways of exploring, using let us say apprenticeships, there are now more effective ways of doing that, too. For example, you used to have to hunt hard to even find where apprenticeships were. Now such information is online. For a list of apprenticeships in your area, see American Job Center's website at http://tinyurl.com/d3pbzc5. If you are a veteran looking for an apprenticeship, see http://tinyurl.com/7urwrs3.

Online Universities

URL: www.phoenix.edu; www.kaplan.edu; www.capella.edu

Background: According to Global Language Monitor's July 2010 ranking, the three top online universities are the University of Phoenix, Kaplan University, and Capella University.

General Description: Offer both courses and degree programs, either by yourself or interacting with an instructor or other students online.

Usefulness to Job-Hunters: You can go to school online, get trained in new skills, etc., while still pursuing your job-hunt. For example, you can get trained in such skills as using a computer or particular software programs, accounting, marketing, business plans, etc. You can even get a college degree while job-hunting.

In Closing

For a complete list of social networking sites, go to the entry on Wikipedia, found at http://tinyurl.com/k2jhx. You can click on the little icon immediately to the right of "Registered Users" and get them listed in their order of popularity.

Another list, with monthly updates, is available at Digital Market Ramblings, found at http://tinyurl.com/d3ytpff.

You can stay up-to-date on social media developments by subscribing to the free daily e-mail called SmartBrief on Social Media. Sign up at www.smartbrief.com/socialmedia.

Each social media site has a different scope, a different emphasis, and a different audience. Look for the things that matter to you. Choose a site appropriately. If you have a particular issue, and you just don't know how to find the appropriate social site, do a search on Google. For example, if ex-military who are hunting for help in getting back into civilian life put "ex-military job-hunting" into their Google search engine, they will turn up a number of sites to help them with that job-hunt, such as: www.jobswap.com, www.dol.gov/vets, www .hireds.com, http://fedshirevets.gov, and www.woundedwarriorproject .org. Also, there are military skills translators, a list of which can be found at http://vetsuccess.gov/military_skills_translators.

Now, on to the part of the job-hunt that has moved online the most dramatically: your resume.

He or she who gets hired is not necessarily
The one who can do that job best;
But, the one who knows the most
About how to get hired.

—*Richard Lathrop (1919–2001)*

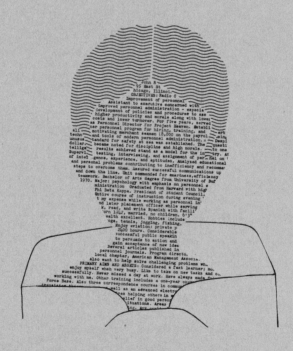

Chapter 2

Google Is Your New Resume

I know what you're thinking. *I'm out of work, I've got to go job-huntin'. So the first thing I have to do is put together my resume.*

Yeah, that used to be true.

In "the old days." Before the Internet became popular with job-hunters.

Back then, the only way an interviewer could learn much about you was from a piece of paper that you yourself wrote—with maybe a little help from your friends—called your resume, or C.V. (an academic term meaning "curriculum vitae").

On that paper was a summary of where you had been and all you had done in the past. From that piece of paper, the employer was supposed to *guess* what kind of person you are in the present and what kind of employee you'd be in the future.

The good thing about this—from your point of view—was that you had absolute control over what went on that piece of paper.

You could omit anything that was embarrassing, or anything from your past that you have long since regretted.

Short of their hiring a private detective, or talking to your previous employers, a prospective employer couldn't find out much else about you.

That was nice. But now those days are gone forever.

Since 2008, and even before, there's been a new resume in town, and it's called Google.

All any employer has to do is type your name into a search engine (such as Google), and bammo! If you've been anywhere near the

Internet—and over 80% of us in the U.S. have[1]—and if you've posted anything on Facebook, Twitter, MySpace, Pinterest, or YouTube, or if you have your own website or webcasts or photo album or blog, or if you've been on anyone else's Facebook page, every aspect of you may be revealed (depending on your privacy controls).

So naturally, a vast majority of employers now *Google* your name— yes, *Google* has become both noun and verb—before they'll consider hiring you. There's your new resume, using the word *resume* loosely. Bye, bye, control.

Statistics are hard to come by, and they tend to be all over the map. Some are from very old surveys or very limited surveys (such as *100 employers*). What we know for sure is that somewhere between 35% and 70% of employers now report that they have rejected applicants on the basis of what they found through Google. Things that can get you rejected: bad grammar or gross misspelling on your Facebook or LinkedIn profile; anything indicating you lied on your resume; any badmouthing of previous employers; any signs of racism, prejudice, or screwy opinions about stuff; anything indicating alcohol or drug abuse; and any—to put it delicately—*inappropriate content*, etc.

What is sometimes forgotten is that this works both ways. Sometimes— 29% of the time, it is claimed—an employer will offer you a job because they were impressed by what Google turned up about you. Things like the creativity or professionalism you demonstrate online; your expressing yourself extremely well online; their overall impression of your personality online; the wide range of interests you exhibit online; and evidence online that you get along well and communicate well with other people.

But what you want to know is how to manage or remove anything online that would cause a prospective employer to reject you.

Is there anything you can do about this new Google resume of yours? Well, yes actually, there are four things you can do.

You can edit, fill in, expand, and add. Let's see what each of these involves.

---

1. Of U.S. households, 71% have Internet access at home plus 9% elsewhere, for a total of 80%. But this is only the average. According to the latest U.S. census (2010), 99% of households making $150,000 or more have Internet access, but only 57% of households making $15,000 or less do.

1. Edit.

First of all, think of how you would like to come across, when you are being considered for a job. Make a list of adjectives you'd like the employer to think of, when they consider hiring you. For example, how about: professional? experienced? inventive? hard working? disciplined? honest? trustworthy? kind? What else? Make a list.

Then Google yourself and read over everything the search engine pulls up about you. Go over any pages you have put up on social sites like Facebook, LinkedIn, Plaxo, MySpace, Pinterest, or YouTube, and remove anything you posted there, or allowed others to post, that contradicts the impression you would like to make, anything that might cause a would-be employer to think, *"Uh, let's not call them in, after all."* You have the list, above, of what to look for.

If you don't know how to remove an item from a particular site, type or speak the following into a search engine like Google: "How to remove an item from *Facebook"* or whatever.

The site itself may not tell you, but using your favorite search engine, you should have no trouble finding somebody's detailed, step-by-step instructions for scrubbing any site.

I guarantee you're hardly the first one with this need, so someone clever has already figured out how to do it, and posted the answer. But you want current instructions, so look at the date on the list of items the search engine pops up. Pick the most recent, and do what they say.

If you want to be thorough, you should do this editing on any and all sites that you find you're on.

Now to the second of the four things you can do about your new Google resume (so to speak):

2. Fill In.

On any of these sites, but on LinkedIn or Plaxo in particular, if they allow you to fill out a profile, fill it out completely. I mean *completely*; cross every t, and dot every i, have someone check your spelling. Leave no part of the profile blank unless you have a very good reason. If you're on Twitter, fill out your profile completely there, too. For help, see such sites as http://blazingminds.co.uk/write-twitter-bio-gains-followers or https://support.twitter.com/articles/20005336-promoting-your-profile#.

More importantly, be sure to keep each profile up-to-date. Really up-to-date. There is nothing that makes you look less professional than having an obviously outdated profile.

Last thought here: I mentioned LinkedIn; be sure to get on it, if you're not already. More than 200 million other people have, and it became the first social media site to go public. It's the site of first resort when some employer is curious about you. It allows corporate and agency head-hunters to avoid advertising an open position, but nonetheless to go "trolling" on LinkedIn for what employers call "passive job-seekers." You ain't lookin' for them, but they are lookin' for you. Of course you have no control over whether they find you, except for being sure you have a completely filled-out profile. (They search by keywords.)

Now to the third thing you can do about your new Google resume:

3. Expand.

Expand your presence on the Internet. How to do this? Several ways:

Forums. Professional sites like LinkedIn have forums, or groups, organized by subject matter. Other social networking sites, like Facebook, have pages devoted to particular subjects. Look through the directory of those groups or forums, choose one or two that are related to your industry or interests, and after signing up, speak up regularly whenever you have something to say that will quietly demonstrate you are an expert in your chosen subject area. Other-wise, keep quiet. Don't speak up about just anything. You want to be seen as a specialist—knowledgeable and focused. You want to get noticed by employers when they're searching for expert talent in your field or specialty.

Blogs. Start a blog (*that's short for "web log," which most people now don't remember*), if you don't already have one. It doesn't matter what your expertise is; if it's related to the job you are looking for, do a blog, and update it regularly. And if you don't know how to

blog, there are helpful sites such as Blogger.com, at http://tinyurl
.com/294vgzr, which give you detailed instructions. Incidentally,
there are over 181 million blogs on the Internet. Figure out how to
make yours stand out.

If you already have a blog, but it roams all over the country-
side in terms of subject matter, then start a new blog that is more
narrowly preoccupied with your particular area of expertise. Post
helpful articles there, focused on action steps, not just thoughts.
Let's say you are an expert plumber; you can post entries on your
blog that deal with such problems as "how to fix a leaky toilet,"
etc. Generally speaking, employers are looking for blogs that deal
with concrete action, rather than lofty philosophical thought.
Unless, of course, they represent a think tank.

Twitter. Some experts claim that blogs are so *yesterday.* Communication, they say, is moving toward brief, and briefer. Texting has
become hugely, hugely, popular. So has Twitter. Twitter now has
over 500 million users, who post over 400 million "tweets" a day.[2]
Twitter's advantage is that it has hashtags,[3] and Google is index-
ing all those tags and "tweets." Savvy employers know how to do
Twitter searches on Google (or on Twitter itself, for that matter).
All you have to figure out is which hashtags employers are likely
to look for, when they want to find someone with your expertise
and experience.

Videos. Presentation is moving strongly these days toward the
visual. People like to *see* you, not just *read* you. Expensive equipment not required. The Flip video camcorder used to be the most
popular and inexpensive way to record yourself; but that is ancient
history, now. It was displaced, as you might guess, by smartphones, which usually can do video, and sometimes rather sur-
prisingly good video.

As for where to post your video, once you've shot and edited it,
the champion of course is YouTube—1 billion users, 4 billion views
per day. But there are other choices: see PCGDigitalMarketing's
list, found at http://tinyurl.com/8owtlbo.

2. Most statistics (up-to-date at the time of writing) in this chapter are from Craig Smith's wonderful monthly updates called "Digital Marketing Ramblings," found at http://tinyurl.com/d3ytpff.
3. For more on hashtags, see both http://tinyurl.com/c2862re *and* http://tinyurl.com/d5nt87.

Now to the fourth and final thing you can do about your new Google resume:

4. Add.

The kind of resume everyone thinks of when they hear the word (the pre-Google resume) still has its uses. It will take any employer or HR department some time to sift through all the stuff about you that may appear when they do a Google search. You would help them by summarizing and organizing the pertinent information about yourself. You do this by—*surprise!*—composing an old type resume. And you can post it on the Internet (where Google will find it), as well as taking or sending it to an interested employer.

You wanna do this? Of course you do. Here's an outline you may find useful for gathering that information about yourself.

Since a resume is about your past, this gives you a framework for recalling that past.

A Starter Kit for Writing Your Resume[4]

Think of your working and personal skills that you believe you possess innately, or have picked up along the way. Which ones are you proud of? What things have you done in your life or work experience that no one else has done, in quite the same way? Take some blank sheets of paper and fill in any answers that occur to you.

It is important to be quantitative when you do this (e.g., mention dates, percentages, dollars, money or time saved, brand names, etc.).

Volunteer, Community, and Unpaid Work

1. Have you completed any voluntary or unpaid work for any organization or company? (e.g., church, synagogue, mosque, school, community service, or special needs organization)

---

4. This is adapted, with the written permission of my friend Tom O'Neil, from an original document of his, which was and is copyright protected under the New Zealand Copyright Act (1994) © cv.co.nz 2001. You may contact Tom at www.cv.co.nz.

Educational

2. Did you work while you were studying? If so, did you receive any promotions or achievements in that role?

3. Did you gain any scholarships?

4. Were you involved in any committees, etc.?

5. Did you win any awards for study?

6. Did you have any high (e.g., A or A+) grades? If so, what were the subjects—and grades?

Sales or Account Management

Have you ever been in sales? If so, what were some of your achievements? For example:

7. Have you ever consistently exceeded your set budget in that role? If so, by what percent or dollar value?

8. Have you exceeded your set budget in a particular month(s)/ quarter(s) in a role? If so, by what percent or dollar value?

9. What level were you, compared to other sales professionals in your company? (e.g., "Number three out of twenty on the sales team.")

10. Have you ever increased market share for your company? If so, by what percent or dollar value?

11. Have you ever brought in any major clients to your company?

12. What major clients are/were you responsible for managing and selling to?

13. Did you ever manage to generate repeat business or increase current business? If so, by what percent or dollar value?

14. Have you won any internal or external sales awards?

15. Did you develop any new successful promotional or marketing ideas that increased sales?

Administration, Customer Service, and Accounts

Have you ever been in customer service or helped run a business unit? If so:

16. Did you assist in reducing customer complaints, etc.?

17. Did you set up or improve any systems and/or processes?

18. Was there a quantifiable difference in the company or business unit when you first joined the business or project and when you completed the project or left the business?

19. Did you take any old administration or paperwork-based systems and convert them into an IT-based system?

Responsibility

20. Have you ever been responsible for the purchase of any goods or services in some job? (e.g., air travel or PC acquisition)

21. Have you ever had any budget responsibility? If so, to what level? (e.g., "Responsible for division budget of $200,000 per annum.")

22. Have you ever been responsible for any staff oversight? If so, in what capacity and/or how many staff members were you responsible for?

23. Were you responsible for any official or unofficial training? If so, what type, for whom, and how many people have you trained? (e.g., "Responsible for training twelve new staff in customer service as well as in using the in-house computer system.")

24. Were you responsible for any official or unofficial coaching or mentoring of other staff?

Events or Conference Planning or Logistical Management

25. Have you organized any events or conferences? If so, how large were they (both people attending and total budget if possible) and where and when was the event(s) held?

26. Have you been involved in any major relocation projects?

27. Have you had responsibility with regard to any major suppliers? If so, who?

Computers

28. What systems, software, and hardware experience do you have? Desktop, notebook, mobile, smartphones? Mac OS, Android, or Windows? And how deep is your expertise with any of these?

29. What software have you utilized? Or what software have you developed? Mobile apps? Systems software?

30. Have you developed any websites? If so, what were they, and did they positively affect any business you were doing? Are you on LinkedIn, Plaxo, Twitter, Facebook, YouTube, etc., and if so how deep an expertise do you have with any of these sites?

31. Were you involved in any special projects that were outside of your job description?

Mechanical

32. Other than computers, have you had experience on any kinds of machines or equipment? Please list them together with the number of years.

33. If you ever worked on transportation devices, what were the airplane, farm equipment, truck, car, machine, or bike brands that you serviced, maintained, or repaired?

College of the Ouachitas

Building, Construction, Electrical, and Plumbing

34. If you ever worked in those fields, were there any major projects you worked on? How much did the project(s) cost? (e.g., "Reception refurbishment—ABC Bank [Auckland Central Head Office] $1.2m.")

General

35. How long have you spent within any industry? (e.g., "Twelve years' experience within the fashion industry.")

36. Were you promoted in any of your roles? If so, in what years and to which roles?

37. Was extra authority awarded to you after a period of time within a role? (e.g., "Commenced as receptionist; then, after three months, awarded by being given further clerical responsibilities including data entry and accounts payable.") It is not necessary that these responsibilities awarded to you should have changed your job title and/or salary.

38. Have you been asked to take part in, or lead, any trainee management courses or management development programs?

39. Were you asked to get involved in any special projects outside your job description? Or, did you ever volunteer for such? What was the result?

Positive Feedback

40. Have you ever received any written or verbal client, customer, or managerial commendations or letters of praise?

41. Can you think of any occasions where you gave excellent customer service? If so, how did you know the customer was satisfied? (Also: What was the outcome? How did it benefit the company?)

42. Did you receive any awards within your company or industry? (e.g., "Acknowledged for support or service of clients or staff, etc.")

Memberships

43. Have you been a representative on any committees (e.g., health and safety committee)? Any special responsibilities there?

44. Do you belong or have you belonged to any professional clubs such as Toastmasters, Lions, or Rotary?

Published or Presented Work

45. Have you had any articles, papers, or features published in any magazines, journals, or books? If so, what publications and when? Have you written any books?

46. Have you presented any topics at any conferences or completed any public speaking? If so, what subjects have you talked about and how large was the audience? List in detail.

Looking Ahead

47. What value do you think you would add to a potential employer's business? How would you be "a resource" or even "a resource-broker" for them, rather than just "a job beggar"? What kind of problems are you good at solving?

48. How do you think you would stand out compared to other applicants who have about the same qualifications as you have?

That should give you a good start. Modify the list any way you want to—add items and questions to it, change the wording, whatever.

If you need additional guidance, search Google for the topic "keywords on an electronic resume" or "examples of resumes." Or "how to write a resume," or "tips on writing a resume." This will not only turn up free resources and advice on the Internet and for-fee resources, such as professional resume writers, but also the names of books, if you want to get *very* thorough.[5]

---

5. Books that I like: *Resume 101* by Quentin J. Schultze, PhD; *Resume Magic: Trade Secrets of a Professional Resume Writer* by Susan Britton Whitcomb; *Federal Resume Guidebook: Strategies for Writing a Winning Federal Resume* by Kathryn Kraemer Troutman; and *Knock 'em Dead Resumes* by Martin Yate. Returning vets from Iraq and Afghanistan will find help on such sites as job-hunt.org (http://tinyurl.com/86a8rkn), Real Warriors (http://tinyurl.com/6u3vawm), and MyNextMove.org, maintained by the government's O*Net Online site.

As for what is the proper form for a resume, there are no rules. The only question is: is there a particular place or kind of place where you'd like to work, and if so, will the person there who has the power to hire you for the kind of job you want, be persuaded by your resume to invite you in? If the answer is, Yes, then it matters not what form your resume takes.

To illustrate my point, I used to have a hobby of collecting "winning" resumes—that is, resumes that had actually gotten someone an interview and, ultimately, a job. Being playful by nature, I would show these without comment, to employer friends of mine, over lunch. Many of them didn't like these winning resumes at all. "That resume will never get anyone a job," they would say. Then I would reply, "Sorry, you're wrong. It already has. I think what you mean is that it wouldn't get them a job with *you*."

The resume reproduced on the opposite page is a good example of what I mean; it's dated, but it's still my favorite.

Like the employer who hired him, I loved this resume. Yet some of the employers I showed it to (over lunch, as I said) criticized it for using a picture or for being too long, or for being too short, etc. In other words, had Jim sent that resume to them, they wouldn't have invited him in for an interview.

The brutal truth is, no matter how skillfully you write and post your resume, some employers will like it, some won't. Trouble is, if you're interested in some employer, you don't know which category they fit into. That's why many job-hunters, if they use resumes, pray as they post their resume: *Please, dear God, let them be employers who like resumes in general, and may the form of my resume appeal to those employers I care about, in particular.*

Whatever form you decide on, write the resume and then post it everywhere you can, online: on the omnibus job boards, famous job boards, community bulletin boards, and niche sites. For lists of such sites, go to Quintessential Careers' great website, which you can find at http://tinyurl.com/3nnqhse.

Incidentally, if this all seems like just too much trouble, there are resume distribution services that will do this blanket posting for you, if you wish, sometimes without a fee, but most often for fees ranging from fifty to one hundred bucks (see www.forwardyourresume.com

E-J Dyer   **Street, City, Zip**   **Telephone No.**

**I SPEAK THE
LANGUAGE OF
MEN, MACHINERY,
AND MANAGEMENT . . .**

OBJECTIVE	Sales of Heavy Equipment
QUALIFICATIONS	• Knowledge of heavy equipment, its use and maintenance.
	• Ability to communicate with management and with men in the field.
	• Ability to favorably introduce change in the form of new equipment or new ideas . . . the ability to sell.
EXPERIENCE	• Maintained, shipped, budgeted and set allocation priorities for 85 pieces of heavy equipment as head of a 500-man organization (1975–1977).
Men and Machinery	• Constructed twelve field operation support complexes, employing a 100-man crew and 19 pieces of heavy equipment (1965–1967).
	• Jack-hammer operator, heavy construction (summers 1956–1957–1958).
Management	• Planned, negotiated and executed large-scale equipment purchases on a nation-to-nation level (1972–1974).
Sales	• Achieved field customer acceptance of two major new computer-based systems:
	—Equipment inventory control and repair parts expedite system (1968–1971)
	—Decision makers' training system (1977–1979)
	• Proven leader . . . repeatedly elected or appointed to senior posts.
EDUCATION	B.A. Benedictine College, 1959 (Class President; Yearbook Editor; "Who's Who in American Colleges")
	• Naval War College, 1975 (Class President; Graduated "With Highest Distinction")
	• University of Maryland, 1973–1974 (Chinese Language)
	• Middle Level Management Training Course, 1967–1968 (Class Standing: 1 of 97)
PERSONAL	Family: Sharon and our sons Jim (11), Andy (8) and Matt (5) desire to locate in a Mountain State by 1982; however, in the interim will consider a position elsewhere in or outside the United States . . . Health: Excellent . . . Birthdate: December 9, 1937 . . . Completing Military Service with the rank of Lieutenant Colonel, U.S. Marine Corps.
SUMMARY	A seeker of challenge . . . experienced, proven and confident of closing the sales for profit.

for very useful evaluations of the top ten such services). Whether it will pay you or not to use one of these services is, in my opinion, largely a matter of luck. Blind, dumb, luck. Personally, I'd always try to do this myself before giving money to anyone else.

If you decide to do this for yourself, my advice is: post it right on the actual website of companies that interest you, if they have a site, and if their site permits that. This, of course, assumes you have figured out where you would most like to work, if they'll have you (more on this later in the book). In this post-2008 period, I recommend you pay particular attention to small employers (25 or fewer employees, 50 or fewer, 100 or fewer), and newer organizations (7 years old or less).

If you post your resume on the sites of particular employers, large or small, don't count on any acknowledgment or reply. Just post the thing, cross your fingers, and pray it arrives at the right time, at the right place, into the hands of the right person: the one who actually has the power to hire you.

Alternatives to the Classic Resume

A cover letter was, for decades, something you sent along with your resume. Now, many employers prefer a cover letter *instead* of your resume. That brief cover letter can summarize all that a longer resume might have covered. I get this kind of report all the time, from success-ful job-hunters: *"Cover letter. Make it personal and specific to THAT job. I was directly told in two interviews that my unique cover letter got me in the door. I researched the companies. . . ."*

If you don't know what a cover letter is, or how to write it, the Inter-net can rescue you handily. Just type "cover letters" into your favorite search engine. You'll be surprised at how many tips, examples, etc., you find. Look especially for Susan Ireland's Cover Letter Guide at http://susanireland.com/letter/how-to. It's good, and it's free.

Incidentally, recent surveys have revealed that many employers *pre-fer* a cover letter to a resume.

Another alternative to a classic resume is a Job or Career Portfolio. A portfolio may be electronic (posted on the Internet) or on paper/in a notebook/in a large display case (as with artists), demonstrating your accomplishments, experience, training, commendations, or awards, from the past. Artists have a portfolio, with samples of their work. You probably knew that. But portfolios are equally apt in other fields.

Instead of "portfolio" we might just call them, "Evidence of What I Can Do and Have Done," or "Proof of Performance." For guidance on how to prepare a job portfolio, and what to include, simply type "job or career portfolio" into Google; you'll get a wealth of tips and information.

Some Friendly Reminders About Your "Pre-Google Resume"

1. If you're blanketing the Internet with that resume, be cautious about including any stuff on the resume that would help someone find out where you live or work, particularly if you're a female. No, I'm not being sexist. It's just that there are some sick people out there. Sick in the head, that is. If I were you, I'd be sure to leave out my address and home phone number. Just an e-mail address should more than suffice.

2. If you are targeting particular employers, rather than or in addition to broad job-sites, keep in mind that a resume is best not sent solely by e-mail, particularly if it's an attachment, and not embedded in the body of the e-mail. Many employers, leery of viruses, will not even open e-mail attachments (and that includes your resume). Send it by e-mail if you must, but always send a nicer version of it by the postal service, or UPS, or FedEx, etc.

3. If you're going to snail-mail a resume to a target employer, pay attention to the paper you write or print it on. Picture this scenario: an employer is going through a whole stack of resumes, and on average he or she is giving each resume about eight seconds of their time (true: we checked!). Then that resume goes either into a pile we might call "Forgeddit," or a pile we might call "Bears further investigation." And what determines which pile? The feel of the paper. Yes, that employer's first contact with

your resume is with their fingers. By the pleasure or displeasure of their fingers, they are prejudiced in your favor before they even start reading, or prejudiced against you. Usually they are not even aware of this. Anyway, this is why you want the paper to feel good. That usually means using paper weighing at least 28 pounds (a paper's weight is on the outside of every package). And you want it to be easy to read—so be sure it's nicely laid out or formatted, using a decent-sized font, size 12 or even 14, etc.

4. A resume should have a purpose, at least in *your* mind. It might be that you're posting it online, just to collect and organize all pertinent information about yourself in one place, so that when an employer Googles you they find *this*, nice and concise, in contrast to all the other stuff about you that Google will find, scattered all over the Internet.

5. Your purpose, for your resume, if you're targeting individual employers, is to get yourself invited in for an interview. Period. This truth, unfortunately, is not widely known. Most job-hunters (and more than a few resume writers) assume a resume's pur-pose is to "sell you," or secure you a job. It does happen. But mostly the purpose of a resume is just to get invited in for an interview, where it will then be time for you to sell yourself. In person. Face to face. Not on paper. So, read over every single sentence in your resume and evaluate it by this one standard: *"Will this item help to get me invited in? Or will this item seem too puzzling, or off-putting, or a red flag?"* If you doubt a particular sentence will help get you invited in for an interview, then omit that sentence. If it's important to you, give yourself a note to be sure to cover it in the interview. And if there is something you feel you will ultimately need to explain, or expand upon, save that explanation also for the interview. Your resume is, above all, no place for "true confessions." ("I kind of botched up, at the end, in that job; that's why they let me go, as I'm sure they'll tell you when you check my references.") If you want the interviewer to know that, in the interest of full disclosure, don't put it in your resume. Save true confessions for the end of the

interview, and only if you're confident at that point that they
really want you, and you really want them.

6. The same advice applies to discussing any non-visible or non-
obvious handicap you may have. Generally speaking—there
are exceptions—don't mention it as early as the resume. And
even when you're in the interview, don't discuss right off the
bat what you *can't* do. Focus all their attention, initially, on what
you can do—that you can perform all the tasks required in this
job. Save what you can't do for the moment when they say they
really want you.

7. If you're coming out of some subculture that has its own language (*military, clergy, etc.*) get some help in translating your
experience into the language of employers. For example,
"preached" should be replaced by "taught." "Commanded"
should be replaced by "supervised," etc.

8. "Keywords" are important if you're posting your resume without specific employers in mind. A good article about keywords—
what they are, how to insert them in your resume—can be found
in SqualkFox's article, "8 Keywords That Set Your Resume on
Fire," at http://tinyurl.com/d9k4ns.

9. Finally, don't include references on your resume. Some career
counselors and resume writers will disagree with me on this,
but I think references are better offered after prospective
employers have had a chance to see and talk with you. And
please, please, please, never list somebody as a reference, at
any time in your job-hunt, without first getting their written
permission to do so. Be aware that your references, if they are
checked out, will often be checked out over the phone, rather
than in writing. But in case you may need something in writing, if your references permit you to use their name, ask them
to give the letter of recommendation to *you.* You want to screen
your references, believe me you do! *Don't assume they'll give you a
raving recommendation.* Some of your preferred reference writers
may turn out to be people who are by nature brutally honest. If
they've never actually seen you at work, for example, they may
say so, and decline to say whether you'd be an asset or not. That

kind of "recommendation" is honest, but it won't do you any good. You want to find this out before any prospective employer sees it. Then you can decide whether you want to use it or deep-six it, before you go into the interview.

10. Hard fact to learn, but you must learn it: some employers *hate* resumes. Why should that be any surprise? Currently, according to experts, 82% of all resumes have to be checked out, concerning the facts stated or the experience claimed. Lies are spreading like a plague, on resumes. Another hard fact: some employers *love* resumes. Unfortunately, it's not for the reasons you think. They love them because they offer an easy way to cut down the time they have to spend interviewing candidates for a vacancy. Don't forget this: for an employer, hiring is essentially *an elimination game*. Particularly where a lot of people are applying, they're reading over your resume looking for one thing: a reason—any reason—to eliminate you, so they can cut that stack of resumes down to a manageable number for face-to-face interviewing (say, three to eight). Surveys show it only takes a skilled human resources person about eight seconds to scan a resume (thirty seconds, if they're really dawdling), so getting rid of fifty job-hunters—I mean getting rid of fifty resumes— takes only half an hour or less. Whereas, interviewing those fifty job-hunters in person would have required a minimum of twenty-five hours. Great time savings—for them! No wonder employers invented resumes!

Where You Post Your Resume Makes a Difference

This should guide you in your resume strategy, if you're going to post a resume to supplement what else they'll find online about you, with Google.

The number of interviews employers need to conduct to find a hire, stays pretty constant—around 5.4—once they've sifted through all the resumes or applications. So, to conserve their energy, they ask themselves, "Where would I have to read or sift through the least number of resumes, before I decide who to do those 5.4 interviews with?" Fortunately, we know the answer. Somebody did a study.[6]

If employers post their vacancy on a job-board such as CareerBuilder .com or Monster.com, they have to look through 219 resumes from job-hunters who respond, before they find someone to interview and hire.

If employers consider resumes from job-hunters who come through social media sites, such as LinkedIn or Facebook, they have to look through 116 resumes, before they find someone to interview and hire.

If employers post their vacancy on their own website, they have to look through 33 resumes from job-hunters who respond, before they find someone to interview and hire.

If the job-hunter takes the initiative to find a very specific job, rather than waiting to find a vacancy, and does this, say, by typing the name of that kind of job into a search engine, then sending resumes to any companies whose name turns up, employers only have to look through 32 applications, before they find someone to interview and hire.

And if the job-hunter takes even more initiative, chooses a company where they'd like to work, and gets a referral (i.e., gets some employee within that company to recommend them), employers have to look through only 10 such candidates, before they find someone to interview and hire.

Summary

Okay, one more time: ever since 2008, *do you need a resume?*

Well, no you don't, and yes you do.

You already have a kind of resume without lifting a finger, if you've been posting anything on the Internet. Google is your new resume. What an employer finds out about you simply by *Googling* your name, helps determine whether you get hired or not.

---

6. From an analysis, released in April 2011, by Jobs2web Inc., of 1,300,000 job applications and 26,000 hires in 2010.

You've got to clean up what they'll find, before they find it. Edit, fill in, expand, and add to it, before they see it.

But that, alone, is not enough. You need to summarize and organize the information about yourself in one place, online or off. And that means, you need to write the old kind of resume, that you did pre-2008.

Once written, you can go two ways with it. The first way is just to post it everywhere on the Internet, which is akin to nailing it to a tree in the town square, where everyone can see it. You just post it *as is.*

The second way is to send it to particular employers whom you have targeted, hoping that resume will get you an interview. Here you will need to *edit it,* before sending it to any employer. You will need to weigh every sentence in it by one criterion and one only: will this help get me invited in, for an interview? If the answer is *No,* you must edit or remove that sentence.

Because, these are the most fundamental truths about approaching individual employers:

The primary purpose of a resume is *to get yourself invited in for an interview.*

The primary purpose of that interview is *to get yourself invited back* for a second interview.

The primary purpose of the second and subsequent interviews there, is *to help them decide that they like you and want you,* once you've decided that you like them, and could do some of your best work there.

Wild Life, by John Kovalic, ©1989 Shetland Productions. Reprinted with permission.

God grant me the serenity
To accept the things I cannot change,
The courage to change the things I can,
And the wisdom to know the difference.

—*Reinhold Niebuhr (1892–1971)*

Chapter 3

There Are Seven Million Vacancies This Month

The Good News: The Job-Hunt Hasn't Really Changed At All Since 2008

Yes, I know this contradicts what I said in the first chapter. But there you have it. Both things are true: the job-hunt has changed dramatically since 2008, yet the job-hunt hasn't really changed at all since 2008.

How can they both be true? The answer lies in the distinction between inner essence and surface behavior.

The surface *behavior* of the job-hunt is always changing, often dramatically, as we saw in the first and second chapters. This, because job-hunt *behavior* at any given time is determined by technology. And when a new technology arises—think *computers*, think *Internet*, think *smartphone*, think *digital* resumes—job-hunting alters. On the surface.

But beneath all surface change, the *essence* of the job-hunt never really changes. Job-hunting is all about human nature, and in its essence is most like another human activity that we call *dating*. Both shake down to: "Do you like me?" and "Do I like you?" If the answer to both is "Yes," then it's "Do you want to try goin' steady?" In dating. In job-hunting. So, if you focus on *essence* rather than *form*, the job-hunt remains constant year after year.

First question: *"Do you like me?"* In the job-interview that means "Hey employer, you are looking for someone who can do this thing that you want done, and can get along with you and the other people here. So, given that, do you like me?"

Second question: *"Do I like you?"* In the job-interview that means "Are you going to give me a work environment that will enable me to be at my most productive and most effective level, where I feel useful and appreciated, and can make a difference?"

Both questions are equally important, and permissible to ask. But that second question needs to be emphasized, underlined, and written in large letters because when we are job-hunting we are so prone to think all power belongs to employers. They have every right to ask their question. We have no right to ask ours—or so street-wisdom claims.

But wait a minute. Meditate on why we have the word *quit* in our vocabulary, as in *"I quit,"* and you will realize that the job-hunt *and job* are always a matter of the job-hunter or worker asking themselves "Do I like you?" And if you conclude, "No I don't really like you," or "I really hate it here," then eventually you quit.

Your big decision is, do I wait three years to find out the answer to my question, or do I try to find it out now, during the job-hunt in general, during the job-interview in particular?

The job-hunt is a conversation—a two-way conversation—wherein your opinion matters as much as the employer's. That always has been true. Always will be.

You Are Not As Powerless as You Think

If you're currently out of work, and looking for a job, you have every reason in the world to think you are up against overwhelming forces and the situation you face is rather hopeless. You may have struck out, again and again. The media is always filled with bad news, about the unemployed, since 2008. But the situation you face is not hopeless. In the world today, you have more power than you think, even with all the bad news and these great forces that you are up against since 2008. It may not be a lot of power, but . . . well, let me tell you a story.

Some years ago, when I was doing a lot of counseling, not just about careers, a friend of mine asked me if I would be willing to see someone he knew. Her name was Mary. She had been diagnosed with multiple sclerosis, or MS. She had been to a wide range of medical specialists: neurologist, psychologist, internist, you name it. They all had declared there was nothing they could do to help her with the disease. My friend said, "Would you see her?" "Sure," I said, "but I'm not sure there's anything I can do."

The next day my friend brought her over. She walked very stiffly up the front sidewalk, came in, sat down, and after exchanging a few pleasantries, I got down to business. "Mary," I said, "what is multiple sclerosis?"

Mary's and my discussion was a philosophical one. We both knew how the disease is generally described: a disease that attacks the central nervous system. My question to her was deeper, and I knew she understood what I was getting at: What causes MS? How much control do we have over its progression? What hastens or slows its rise and fall in the individual? Etc.

"I don't know," she said, in a dull, emotionless voice. "Well then," I said, "that makes us even; because I don't know, either. But here's what I propose. I'm sure that a huge proportion of whatever MS is, is out of your control. There's nothing you can do about it. But that proportion can't be 100%. There's got to be some proportion—let's say it's even just 2%, or 5%—that is within your control. We could work on that. Do you want to begin that journey?" She said yes. Over the next few weeks she improved, and finally was free of all symptoms (typical of the disease for a spell, but this lasted for a very long time), and now—free of all stiffness—she became a model on 57th Street in New York City.

So it is, that in any situation you find yourself, no matter how overwhelmed you may feel, no matter how much you may feel you're at the mercy of huge forces that are beyond your control, some part of it *is* within your control: maybe 2%, 5%, who knows? There is always *something* you can work on. Something that is within your power. And often, changing that little bit results in changing a whole lot. Maybe not as dramatic a change as with Mary; but change nonetheless.

You are not powerless during the job-hunt. Maybe the employer has an overwhelming amount of power in the whole job-hunt. But the employer does not hold all the cards.

That is what never changes.

Of course, you will object, "Well, that may be true during normal times, but these ain't normal times. I cannot afford to be picky. There are very few vacancies out there."

Where did we get *that* idea? From the media, that's where. Two reports come out each month in the U.S., about the state of the job-market. One of those reports is usually hopeful. One of them is usually depressing. Both of them are put out by the federal government. The media choose to emphasize one of those reports, but not the other.

The first report comes out on the first Friday of each month, with rare exception. It is typically called "news about the unemployment rate," though it is more accurate to think of it as "the monthly measure of the *net change* in the size of the working workforce in the U.S." Its technical name is the Current Population Survey.[1] It said that in the month of February, 2013, only 236,000 jobs were added to the economy. With twelve million looking for work that month, that was not good news.

But, there was that other report. It comes out about two months later. It's called JOLT, which stands for *Job Openings and Labor Turnover.*[2] It said that during that month of February 2013, 4,418,000 people found work, and even so, 3,925,000 vacancies remained unfilled by the end of that month. You do the math. That's a total of 8,343,000 jobs available in the U.S. during the month of February. And this is typical, in the U.S., month in and month out.

What's going on, here? Well, let me give you a parallel situation.

Suppose I own a dress shop. You come in to visit me, and for fun you count the number of dresses I have in the shop. It turns out I have 100. You leave that day, and you don't return for a month. You count, again for fun, how many dresses I have in the shop one month later. I have 95. So you say to me, "Oh, I see you only sold 5 dresses this month. Poor you."

"No," I reply, "I added to the inventory during the month." "How many," you ask. "50," I say.

You stop, and calculate: "Oh, so you actually sold 55 dresses this past month." I say, "Right."

1. www.bls.gov/cps
2. www.bls.gov/jlt

5 vs. 55. You get the one figure, as the net change in the size of the inventory in my shop, with visits a month apart; you get the other figure as the actual change in the number of dresses sold, during the month.

It's the same with the two government reports. Not 5 vs. 55, but 236,000 vs. 8,343,000.

Of course, the question for us when we're out of work is, "If there are typically seven or eight million jobs available each month, why didn't I get one of them?"

More importantly, this wipes out the impression that things are so bad, it doesn't matter what you want. *Nonsense!*

The job-hunt is always a two-way conversation. That never changes. What the employer wants, matters. But also what you want, matters.

Certain other facts about the job-hunt in this country never change. Here are ten of them, that have remained the same since the first edition of this book was published, and throughout the forty-two yearly editions since.

1. You must take charge of your own job-hunt, and determine not to conduct a traditional job-hunt ("this is the way it has always been done and must be done"), but rather, a creative one.

2. To do a creative job-hunt, there are three questions you must find out the answer to: they are What, Where and How. WHAT are your skills that you most love to use? WHERE would you most love to use these skills? (In terms of field, purpose of the company or organization, location, style of working, kinds of people you work with, etc.) And finally, HOW do you go about finding such places?

3. You must devote as much time to your job-hunt as you possibly can. If you want to devote as little time to your job-hunt as possible, then fine; try it. But if that doesn't lead to a job, then you are going to have to devote more time to it.

4. If your job-hunt isn't working, then you must take the time to find out as much up-to-date information as you possibly can about the job-hunt itself, and not just about the job-market. Effective job-hunting techniques keep evolving.

5. If your job-hunt isn't working, then you must take the time to do a thorough survey of yourself before you do a survey of the job-market (like, finding out what are "the hot jobs").

6. You must approach organizations, companies, or institutions that interest you, whether or not they have a known vacancy. Go after smaller, newer companies in particular. Sometimes vacancies develop in a day and a night, and do not immediately get advertised or published.

7. Job-hunting is not a science; it is an art. Some job-hunters know instinctively how to do it; in some cases, they were born knowing how to do it. Others of us sometimes have a harder time with it, but fortunately for us in the U.S. and elsewhere in the world, there is help, coaching, counseling, and advice—online and off.

8. Job-hunting is always mysterious. Sometimes mind-bogglingly mysterious. You may never understand why things sometimes work, and sometimes do not.

9. There is no "always wrong" way to hunt for a job or to change careers. Anything may work under certain circumstances, or at certain times, or with certain employers. There are only degrees of likelihood of certain job-hunting techniques working or not working. But it is crucial to know that likelihood (see chapter 6).

10. There is no "always right" way to hunt for a job or to change careers. Anything may fail to work under certain circumstances, or at certain times, or with certain employers. There are only degrees of likelihood of certain job-hunting techniques working or not working. But it is crucial to know that likelihood, as we just saw. Job-hunting always depends on some amount of luck. Luck, pure luck. Having advanced job-hunting skills doesn't mean absolutely, positively, you will always be able to find a job. It does mean that you can get good at reducing the amount that depends on luck, to as small a proportion as possible.

As I said, some things about the job-hunt have not changed since 2008. In fact, they have not changed since 1970.

THE TEN GREATEST MISTAKES
MADE IN JOB INTERVIEWS

Whereby Your Chances of Finding a Job Are Greatly Decreased

I.   Going after large organizations only (such as the Fortune 500).

II. Hunting all by yourself for places to visit.

III. Doing no homework on an organization before going there.

IV. Allowing the Human Resources department to interview you (their primary function is to look for reasons to screen you OUT).

V.   Setting no time limit when you first begin the interview, and then overstaying your welcome.

VI. Letting your resume be the only agenda discussed during the job-interview.

VII. Talking primarily about yourself throughout the interview, and what benefit the job will be for you.

VIII. Failing to give examples of the skills you claim you have.

IX. Basically approaching the employer as if you were a job-beggar, hoping they will offer you any kind of a job, however humble.

X.   Not sending a thank-you note right after the interview.

Chapter 4

Sixteen Tips About Interviewing for a Job

I say "for a job," because actually there are three types of interviews that you may come across, during your job-hunt. They are distinguished from each other by *what you are looking for,* and more importantly, *who you are talking to:*

1. Interviews for fun or practice, *where you are talking with people who are passionate about the same thing you are, be it Cancun, scrapbooks, travel, physical fitness, running, or whatever;*

2. Interviews for information, *where you are talking with employees who did or do the job you are exploring; or maybe you're talking here with information specialists, or with experts in the industry that interests you;*

3. Interviews for a job, *where you are talking with employers, and most particularly not with the HR department but with the person who actually has the power to hire you for the job you want.*

This chapter is about this third kind of interview, *the one for a job.*[1] Here are sixteen tips about that kind of interview.

---

1. The other two are discussed at the end of chapter 9 (pages 222–28).

Tip #1

There is no such thing as "employers." I'm referring to the way job-hunters use that word, in describing their conclusions after just two interviews: *"Employers just won't hire me or someone with my background or someone with my handicap,"* or nonsense like that. My friend, you're reaching way beyond the facts.

Fact: You interviewed with two employers (or six, or twelve) and they wouldn't hire you. Those two. Those six. Or those twelve. They hardly speak for all employers.

Fact: "Employers" are individuals, as different from one another as night and day. "Employers" span a wide range of attitudes, wildly different ideas about how to hire, a wide range of ways to conduct hiring interviews, and as many different attitudes toward handicaps as you can possibly think of. You cannot possibly predict the attitude of one employer from the attitude of another. All generalizations about "employers" (*including those in this book*) are just mental *conveniences*.

Fact: There are millions of separate, distinct, unrelated employers out there with very different requirements for hiring. Unless you look dirty, wild, and disreputable, and smell really bad, if you know what your *talent* is, I guarantee some employer is looking for *you*. Even if you're crazy, there's some employer crazier than you. You have to keep going. Some employers out there *do* want you, no matter what the others think. Your job is to find *them*.

Fact: There is a big difference between large employers (those with hundreds or thousands of employees) and small employers (alternately defined as those with 25 or fewer employees, those with 50 or fewer employees, or—the most common definition—those with 100 or fewer employees). The chief difference is that large employers are harder to reach, especially if the-person-who-has-the-power-to-hire-you (for the job you want) is in some deep inner chamber of that company, and the company's phone has a voice menu with eighteen impenetrable layers. Don't think your interviewing experience with small employers will necessarily be at all like the rejection you encountered with large ones.

Fact: There is a big difference between new companies or enterprises, and those that have been around for some time, so far as hiring is concerned. A study reported in *TIME* magazine found that newer small companies (100 or fewer employees) that were less than six years old, created 4.7 million jobs in the year studied, while older small firms created only 3.2 million jobs.[2] So when hiring is tight, you will want to concentrate on small firms, and *newer* small firms, at that. Don't think your interviewing experience with new companies will necessarily be at all like the rejection you had with old ones.

Moral: Don't get discouraged by your interview history. Job expert Tom Jackson[3] accurately described the job-hunt as a series:

NO NO NO NO NO NO NO NO NO NO NO NO NO NO
NO NO NO NO NO NO NO NO NO NO NO YES YES

Every "NO" you get out of the way, you're one step closer to YES.

Tip #2

An interview should be prepared for, before you ever go in. Naturally, you wanted to go into the interview with the employer curious to know more about you, but the employer is first of all curious about what you know about them. Do a lot of research on them before you go in. Why? Because organizations love to be loved. If you've gone to the trouble of finding out as much as you can about them, before you interview with them, they will be flattered and impressed, believe me.

Most job-hunters never go to this amount of trouble. Most just walk in the door, knowing nothing about the organization. I have a friend who ran a large organization in Virginia; he said to me, "I'm so tired of people coming in here, saying, *Uh, what do you do here?* that the next person who comes in here and has done some prior research on us, I'm going to offer a job." He called me a week later to say, "I did it."

So don't skip this step. It may make the difference between your being hired, or not being hired. Find out everything you can about

---

2. "Briefing on the Economy," *Time*, April 11, 2011. The last year for which they had statistics was 2005.

3 Author of *The Perfect Resume: Today's Ultimate Job Search Tool*, 2004.

them. Google them. Go to their website if they have one, and read everything there that is hidden under the heading "About Us." If this organization is local, and your town has a public library, ask your local librarian for help in finding any news clippings or other information about the place. And, finally, ask all your friends if they know anyone who ever worked there, or works there still, so you can take them to lunch or tea or Starbucks and find out any inside stories, before you approach the place. (And, of course, maybe after you hear these stories you'll decide not to explore them any further. Better to know that now, than later.)

Tip #3

Honor agreements. If it was you who asked for the interview, not them, remove their dread of this visit by specifying how much time you are asking of them. You are the one in control of how long the interview lasts. Make it some oddball period, like nineteen minutes (*twenty* sounds vague, *nineteen* sounds precise—like you are really serious).

If they grant you the interview, keep to this commitment as though your life depended on it. If you have a smartphone that allows you to select "Vibrate" without any sound, set its timer before you go to your appointment, to *seventeen* minutes (that leaves you two minutes to wrap up). But don't activate the timer yet. Save that step for the time you enter their office for the actual interview, then activate it by tapping it *on* or *go*. Keep the phone in a pocket or location near you, where you can feel it. At the seventeen-minute vibration warning, tap it off, and prepare to end the interview by saying, "*I said I would only take nineteen minutes of your time, and I like to honor my agreements.*" This will always make a huge impression on an employer! You are a woman, or man, of your word!! In this day and age! How rare!

Don't obsess about time, during the interview; just stay quietly aware of it, in the background of your mind, as you focus sharply on what the employer is saying, or you are.

And at the end, don't stay one minute longer than the nineteen minutes, unless the employer begs you to—and I mean, begs, Begs, BEGS.

A courteous interviewer will say, *"Oh, do you have to?"* But don't mistake that for anything other than what it is: *courtesy.* Go.

Of course, if it was they who invited you in for an interview, they are the ones in control of how long the interview lasts. Still, stay quietly aware of *time,* with regard to such things as the following:

Tip #4

An interview for a job at its best is just a conversation. I remind you of what I said in the previous chapter: The other human activity job-hunting most resembles is *dating,* not *marketing* a used car. This conversation is two people attempting to decide if you both want to "try going steady." (Or maybe it's you plus six or nine others, depending on how many from the employer's team are sitting in, on the interview.)

It should be *a two-way* conversation. What the employer decides is critical, of course; but so is what you decide. This interview is a data-collecting process for the employer. Whether one person or a team is interviewing you, they are using the interview to find out "Do we like you? Do we want you to work here? Do you have the skills, knowledge, or experience that we really need? Do you have the work-ethic that we are looking for? And, how will you fit in with our other employees?"

All well and good. But, this interview is part of *your* data-collecting process, too—the one you have been engaged in, or should have been engaged in, during your whole job-hunt. You are sitting there, now, with the employer or their team, and the question you are trying to find an answer to, is: *"Do I like you all? Do I want to work here, or not?"*

The only time you can't afford to be pondering this question is if you're at the end of your rope, flat broke, starving, and you've got to take *anything* that comes along, at this point. Otherwise, you use this interview to find out *"Do I really want to work here?"* You want to find that out *now,* not three years in. And only when you have concluded "Yes," or "I think so," do you then turn your energy toward *marketing* yourself.

During your half of the conversation, it is a two-step process: gentle questioning about the place, then quiet self-confident marketing of yourself, once you've decided this is the place for you.

Tip #5

Questions to expect from them, questions you can ask. The principal question, the first question, the most important question they are likely to ask you is *"Tell me about yourself."* How you answer that question will determine your fate during the rest of the interview. So, here are some key points to keep in mind about your answer to *Tell me about yourself*:

a. This question is a kind of test. They want to see how you respond to an open-ended, unstructured situation, the kind of challenge that life (and a job) are continually presenting to us.

b. Employers generally feel you have failed the test if you respond with a question. Every job-hunter's favorite—*Well, what do you want to know about me?*—is every employer's least favorite. They interpret this to mean you have no idea what to answer, and are stalling for time.

c. What employers are looking for here, is your answer to a question they did not mention aloud: *What experience, skills, or knowledges do you have, that are relevant to the job I am trying to fill?* It is really *that* question you should try to answer here. Not your personal history such as where you grew up, your tastes, or hobbies. They are interested in your work history here, and more particularly your work history as it relates to this job that you are discussing with them.

d. Employers expect you to have the answer at your fingertips, well-summarized, well-rehearsed. (This is the famous "elevator speech" job coaches are often recommending to job-hunters. In the length of time it takes to ride an elevator up a tall building, you should be able to say your entire answer *to this question*, rehearsed and rehearsed, until you could say it in your sleep.)

Okay, what other questions may you expect from the employer? Books on *interviewing*, of which there are dozens and dozens, often publish long lists of questions employers may ask you, along with some timeworn, semi-clever answers. They recommend that you memorize the answers to all those questions. Their lists include such questions as:

- Tell me about yourself. (Of course.)
- What do you know about this company?
- Why are you applying for this job?
- How would you describe yourself?
- What are your major strengths?
- What is your greatest weakness?
- What type of work do you like to do best?
- What are your interests outside of work?
- What accomplishment gave you the greatest satisfaction?
- Why did you leave your last job?
- Why were you fired (if you were)?
- Where do you see yourself five years from now?
- What are your goals in life?
- How much did you make at your last job?

But really there are only *five basic questions* that you need pay attention to. The people-who-have-the-power-to-hire-you need to discover the answers to these five, which they may ask directly or try to find out without ever mentioning the questions per se:

1. "Why are you here?" This means, *"Why are you knocking on my door, rather than someone else's door?"*

2. "What can you do for us?" This means, *"If I were to hire you, will you help me with the challenges I face? What are your skills, and how much do you know about the subject or field that we are in?"*

3. "What kind of person are you?" This means, *"Will you fit in? Do you have the kind of personality that makes it easy for people to work with you, and do you share the values that we have at this place?"*

4. "What exactly distinguishes you from nineteen or nine hundred other people who are applying for this job?" This means, *"Do you have better work habits than the others, do you show up earlier, stay later, work more thoroughly, work faster, maintain higher standards, go the extra mile, or . . . what?"*

5. "Can I afford you?" This means, *"If we decide we want you here, how much will it take to get you, and are we willing and able to pay that amount—governed, as we are, by our budget, and by our inability to pay you as much as the person who would be next above you, on our organizational chart?"*

These are the five principal questions that employers need to know the answers to. *This is the case, as I said, even if the interview begins and ends with these five questions never once being mentioned explicitly by the employer.* The questions are still *floating* beneath the surface of the conversation, beneath all the things being discussed. Anything you can do, during the interview, to help the employer answer these five questions, will make you stand out, in the employer's mind.

Of course, it's not just the employer who has questions. This is a two-way conversation, remember? You have questions too. And—surprise!—they are the same questions (in only slightly different form) *as the employer's*. Here is what you should be asking yourself (or them) during your half of the conversation:

1. "What does this job involve?" *You want to understand exactly what tasks will be asked of you, so that you can determine if these are the kinds of tasks you would really like to do, and can do.*

2. "What are the skills a top employee in this job would have to have?" *You want to find out if your skills match those that the employer thinks a top employee in this job has to have, in order to do this job well.*

3. "Are these the kinds of people I would like to work with, or not?" *Do not ignore your intuition if it tells you that you would not be comfortable working with these people! You want to know if they have the kind of personalities that would enable you to accomplish your best work. If these people aren't it, keep looking!*

4. "If we like each other, and we both want to work together, can I persuade them there is something unique about me, that makes me different from nineteen or nine hundred other people who are applying for this job?" *You need to think out, way ahead of time, what does make you different from other people*

who can do the same job. For example, if you are good at analyzing problems, how do you do that? (1) Painstakingly? (2) Intuitively, in a flash? Or (3) By consulting with greater authorities in the field? You see the point. You are trying to put your finger on the "style" or "manner" in which you do your work, that is distinctive and hopefully appealing, to this employer, so that they choose you over other people they are interviewing.

5. **"Can I persuade them to hire me at the salary I need or want?"** This requires some knowledge on your part of how to conduct salary negotiation. (Key things to know: it should always take place at the end of the interviews there, and whoever mentions a salary figure first, generally loses, in the negotiation.) That's covered in the next chapter.

You will probably want to ask questions one and two out loud. You will *observe* quietly the answer to question three. You will be prepared to make the case for questions four and five, when the *appropriate* time in the interview arises.

Further questions you may want to ask:

- What significant changes has this company gone through in the past five years?
- What values are sacred to this company?
- What characterizes the most successful employees this company has?
- What future changes do you see in the work here?
- Who do you see as your allies, colleagues, or competitors in this business?

How do you first raise these questions of yours, if you initiated the interview? Well, you might begin by reporting just exactly how you've been conducting your job-hunt, and what impressed you so much about *this* organization during your research, that you decided to come in and talk to them about a job. From there, and thereafter, you can fix your attention on the five questions that are inevitably on the employer's mind.

Incidentally, these five questions pop up (yet again), if you're there to talk *not* about a job that already exists, but rather, a job that you hope they will *create* for you. In that case, these five questions change form only slightly. They get changed into five *statements,* that you make to the person-who-has-the-power-to-*create*-this-job.

1. You tell them what you like about this organization.

2. You tell them what sorts of needs you find intriguing in this field, in general, and in this organization, in particular (by the way, unless you first hear the word coming out of their mouth, don't use the word *"problems,"* as most employers prefer synonyms that sound gentler to their ears, such as *"challenges"* or *"needs"*).

3. You tell them what skills seem to you to be necessary in order to meet such needs, and stories from your past experience that demonstrate you have those very skills. Employers, in these days of "behavioral interviews," are looking for *examples* from your past performance and achievement—your behavior—not just vague statements like: "I'm good at. . . ." They want concrete examples, specifically of any transferable skills, work content skills, or self-management skills, i.e., traits, that you claim to have. It's helpful to pose the question to yourself before you ever go in there: "What are *the three most important* competencies, for this job?" Then, of course, you need to demonstrate during the interview that you *have* those three—for the job that you·want them to create.

4. You tell them what is unique about the way *you* perform those skills. Every prospective employer wants to know *what makes you different* from nineteen or nine hundred other people who can do the same kind of work as you. You *have* to know what that is. And then not merely talk about it, but actually demonstrate it by the way you conduct your side of the hiring-interview.

5. And you tell them how the hiring of you will not cost them, in the long run. You need to be prepared to demonstrate that you will, in the long run, end up costing them nothing, as you will bring in more money than the salary they pay you. Emphasize this!

Tip #6

During the interview, determine to observe "the 50-50 Rule." Studies have revealed that, in general, the people who get hired are those who mix speaking and listening fifty-fifty in the interview. That is, half the time they let the employer do the talking, half the time in the interview they do the talking. People who didn't follow that mix, were the ones who didn't get hired, according to the study.[4] My hunch as to the reason why this is so, is that if you talk too much about yourself, you come across as one who would ignore the needs of the organization; if you talk too little, you come across as trying to hide something about your background.

Tip #7

In answering the employer's questions, observe "the twenty-second to two-minute rule." Studies have revealed that when it is your turn to speak or answer a question, you should plan not to speak any longer than two minutes at a time, if you want to make the best impression.[5] In fact, a good answer to an employer's question sometimes only takes twenty seconds to give. (But not less than that, else you will be assumed to be "a grunter," lacking any communication skills.)

Tip #8

The employer is primarily concerned about risk. Employers hate risks. Because if they don't pan out, they will cost the employer a lot of money. Put the search term "cost of a bad hire" into your favorite Internet search engine (Google?), and see what it turns up. As you can see, the cost of hiring the wrong person can cost the employer one to five times the *bad hire's* annual salary, or more.

---

4. This one was done by a researcher at Massachusetts Institute of Technology, whose name has been lost in the mists of time.
5. This one was conducted by my friend and colleague, Daniel Porot, of Geneva, Swtizerland.

So, you may think you are sitting there, scared to death, while the employer (individual or team) is sitting there, blasé and confident. But in actual fact you and they may both be quite anxious.

The employer's anxieties include any or all of the following:

a. That if hired, you won't be able to do the job: that you lack the necessary skills or experience, and the hiring-interview didn't uncover this.

b. That if hired, you won't put in a full working day, more often than not.

c. That if hired, you'll take frequent sick days, on one pretext or another.

d. That if hired, you'll only stay around for a few weeks or at most a few months, until you find a better job.

e. That if hired, it may take you too long to master the job, and thus it will be too long before you turn a profit for that organization.

f. That you won't get along with the other workers there, or that you will develop a personality conflict with the boss.

g. That you will only do the minimum that you can get away with, rather than the maximum that the boss was hoping for. Since every boss these days is trying to keep their workforce smaller than it was before 2008, they are hoping for the maximum productivity from each new hire post-2008.

h. That you will always have to be told what to do next, rather than displaying initiative.

i. That you will turn out to have a disastrous character flaw not evident in the interview, and ultimately reveal yourself to be either dishonest, or irresponsible, a spreader of dissension at work, lazy, an embezzler, a gossip, a sexual harasser, a drunk, a drug-user or substance abuser, a liar, incompetent, or to put it bluntly, an employer's worst nightmare.

j. *(If this is a large organization, and your would-be boss is not the top person there)* that you will bring discredit upon them, and upon their department/section/division, etc., for ever hiring you in the first place—making them lose face, possibly also costing them a raise or a promotion, from the boss upstairs.

In the end, what employers want to hire are people who can bring in more money than they are paid. Every organization has two main preoccupations for its day-by-day work: the problems—they generally prefer "challenges"—they are facing, and what solutions to those challenges their employees and management are coming up with. Therefore, the main thing the employer is trying to figure out during the hiring-interview with you, is: will you be part of the solution there, or just another part of the *problem.*

In trying to allay their worries here, you should figure out prior to the interview how a *bad* employee would "screw up," in the position you are discussing with the employer, individual or team—such things as *come in late, take too much time off, follow his or her own agenda instead of the employer's, etc.* Then plan to emphasize to the employer during the interview how much you are the very opposite: your sole goal "is to increase the organization's effectiveness, service, and bottom line."

Tip #9

It's the small things that are the killers, in a job interview. Okay, you're in the interview. You're ready with your carefully rehearsed summary of your experience, skills, and knowledges. *But the employer isn't listening.* Because, sitting across from you, they are noticing things about you, that will kill the interview. And the job offer.

I think of this as losing to mosquitoes when you were prepared to fight dragons. And losing in the first two minutes (*ouch*).

So what's going on? Simply this.

The best of interviewers operate intuitively on the principle of microcosm reveals macrocosm. They believe that what you do in some small "universe" reveals how you would and will act in a larger "universe."

They watch you carefully, during the small universe of the interview, because they assume that each of your behaviors there reveals how you would act in a larger "universe"—like: the job!

They scrutinize your past, as in your resume, for the same reason: *microcosm* (your behavior in the past) *reveals macrocosm* (your likely behavior in the future).

So let us look at what mosquitoes (as it were) can fly in, during the first thirty seconds to two minutes of your interview so that the person-who-has-the-power-to-hire-you starts muttering to themselves, "I sure hope we have some other candidates besides this one":

1. Your appearance and personal habits. Survey after survey has revealed that you are much more likely to get the job if:

- you have obviously freshly bathed; if a male that you have your face freshly shaved or your hair and beard freshly trimmed, have clean fingernails, and are using a deodorant; if a female that you have not got tons of makeup on your face, have had your hair newly cut or styled, have clean or nicely manicured fingernails that don't stick out ten inches from your fingers, are using deodorant, and are not wearing clothes so daring that they call a lot of attention to themselves; and that

- you have on freshly laundered clothes, pants, or pantsuits with a sharp crease, and shoes, not flip-flops, freshly polished; and

- you do not have bad breath, do not dispense the odor of garlic, onion, stale tobacco, or strong drink, into the enclosed office air, but have brushed and flossed your teeth; and equally

- you are not wafting tons of aftershave cologne or overwhelming perfume fifteen feet ahead of you, as you enter the room. Employers are super-sensitive these days to the fact that many of their employees are allergic.

2. Nervous mannerisms. It is a turnoff for many employers if:

- you continually avoid eye contact with the employer (in fact, this is a big, big no-no), or

- you give a limp handshake, or

- you slouch in your chair, or endlessly fidget with your hands, or crack your knuckles, or constantly play with your hair during the interview.

3. **Lack of self-confidence.** It is a turnoff for many employers if:

- you are speaking so softly you cannot be heard, or so loudly you can be heard two rooms away, or
- you are giving answers in an extremely hesitant fashion, or
- you are giving only one-word answers (no, yes, maybe, not yet, I think so) to all the employer's questions, or
- you are constantly interrupting the employer, or
- you are downplaying your achievements or abilities, or are continuously being self-critical in comments you make about yourself during the interview.

4. **The consideration you show to other people.** It is a turnoff for many employers if:

- you show a lack of courtesy to the receptionist, secretary, and (if at lunch) to the waiter or waitress, or
- you display extreme criticalness toward your previous employers and places of work, or
- you drink strong stuff during the interview process. Ordering a drink if the employer takes you to lunch is always a no-no, as it raises the question in the employer's mind, *"Do they normally stop with one, or do they normally keep on going?"* Don't . . . do . . . it! . . . even if they do; or
- you forget to thank the interviewer as you're leaving, or forget to send a thank-you note afterward. Says one human resources expert: *"A prompt, brief... letter thanking me for my time along with a (brief!) synopsis of his/her unique qualities communicates to me that this person is an assertive, motivated, customer-service-oriented salesperson who utilizes technology and knows the rules of the 'game.' These are qualities I am looking for. . . . At the moment I receive approximately one such letter . . . for every fifteen candidates interviewed."*

5. Your values. It is a complete turnoff for many employers, if they see in you:

- any sign of arrogance or excessive aggressiveness; any sign of tardiness or failure to keep appointments and commitments on time, including this interview; or
- any sign of laziness or lack of motivation; or
- any sign of constant complaining or blaming things on others; or
- any signs of dishonesty or lying—especially on your resume or during the interview; or
- any signs of irresponsibility or tendency to goof off; or
- any sign of not following instructions or obeying rules; or
- any sign of a lack of enthusiasm for this organization and what it is trying to do; or
- any sign of instability, inappropriate response, and the like; or
- the other ways in which you evidence your values, such as: what things impress you or don't impress you in their office; or what you are willing to sacrifice in order to get this job and what you are not willing to sacrifice in order to get this job; or your enthusiasm for work; or the carefulness with which you did or didn't research this company before you came in; and blah, blah, blah.
- Incidentally, many an employer will watch to see if you smoke, either in the office or at lunch. In a race between two equally qualified people, the nonsmoker will win out over the smoker 94% of the time, according to a study done by a professor of business at Seattle University. Sorry to report this, but there it is!

So, there you have it: these are the *metaphorical* mosquitoes that can kill you, when you're on the watch for dragons, during the hiring-interview.

One favor I ask of you: do not write me, telling me how picayune or asinine some of this is. I know that. I'm not reporting the world *as it should be*, and certainly not *as I would like it to be*. I'm only reporting what study after study has revealed about the world *as it is*. And how it affects your chances of getting hired.

But here's the good news, when all is said and done: you can kill all these mosquitoes. Yes, you control and can change every one of these factors. Go back and read the list and see!

Tip #10

Be aware of the skills most employers are looking for, these days, regardless of the position you are seeking.
They are looking for employees:

- who are punctual, arriving at work on time or better yet, early; who stay until quitting time, or even leave late;
- who are dependable;
- who have a good attitude;
- who have drive, energy, and enthusiasm;
- who want more than a paycheck;
- who are self-disciplined, well-organized, highly motivated, and good at managing their time;
- who can handle people well;
- who can use language effectively;
- who can work on a computer;
- who are committed to teamwork;
- who are flexible, and can respond to novel situations, or adapt when circumstances at work change;
- who are trainable, and love to learn;
- who are project-oriented, and goal-oriented;
- who have creativity and are good at problem solving;
- who have integrity;
- who are loyal to the organization; and
- who are able to identify opportunities, markets, and coming trends.

So, plan on claiming all of these that you **legitimately** can, and prior to the interview, sit down, make a list, and jot down some experience you have had, for each, that proves you have that skill.

Tip #11

Try to think of some way to bring evidence of your skills, to the hiring-interview. For example, if you are an artist, a craftsperson, or anyone who produces a product, try to bring a sample of what you have made or produced—in scrapbook or portfolio form, on a flashdrive, on YouTube, in photos, or if you are a programmer, examples of your code. And so on.

Tip #12

Do not bad-mouth your previous employer(s) during the interview, even if they were terrible people. Employers sometimes feel as though they are a fraternity or sorority. During the interview you want to come across as one who displays courtesy toward *all* members of that fraternity or sorority. Bad-mouthing a previous employer only makes this employer who is interviewing you, worry about what you would say about *them*, after they hire you.

(I learned this in my own experience. I once spoke graciously about a previous employer during a job-interview. Unbeknownst to me, the interviewer already knew that my previous employer had badly mistreated me. He therefore thought very highly of me because I didn't bad-mouth the guy. In fact, he never forgot this incident; talked about it for years afterward.)

Plan on saying something nice about any previous employer, or if you are pretty sure that the fact you and they didn't get along will surely come out, then try to nullify this ahead of time, by saying something simple like, "I usually get along with everybody; but for some reason, my past employer and I just didn't get along. Don't know why. It's never happened to me before. Hope it never happens again."

Tip #13

Throughout the interview, keep in mind: employers don't really care about your past; they only ask about it, in order to try to predict your future (behavior) with them, if they decide to hire you. They have fears, of course; don't we all?

Legally, U.S. employers may only ask you questions that are related to the requirements and expectations of the job. They cannot ask about such things as your creed, religion, race, age, sexual orientation, or marital status. But, any other questions about your past are *fair game*. And they *will* ask them, if they know what they're doing.

Therefore, during the hiring-interview, before you answer any question the employer asks you about your past, you should pause to think, "What fear about the *future* caused them to ask this question about my past?" and then address *that fear*, obliquely or directly.

Here are some *examples*:

Employer's Question	The Fear Behind the Question	The Point You Try to Get Across	Phrases You Might Use to Get This Across
"Tell me about yourself."	The employer is afraid he/she isn't going to conduct a very good interview, by failing to ask the right questions. Or is afraid there is something wrong with you, and is hoping you will blurt it out.	You are a good employee, as you have proved in the past at your other jobs. (Give the briefest history of who you are, where born and raised, interests, hobbies, and kind of work you have enjoyed the most to date.) Keep it to two minutes, max.	In describing your work history, use any honest phrases you can about your work history, that are self-complimentary: "Hard worker." "Came in early, left late." "Always did more than was expected of me." Etc.

Employer's Question	The Fear Behind the Question	The Point You Try to Get Across	Phrases You Might Use to Get This Across
"What kind of work are you looking for?"	The employer is afraid that you are looking for a different job than that which the employer is trying to fill. E.g., he/she wants an assistant, but you want to be an office supervisor, etc.	You are looking for precisely the kind of work the employer is offering (but don't say that, if it isn't true). Repeat back to the employer, in your own words, what he/she has said about the job, and emphasize the skills you have to do that.	If the employer hasn't described the job at all, say, "I'd be happy to answer that, but first I need to understand exactly what kind of work this job involves." Then answer, as at left.
"Have you ever done this kind of work before?"	The employer is afraid you don't possess the necessary skills and experience to do this job.	You have skills that are transferable, from whatever you used to do; and you did it well.	"I pick up stuff very quickly." "I have quickly mastered any job I have ever done."
"Why did you leave your last job?"—or "How did you get along with your former boss and co-workers?"	The employer is afraid you don't get along well with people, especially bosses, and is just waiting for you to "bad-mouth" your previous boss or co-workers, as proof of that.	Say whatever positive things you possibly can about your former boss and co-workers (without telling lies). Emphasize you usually get along very well with people—and then let your gracious attitude toward your previous boss(es) and co-workers prove it, right before this employer's very eyes (and ears).	If you left voluntarily: "My boss and I both felt I would be happier and more effective in a job where [here describe your strong points, such as] I would have more room to use my initiative and creativity." If you were fired: "Usually, I get along well with everyone, but in this particular case the boss and I just didn't get along with each other. Difficult to say why." You don't need to say anything more than that. If you were laid off and your job wasn't filled after you left: "My job was terminated."

Employer's Question	The Fear Behind the Question	The Point You Try to Get Across	Phrases You Might Use to Get This Across
"How is your health?"—or "How much were you absent from work during your last job?"	The employer is afraid you will be absent from work a lot, if they hire you. Unfortunately for them, and fortunately for you, this is a question they cannot legally ask you.	Just because the question is illegal, doesn't mean you can't address their hidden fear. Even if they never mention it, you can try to disarm that fear.	You can find a way to say, "My productivity always exceeded other workers, in my previous jobs."
"Can you explain why you've been out of work so long?"—or "Can you tell me why there are these gaps in your work history?" (Usually said after studying your resume.)	The employer is afraid that you are the kind of person who quits a job the minute he/she doesn't like something at it; in other words, that you have no "stick-to-it-iveness."	You love to work, and you regard times when things aren't going well as challenges, which you enjoy learning how to conquer.	"During the gaps in my work record, I was studying/doing volunteer work/doing some hard thinking about my mission in life/finding redirection." (Choose one.)
"Wouldn't this job represent a step down for you?"—or "I think this job would be way beneath your talents and experience."—or "Don't you think you would be underemployed if you took this job?"	The employer is afraid you could command a bigger salary, somewhere else, and will therefore leave him/her as soon as something better turns up.	You will stick with this job as long as you and the employer agree this is where you should be.	"This job isn't a step down for me. It's a step up—from welfare." "We have mutual fears; every employer is afraid a good employee will leave too soon, and every employee is afraid the employer might fire him/her, for no good reason." "I like to work, and I give my best to every job I've ever had."
And, last, "Tell me, what is your greatest weakness?"	The employer is afraid you have some character flaw, and hopes you will now rashly blurt it out, or confess it.	You have limitations just like anyone else, but you work constantly to improve yourself and be a more and more effective worker.	Mention a weakness and then stress its positive aspect, e.g., "I don't like to be over-supervised, because I have a great deal of initiative, and I like to anticipate problems before they even arise."

Tip #14

As the interview proceeds, you want to quietly notice the time-frame of the questions the employer is asking, because it's a way of measuring how the interview is going. If it's going favorably for you, the timeframe of the employer's questions will often move—*however slowly*—through the following stages.

1. Distant past: *e.g., "Where did you attend high school?"*

2. Immediate past: *e.g., "Tell me about your most recent job."*

3. Present: *e.g., "What kind of a job are you looking for?"*

4. Immediate future: *e.g., "Would you be able to come back for another interview next week?"*

5. Distant future: *e.g., "Where would you like to be five years from now?"*

Well, you get the point. The more the timeframe of the interviewer's questions moves from the past to the future, the more favorably you may assume the interview is going for you. On the other hand, if the interviewer's questions stay firmly in the past, the outlook is not so good. *Ah well, ya can't win them all!*

When the timeframe of the interviewer's questions moves firmly into the future, *then* is the time for you to get more specific about the job in question. Experts say it is essential for you to ask, at that point, these kinds of questions, *if* you don't already know the answers:

- What is the job, specifically, that I am being considered for?

- If I were hired, what duties would I be performing?

- What would you be hiring me to accomplish?

- What responsibilities would I have?

- Would I be working with a team, or group?

- To whom would I report? *(Remember, the communication skills and personal warmth of an employee's supervisor are often crucial in determining the employee's tenure and performance. In fact, recent research shows that the quality of the supervisor may be more important than the experience and individual attributes of the workers themselves.)*

- Whose responsibility is it to see that I get the training I need, here, to get up to speed?

- How would I be evaluated, how often, and by whom?

- What were the strengths and weaknesses of previous people in this position?

- May I meet the persons I would be working with and for (if it isn't you)?

- (Optional) If you don't mind my asking, I'm curious as to why *you* yourself decided to work at this organization?

- (Optional) What do you wish you had known about this company before you started here?

Tip #15

Before you leave the (final) interview there, assuming you have decided that you like them and maybe they like you, there are five questions you should always ask:

1. **"Can you offer me this job?"** I know this seems stupid, but it is astonishing (at least to me) how many job-hunters have secured a job simply by being bold enough to ask for it, at the end of the (final) interview, in language they feel comfortable with. I don't know why this is. I only know that it is. Anyway, if after hearing all about this job at this place, you decide you'd really like to have it, you must ask for it. The worst thing the employer can say is "No," or "We need some time to think about all the interviews we're conducting."

2. **"When may I expect to hear from you?"** If the employer says, "We need some time to think about this," or "We will be calling you for another interview," you don't want to leave this as a vague good intention on the employer's part. You want to nail it down.

3. "Might I ask what would be the latest I can expect to hear from you?" The employer has probably given you their best guess, in answer to your previous question. Now you want to know: what is the worst-case scenario? Incidentally, when I was job-hunting once, and I asked my interviewer when was the latest I might expect to hear from him, he replied, "Never!" I thought he had a great sense of humor. Turned out he was dead serious.

4. "May I contact you after that date, if for any reason you haven't gotten back to me by that time?" Some employers resent this question. You'll know that is the case if they snap at you. But most employers appreciate your offering them what is in essence a safety net. They know they can get busy, become overwhelmed with other things, forget their promise to you. It's reassuring, in such a case, for you to offer to rescue them.

5. (Optional) "Can you think of anyone else who might be interested in my skills and experience?" This question is invoked only if they replied "No," to your first question, above.

Jot down any answers they give you, then stand up, thank them sincerely for their time, give a firm handshake, and leave.

In the following days, rigorously keep to all that you said, and don't contact them except with that mandatory thank-you note, until after the latest deadline you two agreed upon, in answer to question #4. If you do have to contact them after that date, and if they tell you things are still up in the air, you should gently ask questions #2, #3, and #4, all over again.

Tip #16

Every expert on interviewing will tell you two things:

1. **Thank-you notes must be sent after every interview, by every job-hunter; and**

2. **Most job-hunters ignore this advice.**

Indeed, it is safe to say that it is the most overlooked step in the entire job-hunting process.

If you want to stand out from the others applying for the same job, send thank-you notes—to everyone you met there, that day. Ask if they have a business card, and if not, ask them to write out their name and address. Do this with secretaries (who often hold the keys to the kingdom) as well as with your interviewer.

If you need any additional encouragement to send thank-you letters (besides the fact that it may get you the job), here are six more reasons for sending a thank-you note, especially to the one who interviewed you:

First, you were presenting yourself as one who has good skills with people. Your actions with respect to the job-interview must back this claim up. Sending a thank-you note does that. The employer can see you are good with people; you remembered to thank them.

Second, it helps the employer recall who you are. Very helpful if they've seen a dozen people that day.

Third, if a committee will be involved in the hiring process, but only one member was at the first interview, the man or woman who first interviewed you has something to show the others on the committee.

Fourth, if the interview went rather well, and the employer seemed to show an interest in further talks, the thank-you note can reiterate your interest in further talks.

Fifth, the thank-you note gives you an opportunity to correct any wrong impression you left behind. You can add anything you forgot to tell them, that you want them to know. And from among all the things you two discussed, you can underline the two or three points that you most want to stand out in their minds.

Lastly, if the interview did not go well, or you lost all interest in working there, and this thank-you note is sort of "goodbye, and thanks," keep in mind that they may hear of openings elsewhere, that would be of interest to you. In the thank-you note, you can mention this, and ask them to please let you know if they hear of anything anywhere. If this was a kind man or woman who interviewed you, they may send you additional leads.

Conclusion

Hopefully, with these tips you will do well in your interviews. And if you do get hired, make one resolution to yourself right there, on the spot: plan to keep track of your accomplishments at this new job, on a weekly basis—jotting them down, every weekend, in your own private log. Career experts recommend you do this without fail. You can then summarize these accomplishments annually on a one-page sheet, for your boss's eyes, when the question of a raise or promotion comes up.

But despite all your careful preparation, and all your thoughtful questions, you may not be offered the job. Bummer!

I remind you of what I said earlier: the hiring process is more like choosing a mate, than it is like deciding whether or not to buy a car. "Choosing a mate" here is a metaphor. To elaborate upon the metaphor just a bit, it means that the mechanisms by which human nature decides to hire someone, are similar to the mechanisms by which human nature decides whether or not to marry someone. Those mechanisms, of course, are often impulsive, intuitive, nonrational, unfathomable, made on the spur of the moment, and—sometimes—just plain crazy.

There is no magic in job-hunting. No techniques work all the time. I hear regularly from job-hunters who report that they paid attention to all the tips I have mentioned in this chapter and the book, and are quite skilled at securing interviews—but they never get hired. And they want to know what they're doing wrong.

Well, unfortunately, the answer sometimes is: "Maybe you're doing nothing wrong." I don't know how often this happens, but I know it does happen: namely, some employers play despicable tricks on job-hunters, whereby they invite you in for an interview despite the fact that they have already hired someone for the position in question, and they know from the beginning that they have absolutely no intention of hiring you—not in a million years!

You are cheered, of course, by the ease with which you get these interviews. But unbeknownst to you, the manager who is interviewing you (we'll say it's a he) has a personal friend he already agreed to give the job to. Only one small problem remains: the state or the federal government gives funds to this organization, and has mandated that this position be opened to all. So this manager must pretend to interview ten candidates, including his favorite, as though the job opening were still available. But, he intended, from the beginning, to reject the other nine and give the job to his favorite. You were selected for the honor of being among those nine rejectees.

You will, of course, be baffled as to why you got turned down. Trouble is, you will never know.

On the other hand, maybe no games are being played. You are getting rejected, at place after place, because there is something really wrong with the way you are coming across, during these hiring-interviews.

Employers will rarely ever tell you this. You will never hear them say something like, "You came across as just too cocky and arrogant during the interview." You will almost always be left in the dark as to what it is you're doing wrong.

If you feel daring, there is a strategy you can try. If you've been interviewed by a whole bunch of employers, whoever was the friendliest of them all may want to help you. I said *may*.

You can always try phoning, reminding them of who you are, and then asking the following question—deliberately kept generalized, vague, unrelated to just that place, and above all, future-directed. Something like: *"I'd appreciate some advice. I've been on several interviews at several different places now. From what you've seen, is there something about me in an interview, that you think might be causing me not to get hired at those places? If so, I'd really appreciate your giving me some pointers so I can do better in my future hiring-interviews."*

Most of the time they'll duck. Their legal advisor, if they have one, will certainly advise against it. First of all, they're afraid of lawsuits. Second, they don't know how you will use what they might have to say. (Said an old military veteran to me one day, *"I used to think it was my duty to tell everyone the truth. Now I only give it to those who can use it."*)

But occasionally you will run into a compassionate and kind employer who is willing to risk giving you the truth, because they think you will use it wisely. If so, thank them from the bottom of your heart, no matter how painful their feedback is. Such advice, seriously heeded, can bring about just the changes in your interviewing strategy that you most need, in order to win during interviews in the future.

In the absence of any such help from employers who interviewed you, you might want to get a good business friend of yours to role-play a mock hiring-interview with you, in case they immediately see something glaringly wrong with how you're "coming across."

When all else fails, I would recommend you go to a career coach who charges by the hour, and put yourself in their tender knowledgeable hands. Role-play an interview with them, and take their advice seriously (you've just paid for it, after all).

In interviewing, as elsewhere in your job hunt, the secret is to find out anything that is within your control, even if it's only 2%; and change it!

THE TEN COMMANDMENTS
FOR JOB-INTERVIEWS

Whereby Your Chances of Finding a Job Are Vastly Increased

I. Go after new small organizations with twenty or fewer employees, at first, since they create two-thirds of all new jobs. Only if you turn up nothing should you broaden the search to slightly larger organizations, those with fifty employees, then if that doesn't prove to be a successful strategy, organizations with one hundred employees.

II. Hunt for places to interview using the aid of, say, eighty friends and acquaintances—because a job-hunt requires eighty pairs of eyes and ears. But first do homework on yourself so you can tell them exactly what you are looking for. (This is discussed further in chapter 7.)

III. As for who to interview, once you've identified a place that interests you, you really need to find out who has the power to hire you there, for the position you want, and use "bridge-people" (those who know you and also know them) to get an introduction to that person. Employ LinkedIn.com and similar, to find these people. (See chapter 8.)

IV. Do thorough homework on an organization before going there, using Informational Interviews (see chapter 8) plus the Internet to find out as much about them as you possibly can. If you have a public library in town, ask there too.

V. Then prepare for the interview with your own agenda, your own questions and curiosities about whether or not this job fits you. This will always impress employers.

VI. If you initiated the appointment, ask for just nineteen minutes of their time; and keep to your word strictly. Watch your watch.

VII. When answering a question of theirs, talk only between twenty seconds to two minutes, at any one time. Try to be succinct. Don't keep rattling on, out of nervousness.

VIII. Basically approach them not as a "job-beggar" but humbly as a resource person, able to produce better work for that organization than any of the people who worked in that position, previously.

IX. At the end of the interviewing process, ask for the job: "Given all that we have discussed, can you offer me this job?" Salary negotiation should only happen when they have definitely said they want you; prior to that, it's pointless.

X. Always write a thank-you note the same evening as the interview, and mail it at the latest by early next morning. This in addition to e-mailing it. The tendency these days is for job-hunters to only e-mail a thank-you note. You will stand out from the others if you do both.

Students spend four or more years
Learning how to dig data out of the library
And other sources.
But it rarely occurs to them
That they should also apply
Some of the same newfound research skill
To their own benefit—
To looking up information on companies,
Types of professions, sections of the country,
That might interest them.

> —*Professor Albert Shapiro, Ohio State University*
> *(d. 1985)*

Chapter 5

The Six Secrets of Salary Negotiation

"You choose your own salary here. Would you care to work at: 1. No risk; 2. Some risk; 3. High risk; or 4. Are-you-sure-you-want-to-do-this?"

Salary.

It must be discussed, before you agree to take the job.

I hope you know that. I remember talking to a breathless high school graduate, who was elated at having just landed her first job. "How much are they going to pay you?" I asked. She looked startled. "I don't know," she said, "I never asked. I just assume they will pay me a fair wage." Boy! Did she get a rude awakening when she received her first paycheck. It was so miserably low, she couldn't believe her eyes. And thus did she learn, painfully, what you must learn too: Before accepting a job offer, *always* ask about salary.

Indeed, ask and then negotiate.

It's the "negotiate" that throws fear into our hearts. So many of us feel ill prepared to do that.

Well, set your mind at ease; it's not all that difficult.

While whole books can be—and have been—written on this subject, there are basically just six secrets to keep in mind.

The First Secret of Salary Negotiation

Never Discuss Salary Until the End of the Whole Interviewing Process at That Organization, When (and If) They Have Definitely Said They Want You

"The end of the interviewing process" is difficult to define. It's the point at which the employer says, or thinks, "We've got to get this person!" That may be at the end of the first (and therefore the last) interview; or it may be at the end of a whole series of interviews, often with different people within the same company or organization, or with a whole bunch of them all at once.

But assuming things are going favorably for you, whether after the first, or second, or third, or fourth interview, *if you like them* and they increasingly like you, a job offer will be made. Then, and only then, is it time to deal with the question that is inevitably on any employer's mind: *how much is this person going to cost me?* And the question that is on your mind: *how much does this job pay?*

If the employer raises the salary question earlier, say near the beginning of the interview, asking (innocently), *"What kind of salary are you looking for?"* you should have three responses ready—at your fingertips.

Response #1: If the employer seems like a kindly man or woman, your best and most tactful reply might be: *"Until you've decided you definitely want me, and I've decided I definitely could help you with your tasks or projects here, I feel any discussion of salary is premature."*

That will work, in most cases. There are instances, however, where that doesn't work. Then you need:

Response #2: You may be face-to-face with an employer who demands within the first two minutes of the interview to know what salary you are looking for. That is not good, especially since 2008, as some employers can afford to be really picky, since—in their minds—there is a plentiful bunch of job-hunters to choose from. So, here, you may need a backup response, such as: *"I'll gladly answer that, but could you first help me understand what this job involves?"*

That is a good response, in most cases. But what if it doesn't work? Then you'll need to fall back on:

Response #3: The employer with rising voice says, *"Come, come, don't play games with me. I want to know what salary you're looking for."* Okay, that's that. You have to come clean. But you don't have to mention a single figure; instead you can answer in terms of *a range.* For example, *"I'm looking for a salary in the range of $35,000 to $45,000 a year."*

If that still doesn't satisfy them, then clearly you are being interviewed by an employer who has no range in mind. Their beginning figure is their ending figure. No negotiation is possible.[1] This happens, when it does, because many employers since 2008 are making salary their major if not sole criterion for deciding who to hire, and who not to hire. It's an old game: among two equally qualified candidates, the one who is willing to work for the least pay, wins. And *that* is *that!*

If you run into this situation, you may decide this isn't the kind of place you want to work at, for if they're inflexible in this, what else will they be inflexible about, once you take the job? You've been warned. Microcosm equals macrocosm.

On the other hand, if you're flat broke and you need this job—any job—desperately, you will have no choice but to give in. Ask what salary they have in mind, and make your decision. (Of course you can always try postponing your decision a day or so, by saying, "I need a little time, to think about this.")

However, all the foregoing is merely the worst-case scenario. Usually, things won't go this badly, where you feel so powerless.

In most interviews these days, the employer, alone or in a group, *will* be willing to save salary negotiation until they've finally decided they want you (and you've decided you want them). And at that point, the salary will be negotiable. I'll explain *why* in the next Secret.

---

1. One job-hunter said his interviews *always* began with the salary question, and no matter what he answered, that ended the interview. Turned out, this job-hunter was doing all the interviewing over the phone. That was the problem. Once he went face to face, salary was no longer the first thing discussed in the interview.

For now, let me hammer home this first Secret: it is in your best interest to *not* discuss salary until all of the following conditions have been fulfilled:

- Not until they've gotten to know you, at your best, so they can see how you stand out above the other applicants, and therefore how you're worth more than they would pay *them*.
- Not until you've gotten to know them, as completely as you can, so you can tell if this really is a place where you want to work.
- Not until you've found out exactly what the job entails.
- Not until they've had a chance to find out how well you match their job requirements.
- Not until you're in the final interview at that place, for that job.
- Not until you've decided, "I *really* would like to work here."
- Not until they've conveyed to you their feelings, such as: "Well that's good, because we want you." Or, better yet:
- Not until they've conveyed the feeling, "We've *got* to have you."

If you'd prefer this be put in the form of a diagram, here it is:

WHEN TO NEGOTIATE SALARY

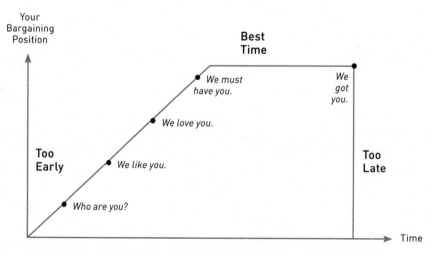

It all boils down to this: if you really shine during the hiring-interview, they may—at the end—offer you a higher salary than they originally had in mind when the interview started. And this is particularly the case when the interview has gone so well, that they're now *determined* to obtain you. .

The Second Secret of Salary Negotiation

The Purpose of Salary Negotiation Is to Uncover the Most That an Employer Is Willing to Pay to Get You

Negotiation. There's the word that strikes terror into the hearts of most job-hunters or career-changers. Why do we have to negotiate?

Simple. It would never be necessary if every employer in every hiring-interview were to mention, right from the start, the top figure they are willing to pay for that position. A few employers do. And that's the end of any salary negotiation. But most employers don't.

They know, from the beginning of the interview, the top figure they're willing to pay for this position under discussion. But. But. They're hoping they'll be able to get you for less. So they *start* the bidding (*for that is what it is*) lower than they're ultimately willing to go.

And this creates a range.

A range between the lowest they're hoping to pay, vs. the highest they can afford to pay. And that range is what the negotiation is all about.

For example, if the employer can afford to pay you $30 an hour, but wants to try to get you for $18 an hour, the range is $18–$30.

You have every right to try to negotiate the highest salary that employer is willing to pay you, *within that range*.

Nothing's wrong with the goals of either of you. The employer's goal is to save money, if possible. Your goal is to bring home to your own household the most money that you can, for the work you will be doing.

The Third Secret of Salary Negotiation

During Salary Discussion, Never Be the First One to Mention a Salary Figure

Where salary negotiation has been successfully kept offstage for much of the interview process, when it finally does come up, you want the employer to be the first one to mention a figure, if you possibly can.

Why? Nobody knows. But it has been observed over the years that where the goals are opposite, as in this case—you are trying to get the employer to pay the most they can, and the employer is trying to pay the least they can—whoever mentions a salary figure first, generally loses. You can speculate from now until the cows come home, as to why this is so. There are a dozen theories. All we really know for sure is that it is true.

Inexperienced employer/interviewers often don't know this strange rule. But experienced ones are very aware of it. That's why they will try to get you to mention a figure first, by asking you some innocent-sounding question, like: *"What kind of salary are you looking for?"*

Well, how kind of them to ask me what I want—you may be thinking. No, no, no. Kindness has nothing to do with it. They are hoping you will be the first to mention a figure, because they know this summary of ten thousand interviews in the past: whoever mentions a salary figure first, generally loses the negotiation, in the end.

Accordingly, if they ask you to be the first to name a figure, the simple countermove you should have at the ready, is: *"Well, you created this position, so you must have some figure in mind, and I'd be interested in first hearing what that figure is."*

The Fourth Secret of Salary Negotiation

Before You Go to the Interview, Do Some Careful Research on Typical Salaries for Your Field and in That Organization

As I said, salary negotiation is required anytime the employer does not open the discussion of salary by naming the top figure they have in mind, but starts instead with a lower figure.

Okay, so here is the $64,000 question: how do you tell whether the figure the employer first offers you is only their starting bid, or is their final final offer? The answer is: by doing some research on the field and that organization, before you ever go in for an interview.

Oh, come on! I can hear you say. *Isn't this more trouble than it's worth?* No, it's not. If you want to win the salary negotiation. There is a financial penalty exacted from those who are too lazy, or in too much of a hurry, to go gather this information. In plain language: if you don't do this research, it'll cost ya!

Let's say it takes you from one to three days to run down this sort of information on the three or four organizations that interest you the most. And let us say that because you've done this research, when you finally come to the end of the final interview for a job there, you are able to ask for and obtain a salary that is—oh, let's say— $15,000 a year *higher* than you would otherwise have gotten. (That's not unrealistic.)

In the next three years, then, you will be earning $45,000 extra because of your salary research. Not bad pay, for just one to three days' work! And it can be even more.

It doesn't always happen; but I know many job-hunters and career-changers to whom it has. It's certainly worth a shot.

Okay, then, how do you do this research? Well, there are two ways to go: online, and off. Let's look at each, in turn.

Salary Research Online

If you have access to the Internet—at home or at your library or at an Internet café[2]—and you want to research salaries for particular geographical regions, positions, occupations, or industries, or even (sometimes) organizations, here are some free sites that may give you just what you're looking for:

- http://jobstar.org/tools/salary/index.cfm: This site is a treasure trove. It links to 300 different sites that maintain salary lists, and joy, joy, it is kept updated. It's one of the largest and most complete lists of salary reviews on the Web, maintained by a genius named Mary Ellen Mort. This is a treasure.

- www.salary.com: The most visited of all the salary-specific job-sites, with a wide variety of information about salaries. It was started by Kent Plunkett, and acquired by Kenexa Corporation in August 2010. It has expanded a lot, over the years. Roll over the green navigation bar at the top to see all its resources.

- www.bls.gov/ooh: The Bureau of Labor Statistics' survey of salaries in individual occupations, from the *Occupational Outlook Handbook* 2012–2013. It lists jobs that are highest paying, and/or jobs that are the fastest growing, and/or jobs that have the highest number of openings.

- http://stats.bls.gov/oes/oes_emp.htm: The Bureau of Labor Statistics' survey of salaries in individual industries (it's a companion piece to the *Occupational Outlook Handbook*). Over a period of three years, it surveys 1.2 million establishments to get their figures.

- MyPlan.com: This site has a list of the 300 highest-paying jobs in America for those without a college degree, found at http://tinyurl.com/bo2a7so.

- www.salaryexpert.com: When you need a salary expert, it makes sense to go to "the Salary Expert." Lots of stuff on the subject of salaries here, including a free "Salary Report" for hundreds of job-titles, varying by area, skill level, and experience.

---

2. For a directory of Internet cafes around the world, see www.cybercafes.com.

It also has some salary calculators. I find the site a little complicated to navigate, but maybe that's just me.

If you "strike out" on all the above sites, then you're going to have to get a little more clever, and work a little harder, and pound the pavement, as I shall describe next.

Salary Research off the Internet

Okay, so how do you do salary research offline? Well, there's a simple rule: *generally speaking, abandon books, and go talk to people.*

Use books and libraries only as a second, or last, resort. You can get much more complete and up-to-date information from people who are doing the kind of job you're interested in, maybe at another company or organization than the one(s) you're interested in.

If you don't know where to find them, talk to people at a nearby university or college who train such people, whatever their department may be. Teachers and professors will usually know what their graduates are making. Also you can go visit actual workplaces.

Let's look at some concrete examples:

First Example: A fast food place. You may not need to do any salary research. They pay what they pay. You can walk in, ask for a job application, and interview with the hiring manager. He or she will usually tell you the pay, outright. It's usually set in concrete. But at least it's easy to discover what the pay is. (*Incidentally, filling out an application, or even having an interview there, doesn't mean you have to take that job—but you probably already know that. Just say, "I need to go home and think about this." You can decline any offer from any place. That's what makes this approach harmless.*)

Second Example: A construction company. This is typical of a place where you can't discover what the pay is, right off the bat. If you're actually going to try to get work at that construction company but you want to research salaries before you go for an interview, the best way to do this research is to go visit a different construction company in the same town or geographical area—one that isn't of much interest to you—and ask what *people* make *there*. Or, if you don't know who to talk to there, fill out one of their applications, and talk to the hiring person about what kinds of jobs they have (or might have in the future)—at which time prospective wages is a legitimate subject of inquiry. Then, having done this research on a place you don't care about, go back to the place that really interests you, and apply. You still don't know exactly what they pay, but you do know what their competitor pays— which will usually be close to what you're trying to find out.

Third Example: A one-person office (besides the boss, obviously), working say as an administrative assistant. Here you can often find useful salary information by perusing the Help Wanted ads in the local newspaper for a week or two, assuming you still have a local paper! Most of the ads won't mention a salary figure, but a few may. Among those that do, note what the lowest salary offering is, and what the highest is, and see if the ad reveals any reasons for the difference. It's interesting how much you can learn about administrative assistants' salaries, with this approach. I know, because I was an administrative assistant myself, once upon a time.

There's a lot you can find out by talking to people. But another way to do salary research—if you're out of work and have time on your hands—is to find a Temporary Work Agency that places different kinds of workers, and let yourself be farmed out to various organizations: the more, the merrier. It's relatively easy to do salary research when you're inside a place. (Study what that place pays the agency, not what the agency pays you after they've taken their "cut.") If you're working temporarily at a place where the other workers really like you, you'll be able to ask questions about a lot of things there, including salary.

The Fifth Secret of Salary Negotiation

Research the Range That the Employer Likely Has in Mind, and Then Define an Interrelated Range for Yourself, Relative to the Employer's Range

Okay, I admit this is a bit sophisticated, and you may not have the stomach to do this much research. But you ought to at least know how this works. It begins by defining your goal, here.

What you want, in your research, is not just one salary figure. As you may recall, you want *a range*: a range defined by what's the least the employer may offer you, and what's the most the employer may be willing to pay to get you. In any organization that has more than five employees, that range is comparatively easy to figure out. It will be less than what the person who would be above you makes, and more than what the person who would be below you makes. Examples:

If the Person Who Would Be Below You Makes	And the Person Who Would Be Above You Makes	The Range for Your Job Would Be
$45,000	$55,000	$47,000–$53,000
$30,000	$35,500	$32,500–$34,000

One teensy-tiny little problem here: how do you find out the salary of those who would be above and below you? Well, first you have to find out their names or the names of their positions.

If it is a small organization you are going after—one with twenty or fewer employees—finding out this information should be easy. Any employee who works there is likely to know the answer, and you can usually get in touch with one of those employees, or even an ex-employee, through your own personal "bridge-people"—people who know you and also know them. Since up to two-thirds of all new jobs are created by small companies of this size, that's the kind of organization you are likely to be researching, anyway.

On the other hand, if you are going after a larger organization, then you fall back on a familiar life preserver, namely *every* person you know (family, friend, relative, business, or spiritual acquaintance) and ask them who they know that might know the company in question, and therefore, the information you seek. LinkedIn should prove immensely helpful to you here, in locating such people. If you're not already on it, get on it. (www.LinkedIn.com.)

Maybe this will be easy. Maybe it won't be: it's possible you'll run into an absolute blank wall at a particular organization (everyone who works there is pledged to secrecy, and they have shipped all their ex-employees to Siberia). In that case, seek out information *on their nearest competitor* in the same geographic area. For example, let us say you were trying to find out managerial salaries at Bank X, and that place was proving to be inscrutable about what they pay their managers. You would then turn to Bank Y as your research base, to see if the information is easier to come by, there. And if it is, you can assume the two may be basically similar in their pay scales, and that what you learned about Bank Y is probably applicable to Bank X.

Note: In your salary research take note of the fact that most governmental agencies have civil service positions paralleling those in private industry—and government job descriptions and pay ranges are available to the public. Go to the nearest city, county, regional, state, or federal civil service office, find the job description nearest the kind of job you are seeking in private industry, and then ask the starting salary.

When this is all done, if you want to be a true expert at this game then you're going to have to do a little bit of math, here.

Suppose you guess that the employer's range for the kind of job you're seeking is $36,500 to $47,200. Before you go in for the interview, anywhere, you figure out an "asking" range for yourself, that you're going to use when and if the interview gets to the salary negotiation part. This asking range is clever, in that it should "hook in" just below that employer's maximum, and then go up from there. This diagram shows you how this works:

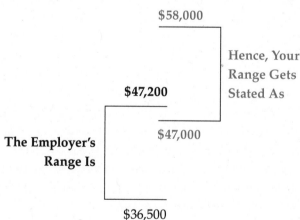

$58,000

Hence, Your
Range Gets
$47,200   Stated As

$47,000

**The Employer's
Range Is**

$36,500

And so, when the employer has stated a figure (probably around their lowest—i.e., $36,500), you will be ready to respond with something along these lines: *"I understand, of course, the constraints under which all organizations are operating these days, but I am confident that my productivity is going to be such, that it will justify a salary"*—and here you mention the range above, where your bottom figure starts just below the top of their range, and goes up from there—*"in the range of $47,000 to $58,000."*

It will help a lot during this discussion, if you are prepared to show in what ways you will make money or in what ways you will save money for that organization, such as would justify precisely this higher salary you are asking for. Even if they accept your offer at the bottom of your range, you are still near the top figure they're willing to pay.

Yes, it's clever. Yes, it's risky. Yes, it takes some work. But you're got the brains to pull it off. You've got the brains to be good at this salary negotiation game.

What if, after all the trouble you went to, this just doesn't work? At least, at that place. The employer has a ceiling they have to work with, it's below what you're asking, and you are unwilling to lower your definition of what you're worth?

Daniel Porot, job-expert from Switzerland, suggests that if you're dying to work there, but they cannot afford the salary you need and deserve, you might consider offering them part of your time.

If you need, and believe you deserve, say $50,000 annually, but they can only afford $30,000, you might consider offering them three days a week of your time for that $30,000 (30/50 = 3/5 of a five-day workweek). This leaves you free to take work elsewhere during those other two days. You will of course determine to produce so much work during those three days per week you are there, that they will be ecstatic about this bargain—won't you?

The Sixth Secret of Salary Negotiation

Know How to Bring the Salary Negotiation to a Close; Don't Leave It "Just Hanging"

Salary negotiation with this employer is not finished until you've addressed more than salary. Unless you're an independent contractor, you want to talk about so-called fringe benefits. "Fringes" such as life insurance, health benefits or health plans, vacation or holiday time, and retirement programs typically add anywhere from 15%–28% to many workers' salaries. That is to say, if an employee receives $3,000 salary per week, the fringe benefits are worth another $450 to $840 per week.

So, before you walk into an interview you should decide what benefits are particularly important to you. And then, after the basic salary discussion is settled, you can go on to ask them what benefits they offer there. If you've given this any thought beforehand, you should have already decided what benefits are most important to you, and be ready to fight for *those*.

And when this all is done, the discussion of the job, the finding out if they like you and if you like them, the salary negotiation, and the concluding discussion of benefits, then you want to get everything they're offering summarized, *in writing*. Believe me you do. In writing, or typing, and *signed*.

Many executives unfortunately "forget" what they told you during the hiring-interview, or even deny they ever said such a thing. It shouldn't happen; but it does. Sometimes they honestly forget what they said.

Other times of course, they're playing a game. Or their successor is, who may disown any *unwritten* promises you claim they made to you at the time of hiring. They may respond with, *"I don't know what caused*

them to say that to you, but they clearly exceeded their authority, and of course we can't be held to that."

I repeat: get it all in writing. And signed. It's called a letter of agreement—or employment contract. If it is a small employer (10 or fewer employees) they may not know how to draw one up. Just put the search term "sample letter of agreement between employer and employee" into your favorite search engine, and you'll get lots of free examples. I particularly like the one from Inc.com. You or the employer can write this up. Then they can sign it.

You have every right to ask for this. If they simply won't give it to you, *beware.*

Conclusion: If Nothing Works

Remember, job-hunting always involves luck, to some degree. But with a little bit of luck, and a lot of hard work, and determination, these instructions thus far in this book, should work for you, as they have worked for so many hundreds of thousands before you.[3]

But. This country is so slow to pull out of the 2008 recession. It was a doozy of a recession. It's changed many employers' hiring patterns. It's increased many employers' reluctance to hire. So, you want to know what to do if none of this works, right?

Good. That's what the rest of this book is about.

---

3. Here is a letter from a job-hunter who had great success:

> Before I read this book, I was depressed and lost in the futile job-hunt using Want Ads only. I did not receive even one phone call from any ad I answered, over a total of four months. I felt that I was the most useless person on earth. I am female, with a two-and-a-half-year-old daughter, a former professor in China, with no working experience at all in the U.S. We came here seven months ago because my husband had a job offer here.
>
> Then, on June 11th of last year, I saw your book in a local bookstore. Subsequently, I spent three weeks, ten hours a day except Sunday, reading every single word of your book and doing all of the flower petals in the Flower Exercise. After getting to know myself much better, I felt I was ready to try the job-hunt again. I used Parachute throughout as my guide, from the very beginning to the very end, namely, salary negotiation.
>
> In just two weeks I secured (you guessed it) two job offers, one of which I am taking, as it is an excellent job, with very good pay. It is (you guessed it again) a small company, with twenty or so employees. It is also a career-change: I was a professor of English; now I am to be a controller!
>
> I am so glad I believed your advice: there are jobs out there, and there are two types of employers out there, and truly there are! I hope you will be happy to hear my story.

It is common sense

To take a method and try it.

If it fails, admit it frankly and try another.

But above all, try something.

—Franklin D. Roosevelt (1882–1945)

Chapter 6

What to Do When Your Job-Hunt Just Isn't Working

We are hoping, of course, that all the strategies I have described thus far will lead to a happy outcome for you, in finding and obtaining a wonderful job or career.

But we all know that isn't how life works.

Sometimes, anyway.

Sometimes you work hard at the task, whatever it is.

You do everything just right.

And yet it doesn't solve your problem or resolve your dilemma. You are left right where you were. Plus now, on top of that, you're really frustrated. And depressed.

We've all been there.

And, since 2008 at least, the job-hunt has gotten more frustrating than ever.

And yet, my friend, your frustrating job-hunt has lessons to teach you.

And they are the lessons of life. They don't apply just to the job-hunt.

The lessons are simple.

Learn them now, if you haven't already.

For they are the secret of a victorious life:

Never give up.

If you're up against huge forces that are beyond your control, figure out what is within your control.

Try a different approach.

Be willing to work harder at this, than you have up to now.

But don't just work harder. Work harder at a different strategy, than you've been following up to now.

Use your brains. Do some hard thinking. You can solve this.

You have a good heart. Believe in yourself.

Okay, now to the task at hand: finding work, or changing a career.

When you're tackling *any* task, and you're not getting results, the first thing you should always do is look at the tools you're using, to see if they're the best tools for the task. If they're not, then find a different, better tool, than the one that you've been using up to now.

I'll give you an example. Suppose you bought a good-sized growing tree that you want to plant near some home: it's four to six feet tall. And the only tool you've got for digging a hole in the ground for the tree's roots is a fork. A solid steel dinner fork. Can you do it? Dig wide enough, and deep enough?

Well, maybe. The fork wasn't made for this job, but maybe with enough time (*Days! Weeks!*) and determination, you can dig the hole with it, and plant the tree.

But the hard truth is: it's not really the right tool, for that job. You need a shovel, at the very least. If the choice is between a fork or a shovel (*for this task*), always choose the shovel.

So it is, with any task: *what tool you use makes a difference.*

This is especially true in the job-hunt. If your job-hunt just isn't working, you need to consider if there's a better tool available than the one that you've been using up to now.

"Tool" may have many meanings in everyday conversation. It may mean an instrument, or an implement, or a utensil, or an appliance, or something regarded as essential to the performance of your occupation. I mean it here in the last sense, where your occupation and preoccupation is *finding work.*

The Two Job-Hunting Tools

It turns out there are basically two tools you can use with your job-hunt. One is the one used by most job-hunters. We call that tool *The Traditional Approach,* or *TA* for short. The newer one is a tool we call *The Creative Approach,* or *CA.*

The primary difference between the two, lies in how you go about identifying which organizations to approach.

With the first, you analyze the needs of the job-market to target where you might work, and then wait until a target organization in that field announces it has a vacancy. At which point you then approach them through *a piece of paper, virtual or real*—your resume.

With the second, you begin by doing a careful inventory of yourself in order to decide what organizations match you. And then you do not wait until they announce they have a vacancy. You approach them anyway, this time through *a person,* specifically a *bridge person*—someone who knows them and also knows you.

Here is a detailed comparison of the two tools, the two approaches to finding work.

	TA **The Traditional Approach**	**CA** **The Creative Approach**
What you are looking for	A job.	A "dream job": one that uses your favorite skills and favorite fields or knowledges.
How you see yourself	As a "job beggar." You will be lucky to get them.	As a "resource." They will be lucky to get you.
Your basic plan	Figure out how to "sell" yourself, before you go out hunting.	Figure out what kind of job you'd die to do, before you go out hunting.
Your preparation	Do research to find out what the job-market wants. *"Fitting in" will carry the day!*	Do homework on yourself, to figure out what you do best, AND most love to do. *Enthusiasm will carry the day!*

	T A **The Traditional** **Approach**	**C A** **The Creative** **Approach**
How you figure out which employers to approach	You wait for them to identify they have a vacancy.	Doing "informational interviews," you figure out which organizations most interest you—in light of your homework—even if they do not have a known vacancy at the time.
How you contact them	Through your resume.	Through a "bridge person" (someone who knows you and also knows them). Use LinkedIn to find them.
What the purpose of your resume is	To sell them on why you should be hired there.	To get an interview with them.
What your main goal is if you get an interview	To sell them on why you should be hired there.	To get another interview there.
What you talk about in the interview	Yourself, your assets, your experience.	50% of the time you let them ask the questions. 50% of the time you ask them the things *you* want to know about the place, and the job there.
What you're trying to find out	Do they want me?	Do I want them? (as well as "Do they want me?")
How you end the final interview there	You ask them: "When may I hope to hear from you?" *(You are leaving things hanging.)*	If you decide you do want to work there, you ask them: "I believe I could be a real asset to you. Given all that we've talked about, can you offer me this job?" *(You are seeking closure.)*
What to do after getting the job, but before you start	Send a thank-you note. Rest, relax, and savor the successful end to your job-hunt.	Send a thank-you note. Keep on job-hunting. (The offer may still fall through before you start, due to unforeseen circumstances there.)

So, which tool should you use, when you're looking for work? That's the question.

And the answer? *It's your call.*

Typically we choose the first tool—TA—*The Traditional Approach.* Most of us know how to use it, or can quickly learn. It doesn't demand much time. Slap together a resume. Post it. Wait to see if you get any responses. Look at the ads online and off for vacancies. Approach those companies via your resume. Send out bushel baskets of resumes. If that doesn't turn up any job offer, send out another 500 to 1,000 more of your resumes. Or, since 2008 at least, post it online. Everywhere.

If this works, great! But then, if it always did, you wouldn't be reading this chapter.

If your job-hunt just isn't working, the first strategy you need to consider is *switching tools.* If you've been using TA—*The Traditional Approach*—and it just isn't working this time, then you need to try using the other tool, CA—*The Creative Approach*—which was outlined in the right-hand column of the chart we just saw.

It's harder to use this tool, this approach.

It requires more of you.

It's more work.

It takes longer.

It asks you to do some hard thinking and reflecting on who you are, and where you're going with your life.

But that is precisely its value. It's not just about work. It forces you to think about your whole life, and what you want out of life.

Does This Tool Really Work?

This all sounds just fine. In theory. But does it actually work? I mean, does it actually help us find a job when all else has failed, up to now?

Yes, it does. Impressively. Most of the time. Not just a job but work we really are looking for.

Here are the comparative statistics for all twelve job-hunting methods, starting with the method that is most effective, and working down from there. As it happens, this means our listing begins with this tool, *The Creative Approach.* It is the best.

THE BEST AND WORST WAYS TO LOOK FOR A JOB

1. **The Creative Approach.** This method works 86% of the time. That means that out of every 100 job-hunters or career-changers who use this job-hunting method, 86 will get lucky and find a job thereby; 14 job-hunters out of the 100 will not—if they use only this method. You have a twelve times better chance of finding work using this method, than if you had just sent out your resume. I described this method in the chart on pages 99–100.

2. **Job Clubs That Meet Five Days a Week from 9-5.** This method works 70% of the time. That's ten times the success rate of sending out resumes. In this method, invented by the late Nathan Azrin, you meet with other job-hunters five days a week, from 9 a.m. to 5 p.m.—using the hours 9–12 noon each day to work on the inventory of yourself, to research companies that interest you, and to contact them; then from 1–5 p.m. you go out into the community, town, or city, and actually visit places, doing informational interviews, or keeping appointments you've set up, to interview about a job.

   During the morning sessions you work with a partner, and each partner takes turns listening to the other on the phone (usually by using an extension phone), and gives them feedback after they hang up. Then, prior to the afternoon, before you go out, each of you shares with the rest of the group what kind of job you are looking for. That means, you have other eyes out there looking for any leads (*rhymes with needs*) that might help *you*. And you of course do the same for them.

   Unfortunately, this is merely a historical note about this method. Many years ago I used to audit groups that used this method, plus similar job clubs in Michigan, Boston, San Diego and Northern California, and I can tell you job clubs worked as well as I have here described. But, the model died. For four reasons: changes in the use of the telephone; the rise of new technologies (the Internet, e-mail, texting, etc.); loss of federal funding for training job-seekers; and—most importantly of all— an increasing unwillingness in Western culture to work this hard. You won't find a single one of these left (so far as I know) anywhere on the face of the Earth. We (Nathan and I) have looked.

What you will find, instead (which is why I have listed job clubs here), is hundreds of job-hunting groups that *call* themselves "job clubs" but they are not. They are far from the Azrin model.[1] They tend to meet only once a week, and then for only a couple of hours, and may more accurately be described as Job-Search Support Groups. Their job-hunting success rate is usually around 10%, if that.

But there are some rare exceptions, with a much higher success rate—50% in fact—particularly if they use this book as their guide.[2]

Still, even "dumbed down," and having a much lower success rate, job-search support groups have one sterling virtue, and that is, they provide community to the otherwise lonely job-hunter. This is very, very valuable. No one should ever have to job-hunt all by themselves, if they can possibly avoid it. We all need encouragement and support, along the way.

A nationwide directory of *job-search support groups* can be found on Susan Joyce's wonderful website, job-hunt.org, located at http://tinyurl.com/7a9xbb.

3. Using the Yellow Pages. This method works 65% of the time. It involves going through the Yellow Pages of your local phone book, or actually, the Index to those Yellow Pages, so you can identify subjects or fields of interest to you. Then you go from the Index to the actual Yellow Pages and look up names of organizations or companies in those fields, in that town or city where

---

1. His detailed manual describing his method, as he used it successfully with ex–mental patients, has been out of print for years; but the desperate, really, really desperate, could find it for $150 on up to $600 on the Alibris website and elsewhere online. Its exact title is *The Job Club Counselor's Manual: A Behavioral Approach to Vocational Counseling.* To be frank, it's not worth anywhere near these prices, inasmuch as Azrin's model would need some thoughtful revision and adaptation to work well in today's world. By the way, the book's price is so high because my friend Nathan died this year (2013), and doubtless people are searching for mementos of him and his ideas.

2. A report of a 50% success rate, from a *Job Search Support Group* in Cupertino, California: "The Cupertino Rotary Job Search Support Group is going strong again this year. Last year we had 154 people come through the Group and exactly 50% found jobs—77 people found the work they were seeking! The '50%' figure has been the 'Rule of Thumb' for the Job Search Support Group.... EVERY year (all 11 years except the first year, which was 43%) the success rate has been 50%! And every year, we use Dick's book as a central 'resource' for encouragement and a practical job-searching guide. Every single person that comes to our Group receives a copy of *What Color Is Your Parachute?* along with a Cupertino Rotary Job Search Support Group binder—and with these resources, it helps people tremendously!"

you want to work. You call them, set up an appointment, go visit them, and explore whether or not they are hiring for the kind of work you do, or the position you are looking for. Of course, in this post-2008 period, it's a lot harder to get employers to consent to see you—in large companies, anyway. Still, you will note that you have a nine times better chance of finding a job with this method, than if you had just depended on your resume.

4. **Knocking on the door of any employer, office, or manufacturing plant.** This method works 47% of the time. It works best with *small* employers (25 or fewer employees) as you might have guessed. Sometimes you blunder into a place where a vacancy has just developed. One job-hunter knocked on the door of an architectural office at 11 a.m. His predecessor (for he did get hired there) had just quit at 10 a.m. that morning. If you try this method and nothing turns up, you broaden your definition of *small employer* to those with 50 or fewer employees. With this method you have an almost seven times better chance of finding a job than if you had just depended on your resume.

5. **Asking for job-leads.** This method works 33% of the time. With this method you ask family members, friends, and people you know in the community (or on LinkedIn) if they know of any place where someone with your talents and background is being sought. It is a simple question: *do you know of any job vacancies at the place where you work—or elsewhere?* Using this method, you have an almost five times better chance of finding a job, than if you had just sent out your resume.

6. **Going to private employment agencies or search firms for help.** This method works 27.8% of the time (at best) on down to 5% (at worse). These agencies used to just place office workers; now it's hard to think of a category of jobs they don't try to place, especially in large metropolitan areas. A directory of these firms in your area can be found at www.yellowpages.com. Into *their* search engine put "Employment agencies" and the name of your local town or city, to get the relevant listings. The wide variation in success rate (5%–27.8%) is due to the fact that these agencies vary greatly in their staffing (ranging from

extremely competent on down to *inept*, or *running a scam*). Still, at their best, agencies are four times more effective than just depending on your resume.

7. Answering local newspaper ads. This method works 24% of the time (at best) on down to 5% (again). With this method, you answer "help wanted ads" in your local newspaper, especially the Sunday edition, assuming your city or town still has a news-paper, online or in print, or both. See the website Job Search Steps found at http://tinyurl.com/d58l8z for how to use them. As for a directory of online newspapers from around the world, your best bet is Newslink, found at www.newslink.org (click on "Newspapers" in the top navigation bar).

The fluctuation between 5% and 24% is due to the level of sal-ary that is being sought; those job-hunters looking for low-level salary jobs find this method works 24% of the time. Those look-ing for a high salary find it works only 5% of the time.

8. Going to places where employers pick up workers. If you're a union member, particularly in the trades or construction, and you have access to a union hiring hall, this method will find you work, up to 22% of the time. What is not stated, however, is how long it may take to get a job at the hall, and how short-lived such a job may be. In the trades, it's often just a few days. Moreover, this is not a job-hunting method that is open to a very large percentage of job-hunters, at all. Only 6.6% of private sector employees are union members these days. (The public sector's comparable figure is 35.9%, and the overall figure for the Ameri-can worker is 11.3%, the lowest level since 1916.)[3]

If you're not a union member, but you like this method (or you're desperate), employers tend to pick up workers (called *day-laborers*) early in the morning, on well-known street corners in your town (ask around). It's called *pick-up work*, it's usually short-term, usually yard work, or work that requires you to use your hands, usually paid to you in cash *that day*, and definitely *temp* work. But no job should be "beneath you" when you're nearly

---

3. These statistics are from a January 25, 2013, report on the WSWS website by Jerry White, found at http://tinyurl.com/czq75rg.

flat-broke. All work like this is honorable. And while such jobs usually don't last long, occasionally they do, or—if the employer is impressed with the quality of your work—they can lead to more permanent employment. Sometimes.

9. Going to the state or federal employment office. This method works 14% of the time. You go to your local federal/state unemployment service office (www.dol.gov/dol/location.htm) or to their CareerOneStop business centers (www.careeronestop.org), now called American Job Centers (www.jobcenter.usa.gov), to get instructions on how to better job-hunt, and find job-leads. (Note: They have a special section for returning veterans.)

10. Answering ads in professional or trade journals, appropriate to your field. This method works 7% of the time. The method consists in looking at professional journals in your profession or field, and answering any ads there that intrigue you (a directory of these associations and their journals is at Susan Joyce's comprehensive site, job-hunt.org (or as she likes to say, "job dash hunt dot org"), found at http://tinyurl.com/d9vxnv4).

11. Posting or mailing out your resume to employers. As you've probably figured out by now, this works at getting you a job (or, more accurately, at getting you an *interview* that leads to a job) 7% of the time. And I'm being generous with this estimate.

This comes as a shock to most job-hunters.

When you're unemployed, and job-hunting, or trying to change careers, *everyone* will tell you: a good resume will get you a job. It's virtually an article of faith among the unemployed (and their helpers).

Why does everyone keep telling us this, when it has such a miserable success record? Oh, you tell me. Why did everyone entrust their money to Bernie Madoff? Or why did so many people buy those incredibly risky financial instruments or mortgages that led to the Great Recession back in 2008? I don't know. I guess if you hear something often enough, and from enough different sources, you start to think it *must* be true.

Anyway, there it stands. Indisputable. The success rate of resumes is only 7%. And actually I'm being generous with that estimate. One study suggested that only 1 out of 1,470 resumes actually resulted in a job. Another study found the figure to be even worse: 1 job offer for every 1,700 resumes floating around out there.

By the way, once you post your resume on the Internet, it gets copied quickly by "spiders" from other sites, and you can never remove it completely from the Internet. There are reportedly now at least 40,000,000 resumes floating around out there in the ether, like lost ships on the Sargasso Sea. Yours, among them. That can come back to haunt you if you ever fibbed (lied?) about anything, once a would-be employer *Googles* you, even years later.

And now, last but not least:

12. Looking for employers' job-postings on the Internet. This method works on average 4% of the time. Yeah, I know, you're somewhere between surprised and shocked at this finding. I was too.

It *is* strange. If you have access to the Internet, and you're out of work, *everyone* will tell you to look for employers' *job-postings* (vacancies)—either on the employer's own website (if you have a particular company or organization in mind), or on specific *job-boards* such as CareerBuilder, Yahoo/Hot Jobs, Monster, LinkUp, Hound, or on *niche sites*[4] for particular industries, such as Dice; or on non-job sites such as Craigslist, or even on LinkedIn, Facebook, Twitter, and other social media sites.

The question is, how helpful is the Internet when you're out of work?

The answer is: *well, that depends.*

The anecdotal evidence is sometimes impressive. You will often hear stories of job-hunters who have been tremendously successful in using the Internet to find a job. Examples:

A job-seeker, a systems administrator in Taos, New Mexico, who wanted to move to San Francisco posted his resume at 10 p.m. on a Monday night, on a San Francisco online site (it

---

4. An impressive directory of niche sites can be found at VetJobs (http://tinyurl.com/28rplc7).

happened to be Craigslist.org). By Wednesday morning he had over seventy responses from employers.

Again, a marketing professional developed her resume following guidance she found on the Internet, posted it to two advertised positions she found there, and within seventy-two hours of posting her electronic resume, both firms contacted her, and she is now working for one of them.

Again, this time from job-hunters' letters: "In May I was very unexpectedly laid off from a company I was with for five years. I did 100% of my job-search and research via the Internet. I found all my leads online, sent all my resumes via e-mail, and had about a 25% response rate that actually led to a phone interview or a face-to-face interview. It was a software company that laid me off, and I am [now] going to work for a publishing company, a position I found online."

And again: "Thanks to the Internet, I found what I believe to be the ideal job in [just] eight weeks—a great job with a great company and great opportunities."

The question is, are these stories just flukes, or is this a universal experience?

Sadly it turns out that this job-search method actually doesn't work for very many who try it. Exception to this: if you are seeking a technical or computer-related job, an IT job, or a job in engineering, finances, or health care, the success rate rises, to somewhere around 10%. But for the other 12,741 job-titles that are out there in the job-market, the success rate reportedly remains at around 4%.

Job-Hunting Methods Were Not Created Equal

So, there you have it. There are twelve job-hunting methods currently, and you can see not only what they are, but what their *comparative* success rate is.[5] These are alternatives for you to pick and choose between; and they were *not* all created equal. Some methods of hunting for work have a pretty good track record, and therefore will repay you well for time spent pursuing them. But other methods have a really terrible track record, and you can waste a lot of time, and energy, on them, with no results.

So, to discuss job-hunting methods is to discuss *conservation of energy. Your* energy. If your job-hunt just hasn't worked so far, look at that list to see if you've been using one of the worst methods to look for work. See if you've been using a method that used to work, but is now more and more ineffective.

If you're feeling stuck, if you've been out of work for months or even years, what you need to do is change job-hunting methods. You need to change tools. The dinner fork will no longer do, to dig there in the job-market. You need the shovel.

That would mean choosing *the* most effective method and tool: *The Creative Approach.* The one with the 86% success rate.

It begins by your doing a self-inventory, in order to understand more fully who you are.

Next chapter.

---

5. The statistics I quoted throughout this chapter do fluctuate somewhat, from year to year, from geographical region to region, from one field to another, from one city, town, or rural area to another. Their best value is how they compare to other job-hunting methods. That tends to remain fairly constant, and predictable, year by year.

You do get to a certain point in life
Where you have to realistically, I think,
Understand that the days are getting shorter.
And you can't put things off,
Thinking you'll get to them someday.
If you really want to do them,
You better do them. . . .
So I'm very much a believer in knowing
What it is that you love doing
So that you can do a great deal of it.

> —*Nora Ephron (1941–2012)*

Chapter 7

You Need to Understand More Fully Who You Are

I know you're probably going to protest that you've lived with yourself all your life, so far, and you don't need to do this inventory. Well, maybe.

But my experience over the past forty years, with literally millions of job-hunters, is that none of us understands fully who we are, and what we have to offer the world.

Oh, we understand part of it, all right. But not the fullness of it. Not the richness of it. Not the uniqueness of who we are.

So you need this, a fresh inventory of what you have to offer the world, before you go back out there. And I mean you need to understand *all* that you have to offer, not just *part* of it. As I said, you already know *part* of it. The problem is that it is only *part*. You need to know it all.

This Is a Job-Hunting Method, and The Most Effective One, at That

Before we get to the inventory, let's get one thing out of the way. This isn't just self-exploration. Though that would be nice, in and of itself. Very popular on the West Coast and places west.

But this is a job-hunting method, as I said in the previous chapter. Or the heart and soul of a job-hunting method, the one that has the best track record of any that are out there.

Of course, the question arises, *Why does this self-inventory work so well in helping you find work, after other methods have failed?* That's important to answer, because the answer may keep you motivated to finish this inventory, when otherwise you might say, *Too much work!* And give up.

So, let's look at this question. There are seven reasons that I have observed:

1. **By doing this homework on yourself, you learn to describe yourself in at least six different ways, and therefore you can approach multiple job-markets.** Retraining, as it is commonly practiced in Western culture, prepares you for only one market. Thus construction workers are retrained, let us say, to be computer repair people. One market. No jobs to be found in that market, once they are trained? Retraining wasted.

   But with this homework, you are embarking on a whole different concept of starting over. You are essentially training or retraining yourself for several markets. This, because you stop identifying yourself by only one job-title. In a tough economy, job-titles like, say, "accountant," just aren't detailed enough. New thinking is called for: you are no longer just "an accountant" or "a construction worker" or whatever. *You are a person who* has these skills and these experiences. If teaching and writing and growing things are your favorite skills, then you can approach the job-market of teaching, or that of writing, or that of gardening. Multiple job-markets are open to you; not just one.

2. **By doing this homework on yourself, you can describe in detail exactly what you are looking for.** This greatly enables your friends, LinkedIn contacts, and family to better help you. You approach them not with, *"Uh, I'm out of work; let me know if you hear of anything,"* but you can describe to them more exactly what kind of "thing," and in what work setting. This greatly increases their helpfulness to you, and therefore your ability to find jobs you would otherwise never find.

3. **By ending up with a picture of a job that would really excite you, you will inevitably pour much more energy and determination into your job-search.** Previously, your job-hunt may have felt more like a duty than anything else. Now, with this vision, you will be *dying* to find *this*. So, you will redouble your efforts, your dedication, and your determination when

otherwise you might tire and give up. Persistence becomes your middle name, once you've identified a prize worth fighting for.

4. **By doing this homework, you will no longer have to wait to approach companies until they say they have a vacancy.** Once done with this homework, you choose places that match who you are, and then it doesn't matter if they have a known vacancy or not. Because they match your vision, you approach them (*through a "bridge person" who knows both you and them*) knowing confidently that you will be an asset there.

5. **When you are facing, let us say, nineteen other competitors for the job you want—equally experienced, equally skilled— you will stand out because you can accurately describe to employers exactly what is unique about you, and what you bring to the table that the others don't.** These will usually turn out to involve adjectives or adverbs, what we normally call *traits*. More on that, later.

6. **If you are contemplating a career-change, maybe—after you inventory yourself—you will see definitely what new career or direction you want for your life.** Maybe. But first, please, please, inventory what you already have. Often you can put together a new career just using what you already know and what you already can do—with much less training or retraining than you thought you would have to do. I'm not talking about a dramatic change, like going from salesperson to doctor: for that, you will need to start over. But most career changes are not that dramatic, as I will show you, in chapter 10.

   It may turn out that the knowledge you need to pick up can be found in a vocational/technical school, or in a (one- or) two-year college. And sometimes, *sometimes* it can be found simply by doing enough *informational interviewing* (more about this in the next chapter).

   Example here: a job-hunter named Bill had worked for a number of years in retail; now he was debating a career-change— working in the oil industry. But he knew virtually nothing about that industry. However, he went from person to person who worked at companies in that industry, just seeking information about the industry. The more of these "informational interviews" he conducted, the more he knew. In fact, coming down the home stretch, just before he got hired in the place of his dreams, he found he now knew more than the people he was visiting, about their competitors and some aspects of the industry.

In other words, with certain kinds of career-change, there is more than one way to pick up the knowledge you need.

7. **Unemployment is an interruption, in most of our lives. And interruptions are opportunities, to pause to think, to assess where we really want to go with our lives.** Martin Luther King Jr. had something to say about this:

> *The major problem of life is learning how to handle the costly inter-ruptions. The door that slams shut, the plan that got sidetracked, the marriage that failed. Or that lovely poem that didn't get written because someone knocked on the door.*

The Creative Approach, with its demand that you do home-work on yourself before you set out on your search for (meaning-ful) work, helps you take advantage of the opportunity that this interruption—being out of work—offers.

So there you have it: the seven reasons why this self-inventory, this *Creative Approach,* performs so much better as a tool for your job-hunt. It is the shovel you were looking for.

Use this opportunity. Make this not only a hunt for a job, but a hunt for a life. A deeper life, a victorious life, a life you're prouder of.

The world currently is filled with workers whose weeklong cry is, "When is the weekend going to be here?" And, then, "Thank God it's Friday!" Their work puts bread on the table but . . . they are bored out of their minds. They've never taken the time to think out what they uniquely can do, and what they uniquely have to offer to the world. The world doesn't need any more bored workers. It needs people will-ing to work hard. It needs passionate people. It needs people excited by their work. It needs people with a sense of high purpose and a sense of mission. So, do this self-inventory. Dream a little. Dream a lot.

One of the saddest pieces of advice in the world is, "Oh come now—be realistic." The best parts of this world were not fashioned by those who were realistic. They were fashioned by those who dared to look hard at their wishes and then gave them horses to ride.

The Inventory:
The Flower Exercise

Okay, let's begin. Begin by mentally stripping yourself of your job-title. You have to stop answering, "Who are you?" with, "Oh, I'm a construction worker, or salesperson, or designer, or writer, or whatever." That locks you into your past. You launch yourself into the future by answering instead: "I am a person who . . ."

"I am a person who . . . has had these experiences."

"I am a person who . . . is skilled at doing this or that."

"I am a person who . . . knows a lot about this or that."

"I am a person who . . . is unusual in this way or that."

Before you answer this question with others, you have to first answer it in your own head. You are a person, not a role. Throughout this self-inventory, you need to keep identifying what kind of person you are, under several headings.

I Am a Person Who . . .
Is Like a Flower

Researchers[1] *tell us that if you are trying to make a decision about yourself and your future, there are Three Rules about where you jot stuff down:*

1. *GATHER.* Put everything you know about yourself on **one piece of paper**.

2. *ORGANIZE.* Put **some kind of graphic** on that piece of paper, in order to organize the information about yourself. A graphic—any graphic—keeps that One Piece of Paper interesting, and not just a flood of words and spaces. It also activates the right side

---

1. Such as (the late) Barbara B. Brown, who was the first to coin the term *biofeedback* and to bring it to the public's awareness back in 1974, with her groundbreaking book (at the time) *New Mind, New Body*. She made these points in a public lecture in 1976. See her bio on www.wikipedia.com.

of your brain, the intuitive side, that looks at a whole bunch of unrelated data and says, "Aha! I see what it all means."

3. *PRIORITIZE.* **Prioritize** all this information, when you have finished organizing it. Don't just leave the data *lying there*; put it in its order of importance *to you*. Always. And every time.

So here you have it, on the next page: an outline—a *practice outline*—of the graphic you are going to fill in when you're done with all the exercises and get to the larger version found on pages 184–85.

We call the graphic *The Flower Diagram,* or *The Flower Exercise.*

I Am a Person Who . . .
Has Seven Sides to Me

This flower representation of *You* has *seven* petals (including the center) because there are seven sides to You, or seven ways of thinking about yourself.

7 Ways of Describing Who You Are

1. You can describe *who you are* in terms of what you know—and what your *favorite* knowledges or fields of interest are, that you have stored in your head (or heart).

2. Or you can describe *who you are* in terms of the kinds of people you most prefer to *work with*, and/or the kinds of people—age span, problems, handicaps, geographical location, etc.—you would most like to *help* or serve.

3. Or you can describe *who you are* in terms of what you can do, and what your *favorite* functional/transferable skills are.

4. Or you can describe *who you are* in terms of your favorite working conditions—indoors/outdoors, small company/ large company, tight ship/loose ship,[2] windows/no windows,

---

2. "Tight ship": you clock in and clock out, work under strict conditions; "loose ship": you have greater leeway about when you come in, or go home, they want your creativity above all else, and there is no time clock or tight supervision of your day.

A Preliminary Outline of The Flower

(A Note Page for Jotting Down Your Idle Thoughts and Hunches[3])

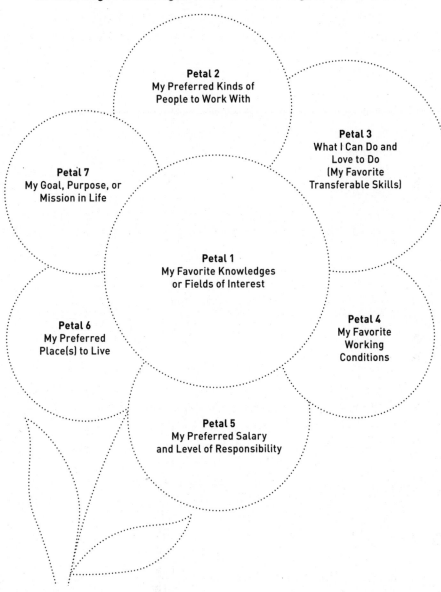

Petal 2
My Preferred Kinds of
People to Work With

Petal 3
What I Can Do and
Love to Do
(My Favorite
Transferable Skills)

Petal 7
My Goal, Purpose, or
Mission in Life

Petal 1
My Favorite Knowledges
or Fields of Interest

Petal 6
My Preferred
Place(s) to Live

Petal 4
My Favorite
Working
Conditions

Petal 5
My Preferred Salary
and Level of Responsibility

3. This page is just for note-taking and jotting down your idle thoughts on each subject. The real Flower is on pages 184–85, and it is there that you enter the final results of each exercise in this chapter.

etc.—because they enable you to work at your top form, and greatest effectiveness.

5. Or you can describe *who you are* in terms of your preferred salary and level of responsibility—working by yourself, or as a member of a team, or supervising others, or running the show—that you feel most fitted for, by experience, temperament, and appetite.

6. Or you can describe *who you are* in terms of your preferred geographical location—here or abroad, warm/cold, north/south, east/west, mountains/coast, urban/suburban/rural/rustic—where you'd be happiest, do your best work, and would most love to live.

7. Or you can describe *who you are* in terms of your goals or sense of mission and purpose for your life. Alternatively, or in addition, you can get more particular and describe the goals or mission you want *the organization* to have, where you decide to work.

I Am a Person Who . . .
Is All These Things

You could choose just one, two, or three of these sides of yourself—let us say, "what you know," "what you can do," and "preferred salary"—as your guide to defining what kind of work would match *You.*

But what the Flower Diagram does is describe who you are in *all seven* ways, joined together on one page, in one graphic. After all, you are not just one of these things; you are *all* of these things. The Flower Diagram is a complete, not partial, picture of *You*.

Believe me, you want the complete picture. I'll tell you why. Let's say there is some job out there that matches only one petal, one side to yourself, one way of defining who you are: for example, let's say this job lets you use your favorite knowledges. Period.

It doesn't let you use your favorite skills, nor does it have you working with the kinds of people you most enjoy, nor does it give you the surroundings where you can do your best work.

What would you call such a job? I think *boring*. You would barely be able to wait for Friday to come around. *Thank God it's Friday!* Some of you have already sung that song. A lot.

But now let us suppose you could instead find another kind of work that matches all seven sides of you. All seven petals. What would you call *that* job? You would call it *your dream job*.

So, your total flower is a picture of who You most fully are. But at the same time it's a picture of a job that would give voice to all that you are. Your dream job. Where you would shine, because it uses the best of Who You Are.

So please fill in your Flower. *And try to keep it a joy rather than a duty.*

For the following exercises you will need several blank sheets of notebook paper ($8^1/_2$ x 11 inches) as your worksheets.

I Am a Person Who . . .
Knows These Particular Things

And *loves* using that knowledge. Or knowledges. Or "know-hows." (Call it what you will.)

First Petal

MY FAVORITE KNOWLEDGES OR FIELDS OF INTEREST

My Favorite Knowledges Petal

Goal in Filling Out This Petal: To summarize all that you stored in your brain. *Required:* From your past, subjects you already know a lot about, and enjoy talking about. *Optional:* For your future, what you would like to learn.

What You Are Looking For: Some guidance as to what field you would most enjoy working in.

Form of the Entries on Your Petal: Basically, they will all turn out to be nouns, but see below.

Example of a Good Petal: *"Graphic design, data analysis, mathematics, how to repair a car, videogames, cooking, music, principles of mechanical engineering, how to run an organization, Chinese, CATIA (Computer Aided Three-dimensional Interactive Application),"* etc.

Example of a Bad Petal: *"Prompt, thorough, analyzing, persistent, communicating."*

> **Why Bad:** Knowledges are always nouns. The words in the bad example above are not. In case you're curious, they are, in order: a trait (adjective), a trait (adjective), a transferable skill (verb), a trait (adjective), and a transferable skill (verb). All in all, that is one mixed bag! All are important, but you want only knowledges on this particular petal.

There are three things traditionally called skills: **knowledges**, as here; **functions**, *also known as transferable skills;* and **traits**. As a general rule throughout this inventory, *knowledges are nouns, transferable skills are verbs,* and *traits are adjectives or adverbs.* If it helps knowing that, great;

if not, forget it. Our overarching principle throughout this book is that if a generalization, or metaphor, or example, helps you, use it. But if it just confuses you, then ignore it!!! Please!

On this Knowledges "petal" (*actually the central part of the Flower*) you will eventually write your final results—your Favorite Knowledges/ Fields of Interest, prioritized in the order of importance to you—on pages 184–85.

Prior to that, you need here, as you will with each petal, a worksheet. Or two. Get blank pieces of notebook or paper to do this on.

WORKSHEET

Notes About My Favorite Knowledges
1. What You Know from Your Previous Jobs
2. What You Know About, Outside of Work
3. What Fields, Careers, or Industries Sound Interesting to You
4. Any Other Hunches, Bright Ideas, Great Ideas, etc.

A worksheet is like a fisherman's net, where you want to cast it into the sea in order to capture the largest haul possible, and then sort out the best of your catch, later.

This worksheet can look sloppy, unorganized, and messy. That's okay. Who cares? Only the final petal is supposed to look organized.

A worksheet is a gathering place, for the results of the exercises you do, but also for every bright idea, every hunch, every remembered dream, every intuition that occurs to you as you are working on that petal. Jot down *everything*.

This is an important petal—very important—so to unearth your favorite knowledges or fields of interest, four exercises are usually needed. We begin with:

1. WHAT YOU KNOW FROM YOUR PREVIOUS JOBS

If you've been out there in the world of work for any time already, you've probably learned a lot of things that you now just take for granted. *"Of course I know that!"* But such knowledges may be important, down the line. So, list them!

Things like: *bookkeeping, handling applications, credit collection of over-due accounts, hiring, international business, management, marketing, sales, merchandizing, packaging, policy development, problem solving, troubleshoot-ing, public speaking, recruiting, conference planning, systems analysis, the culture of other countries, other languages, government contract procedures,* and so on.

To be thorough here, jot down on another piece of paper a list of all the jobs you have ever held, and then *for each job* jot down anything you learned there. For example: "Worked in a warehouse: learned *how to use a forklift and crane, inventory control, logistics automation software, warehouse management systems, JIT (just in time) techniques, teamwork principles,* and *how to supervise employees.*"

Or, again, "Worked at McDonald's: learned *how to prepare and serve food, how to wait on customers, how to make change, how to deal with com-plaints, how to train new employees, etc.*"

Do this with all the jobs you have ever held: where you worked, what you learned there. Then look over everything you've written in *this* exercise, and decide which are your favorite knowledges or interests, that you're glad you picked up. Jot them down on your work-sheet, in the space provided for this exercise.

"I CAN REMEMBER WHEN ALL WE NEEDED WAS SOMEONE WHO COULD CARVE AND SOMEONE WHO COULD SEW."

2. WHAT YOU KNOW ABOUT, OUTSIDE OF WORK

Jot down knowledges you've picked up outside of work, such as: *antiques, gardening, cooking, budgeting, decorating, photography, crafts, spirituality, sports, camping, travel, repairing things, flea markets, scrapbooking, sewing, art appreciation at museums, how to run or work in a volunteer organization*, and so on.

   a. Also think of anything you learned in high school (or college) that you prize knowing today: *keyboarding? Chinese? accounting? geography?* What? Jot it all down.

   b. Think of anything you learned at training seminars, workshops, conferences, and so on, possibly in connection with a job you had at the time. Jot it all down.

   c. Think of anything you studied at home, via online courses, mobile apps, tape programs (likely played in your car while commuting), PBS television programs, etc. Jot it all down.

d. Think of anything you learned out there in the world, such as *how to assemble a flash mob, how to organize a protest, how to fundraise for a particular cause, how to run a marathon, how to repair a toilet,* etc. Jot it all down, in the space provided for this exercise on your worksheet.

3. WHAT FIELDS, CAREERS, OR INDUSTRIES SOUND INTERESTING TO YOU

If you want to pick some career or field from a list of them all, it helps if you start broadly, and then drill down.

Broadly speaking, then, the job-market consists of the following four arenas: *agriculture, manufacturing, information,* and *services.* Any ideas about which of these four is most attractive to you? If so, jot it down, in the space provided for this exercise on your worksheet.

In order to drill down further than that, your best bet is the government's O*Net Online, assuming you have a computer (www.onetonline .org). *Note that is .org, not .com.*

To begin with, this site has various lists of career clusters or industries or job families. Below is a mashup of these. Please read this list over, and check off any of these that you want to explore further (*multiple choice preferred, here, in order to have alternatives and therefore hope*):

- ❏ Accommodation and Food Services
- ❏ Administrative and Support Services
- ❏ Agriculture, Food, and Natural Resources
- ❏ Architecture, Engineering, and Construction
- ❏ Arts, Audio/Video Technology, and Communications
- ❏ Business, Operations, Management, and Administration
- ❏ Community and Social Service
- ❏ Computer and Mathematical
- ❏ Design, Entertainment, Sports, and Media
- ❏ Distribution and Logistics
- ❏ Education, Training, and Library
- ❏ Entertainment and Recreation
- ❏ Farming, Forestry, Fishing, and Hunting

❑ Finance and Insurance

❑ Food Preparation and Serving

❑ Government and Public Administration

❑ Green Industries or Jobs

❑ Health Care, Health Science, and Social Assistance

❑ Hospitality and Tourism

❑ Human Services

❑ Information and Information Technology

❑ Law, Public Safety, Corrections, and Security

❑ Life, Physical, and Social Sciences

❑ Management of Companies and Enterprises

❑ Manufacturing

❑ Marketing, Sales, and Service

❑ Military Related

❑ Mining, Quarrying, and Oil and Gas Extraction

❑ Personal Care and Service

❑ Production

❑ Professional, Scientific, and Technical Services

❑ Protective Services

❑ Real Estate, Rental, and Leasing

❑ Religion, Faith, and Related

❑ Retail Trade, Sales, and Related

❑ Science, Technology, Engineering, and Mathematics

❑ Self-Employment

❑ Transportation, Warehousing, and Material Moving

❑ Utilities

Now, the nice thing about O*Net Online is that once you have chosen anything on the list above, the site has drop-down menus which allow you to go deeper into each *career cluster, industry,* or *job family* that you have checked off. It drills down to career pathways, and then drills down further to individual occupations, and then drills down still further to tasks, tools, technologies, knowledges, skills, abilities, work activities, education, interests, work styles, work values, related occupations, and salary.

The only limitation here, as you will see in chapter 10, "Five Ways to Change Careers," is that O*Net *only does this for about 800 occupations.* Its predecessor, the D.O.T., had 12,741 occupations.[4] So, this does not offer a complete map of the job-market by any means.

And even for those occupations that are listed in O*Net, remember: jobs, industries, and careers are mortal; they are born, they grow, they flourish, they mature, then decline and ultimately die. Sometimes it takes centuries, sometimes merely decades, sometimes even sooner than that. But, eventually, most jobs, industries, and careers are mortal. So, always have a plan B.

Okay, now you're done with the worksheet for this petal. What next? Well, sort them. Copy the diagram below onto a piece of notebook paper, and then sort everything—everything—you have on that worksheet into one of these four bins (well, you can forget bin #4, if you'd rather):

YOUR FAVORITE SUBJECTS MATRIX
HIGH

E X P E R T I S E	3. Subjects for Which You Have Little Enthusiasm but in Which You Have Lots of Expertise	1. Subjects for Which You Have Lots of Enthusiasm and in Which You Have Lots of Expertise BINGO!
	4. Subjects for Which You Have Little Enthusiasm and in Which you Have Little Expertise	2. Subjects for Which You Have Lots of Enthusiasm but in Which You Have Little Expertise

LOW   ENTHUSIASM   **HIGH**

---

4. By the way, if you want to use or visit the D.O.T. it's now online at www.occupationalinfo.org, and can be downloaded to your computer.

Copy the top four or five results from bin #1 and maybe, maybe, an item from bin #2, on to your Favorite Knowledges or Fields of Interest petal, found on page 184–85.

Now you're ready to move on, to consider another side of Who You Are.

I Am a Person Who . . .
Has These Favorite Kinds of People

Second Petal

MY PREFERRED KINDS OF PEOPLE TO WORK WITH

Why do *the people you prefer* matter at all in the larger scheme of things? Because, the people we work with are either energy drainers or energy creators. They either drag us down, and keep us from being our most effective, or they lift us up and help us to be at our best, and perform at our greatest effectiveness. We'll get into that, in a minute.

Keep in mind, "people-environments" are another way of describing jobs or careers. So, we'll cover that here, too. Now, let us begin.

You'll probably need to copy the chart on page 129 to a larger piece of paper—$8^1/_2$ x 11 inches—before you start filling it in. And, by the way, you can fill it out alone, or in company with up to five other job-hunters (recommended, because it's a lot more fun to see how other people are bugged by the same kinds of people that you are).

My Favorite People Petal

Goal in Filling Out This Petal: To avoid past bad experiences with people at work, since who (er, *whom*) you work with can either make the job delightful, or ruin your day, your week, your year.

What You Are Looking For: (1) A better picture in your mind of what kind of people surrounding you at work will enable you to operate at your highest and most effective level. (2) A better picture in your mind of what kind of people you would most like to serve or help: defined by age, problems, geography, and so forth.

Form of the Entries on Your Petal: They can be adjectives describing different kinds of people ("kind," "patient") or it can be types of people, as in the "Holland Code" or "Myers-Briggs" typologies (see pages 135–40 and 147–48).

Example of a Good Petal: (1) *Kind, generous, understanding, fun, smart.* (2) *The unemployed, people struggling with their faith, worldwide, all ages. Holland code: IAS.*

Example of a Bad Petal: *People in trouble, young, smart, in urban settings.* RCI.

> **Why Bad:** It doesn't distinguish between (1) people surrounding me at work and (2) people I want to help or serve. It lumps both together. Not much help. Too vague.

MY FAVORITE PEOPLE CHART

Column 1	Column 2	Column 3	Column 4
Places I Have Worked Thus Far in My Life	Kinds of People There Who Drove Me Nuts (from the first column) (No names, but describe *what about them drove you nuts*; e.g., *bossy, always pestering me with their personal problems, always left early before job was done, etc.* List these in any order; it doesn't matter— at least in *this* column . . .)	Kinds of People I'd Prefer Not to Have to Work With, In Order of Preference (This is now a ranking of the items in the second column, in exact order of: which is worse? next? etc. Use the Prioritizing Grid, page 131, to do this.) 1a.	Kinds of People I'd Most Like to Work With, in Order of Preference (The opposite of those qualities in the third column, in the same order) 1b.
		2a.	2b.
		3a.	3b.
		4a.	4b.
		5a.	5b.

Start, of course, by filling in the first column in the chart, and then the second. This will bring you to the third column, and here you're gonna need some help. How do you look back at that stuff in the second column, and prioritize it? Well, you use:

The Prioritizing Grid

I give you my Prioritizing Grid. It asks you to decide between just two items at a time. There are two forms of it: one prioritizing twenty-four items, the other prioritizing just ten or fewer. I will explain the latter in some detail here. You will then see the twenty-four item grid is done in the same manner.

INSTRUCTIONS FOR USING THE PRIORITIZING GRID

Section A. Write down, in any order, the factors you listed in the second column of the chart. This grid will accommodate up to ten factors. If you originally listed more than ten, take a guess at which ten factors you disliked the most, and list *those ten.*

Section B. Compare just two items at a time. Begin with that little tiny box to the left of factor #1 and factor #2, in which you will see the tiny numbers 1 and 2. The numbers are clearly shorthand for those factors written out in Section A. The question you would frame for yourself, here, would be as follows: Which of these two factors do I dislike the most? Then, in that little tiny box you circle either the tiny number 1 or 2, depending on which factor you dis-like the most.

   In similar manner you work your way down the little boxes *nearest* Section A, which as you can see lie in a diagonal running from northwest to southeast. The next little tiny box has the tiny numbers 2 and 3 in it. Same question, except now it's between factor #2 versus factor #3. Circle the appropriate number in that tiny box. Why *diagonal*, rather than just straight across horizontally or straight down, vertically? Because you can get into a knee-jerk reaction if you do it that way (*"Well, I checked factor #5 each time so far, so I guess I should check factor #5 this next time, too."*) Diagonal defeats knee-jerk reactions.

   So, work your way on down that diagonal direction. When you've reached the little box at the bottom of that first diagonal (containing the little numbers 9 and 10), go back up to the top and work down the next diagonal (beginning with the little box

PRIORITIZING GRID FOR 10 ITEMS OR LESS

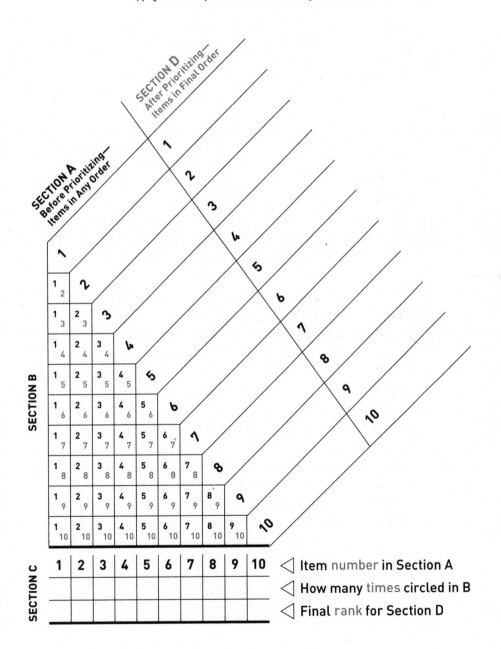

containing 1 and 3; then the little box containing 2 and 4; then the one containing 3 and 5, etc.

When you've reached the box at the bottom of *that* diagonal direction, go back up to the top, and work down the next diagonal (the little box containing 1 and 4, then the box containing 2 and 5, and so on, down to box containing 7 and 10).

Back up to the top to the next diagonal, the box containing 1 and 5, then the box containing 2 and 6, and so on. Keep this up until you've made a decision about every little box (the final one being 1 versus 10).

Section C. The bottom of the grid has three rows to it, as you can see. The first row is already filled in for you: it's the numbers of the factors in Section A. The second row, just below that, asks how many times each number got circled in *all* of the little tiny boxes. Let's say item 1 got circled 7 times. In the row right beneath #1 in the first row of Section C, you enter the number 7. Next, count how many times item 2 got circled; let's say it was 1 time; put the number 1 right below #2. Continue up through item 10.

Look now at the numbers in that second row. If no number is repeated in that second row of Section C, great! Most likely you'll find a tie. That means two items got circled the same number of times—let's say 2 and 10. How do you resolve the tie? Well, you look back at Section B, to find the little tiny box that had 2 and 10 in it, and see which of those two you circled there; let's say it was 2. Well then, in that second row, give #2 an extra half point. Now its "count" is $1^1/_2$. Leave #10 as it is (count just 1). Do this with each two-way tie.

What do you do if you have a three-way tie—three items each got circled the same number of times? This always means that you contradicted yourself somewhere along the way: one time you said *this* was more important, another time you said, no it wasn't. The only way to resolve the three-way tie is to just guess what is the proper order (for you) as to which of the three you dislike the most, which next, which next. Let's say the tie was that 3, 4, and 7 all got circled the same number of times. You dislike #7 the most, #4 next, and #3 next. Okay, so give an extra $^3/_4$ point (*that's three-quarters of a point*) to #7, an extra $^1/_2$ point to #4, and no extra points to factor #3. Now, no two factors or items have the same count in the second line of Section C.

Go down now to the bottom row there in Section C, and now rank the items, according to their circle count in the second row. The factor that got circled the most, let's say it was item #6, must be given *a final rank* of 1. Therefore, write 1 in the third row, down below item #6. Let's say item #8 got the next most circles; write a 2 down below item #8. Let's say item #1 got the next most circles; write a 3 down below it, on the bottom rank line in Section C. And so on. And so forth.

Section D. Recopy the list that you randomly put down in Section A, but now here in Section D put the list in its exact order of *one you disliked the most, next most,* etc.—according to the ranking in the bottom row of Section C. In terms of our examples above, you would copy item #6 as it was called in Section A, and put it on the very top line in Section D, because it got circled the most. You would copy item #8 as it was called in Section A onto the second line in Section D, because it got circled the next most times. And so on, until you've copied all ten factors in exactly the order of "dis-like-ness" (new word) this grid revealed.

Now, what do you end up with, there in Section D? A list of your preferences, regarding people environments: *"I would most prefer not to have to work with . . . and I next most prefer not to have to work with . . ."* etc.

I knew you'd like an example of a finished Prioritizing Grid, which is what you have on page 134. Note that there is a mistake on line 3 in Section D. No matter if you make a mistake. Just cross it out and put the correct information. It's okay not to be perfect.

Now, back to the *chart* on page 129. Copy the first five factors in Section D of the *grid*, into the third column of the *chart*. What you've got there, now, is a *negative* list of what you're trying to avoid. What you want is a *positive* list of what you're trying to find.

So, look at the five negative items you just put up there, in the third column of the *chart,* and write *the opposite,* or something near *the opposite,* directly opposite each item, in the fourth column of the *chart.* By "opposite" I don't necessarily mean "the exact opposite." If one of your

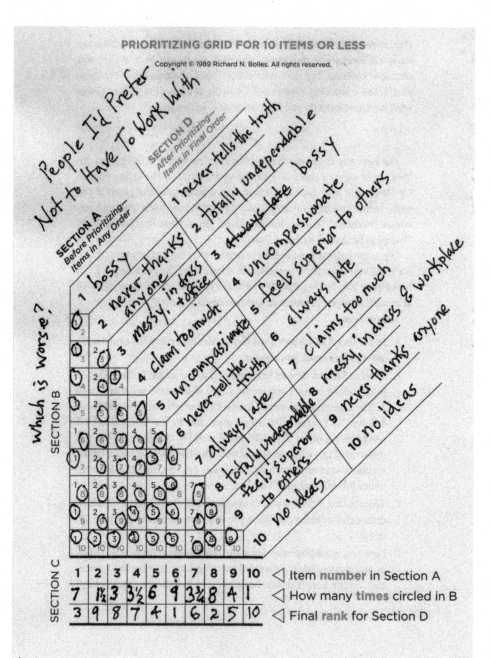

PRIORITIZING GRID FOR 10 ITEMS OR LESS

People I'd Prefer Not to Have To Work With

SECTION A — Before Prioritizing—Items in Any Order

SECTION D — After Prioritizing—Items in Final Order

Which is worse?

SECTION B

SECTION C

1 bossy
2 never thanks anyone
3 messy in dress + office
4 claim too much
5 uncompassionate
6 never tell the truth
7 always late
8 totally undependable
9 feels superior to others
10 no ideas

1 never tells the truth
2 totally undependable
3 always late / bossy
4 uncompassionate
5 feels superior to others
6 always late
7 claims too much
8 messy in dress & workplace
9 never thanks anyone
10 no ideas

SECTION C	1	2	3	4	5	6	7	8	9	10	
	7	1½	3	3½	6	9	3¾	8	4	1	◁ Item **number** in Section A
	3	9	8	7	4	1	6	2	5	10	◁ How many **times** circled in B
											◁ Final **rank** for Section D

complaints in the third column was: "I was micromanaged, supervised every hour of my day," the opposite, in the fourth column, wouldn't necessarily be "No supervision." It might be "Limited supervision" or something like that. Your call.

Note that by first putting your *negative* list in exact order of what you most want to avoid (third column in the chart), your related *positive* list (fourth column) will have its factors in the exact order of what you most want to find in a future job.

You might want, both here and elsewhere in this chapter, a Prioritizing Grid that allows you to work with more than ten items. So, page 136 has a twenty-four item grid, done in the same way as the ten-item. It just takes longer.

Whichever grid you decide to use, when you're done, copy the top five on your *positive* list, onto the petal, My Preferred Kinds of People to Work With, on pages 184–85.

Then we move on, to do the rest of the petal.

The *Party Game* Exercise

This people exercise isn't just a matter of figuring out who irritates you and who doesn't. Though that is important. But, as mentioned earlier, *people* are also a way of identifying careers.

That's because every career has a characteristic people-environment. Tell us what career interests you, and we can tell you, in general terms, what people-environment it will offer—described in terms of six factors.

Or tell us what people-environment you want—in terms of those same six factors—and we can tell you what careers will give you *that*. As I always like to give credit where credit is due, you should know that it was the late Dr. John L. Holland who came up with the system for doing this.[5]

---

5. There is, incidentally, a relationship between the people you like to be surrounded by and your skills and your values. Most of us don't need to go down that road, but if you're curious, you'll need John Holland's book, *Making Vocational Choices* (3rd ed., 1997). You can procure it at your local public library or (if you can afford it) by going to the Psychological Assessment Resources (PAR), Inc., website at www4.parinc.com, and entering the word "Holland" in the search engine there; or by calling 1-800-331-8378. The book is $58.00 at this writing. PAR also has John Holland's instrument, called The Self-Directed Search (or SDS, for short), for discovering what your Holland Code is. PAR lets you take the test online for a small fee ($4.95) at www.self-directed-search.com.

1 1 1 1 1 1 1 1 1 1 1 1 1 1 1 1 1 1 1 1 1 1 1
 2 3 4 5 6 7 8 9 10 11 12 13 14 15 16 17 18 19 20 21 22 23 24

2 2 2 2 2 2 2 2 2 2 2 2 2 2 2 2 2 2 2 2 2 2
 3 4 5 6 7 8 9 10 11 12 13 14 15 16 17 18 19 20 21 22 23 24

3 3 3 3 3 3 3 3 3 3 3 3 3 3 3 3 3 3 3 3 3
 4 5 6 7 8 9 10 11 12 13 14 15 16 17 18 19 20 21 22 23 24

4 4 4 4 4 4 4 4 4 4 4 4 4 4 4 4 4 4 4 4
 5 6 7 8 9 10 11 12 13 14 15 16 17 18 19 20 21 22 23 24

5 5 5 5 5 5 5 5 5 5 5 5 5 5 5 5 5 5 5
 6 7 8 9 10 11 12 13 14 15 16 17 18 19 20 21 22 23 24

6 6 6 6 6 6 6 6 6 6 6 6 6 6 6 6 6 6
 7 8 9 10 11 12 13 14 15 16 17 18 19 20 21 22 23 24

7 7 7 7 7 7 7 7 7 7 7 7 7 7 7 7 7
 8 9 10 11 12 13 14 15 16 17 18 19 20 21 22 23 24

8 8 8 8 8 8 8 8 8 8 8 8 8 8 8 8
 9 10 11 12 13 14 15 16 17 18 19 20 21 22 23 24

9 9 9 9 9 9 9 9 9 9 9 9 9 9 9
 10 11 12 13 14 15 16 17 18 19 20 21 22 23 24

10 10 10 10 10 10 10 10 10 10 10 10 10 10
 11 12 13 14 15 16 17 18 19 20 21 22 23 24

11 11 11 11 11 11 11 11 11 11 11 11 11
 12 13 14 15 16 17 18 19 20 21 22 23 24

12 12 12 12 12 12 12 12 12 12 12 12
 13 14 15 16 17 18 19 20 21 22 23 24

13 13 13 13 13 13 13 13 13 13 13
 14 15 16 17 18 19 20 21 22 23 24

14 14 14 14 14 14 14 14 14 14
 15 16 17 18 19 20 21 22 23 24

15 15 15 15 15 15 15 15 15
 16 17 18 19 20 21 22 23 24

16 16 16 16 16 16 16 16
 17 18 19 20 21 22 23 24

17 17 17 17 17 17 17
 18 19 20 21 22 23 24

18 18 18 18 18 18
 19 20 21 22 23 24

19 19 19 19 19
 20 21 22 23 24

20 20 20 20
 21 22 23 24

21 21 21
 22 23 24

22 22
 23 24

23
 24

PRIORITIZING GRID FOR 24 ITEMS

Total times each number got circled

1	2	3	4	5	6
7	8	9	10	11	12
13	14	15	16	17	18
19	20	21	22	23	24

Surveying the whole job-market, he said there are basically six people-environments. Let's tick them off:

1. Realistic People-Environment: filled with people who prefer activities involving "the explicit, ordered, or systematic manipulation of objects, tools, machines, and animals." "Realistic," incidentally, refers to Plato's conception of "the real" as that which one can apprehend through the senses. ("Knock on wood!")

   I summarize this as: R = people who like nature, or plants, or animals, or athletics, or tools and machinery, or being outdoors.

2. Investigative People-Environment: filled with people who prefer activities involving "the observation and symbolic, systematic, creative investigation of physical, biological, or cultural phenomena."

   I summarize this as: I = people who are very curious, liking to investigate or analyze things, or people, or data.

3. Artistic People-Environment: filled with people who prefer activities involving "ambiguous, free, unsystematized activities and competencies to create art forms or products."

   I summarize this as: A = people who are very artistic, imaginative, and innovative, and don't like time clocks.

4. Social People-Environment: filled with people who prefer activities involving "the manipulation of others to inform, train, develop, cure, or enlighten."

   I summarize this as: S = people who are bent on trying to help, teach, or serve people.

5. Enterprising People-Environment: filled with people who prefer activities involving "the manipulation of others to attain organizational or self-interest goals."

   I summarize this as: E = people who like to start up projects or organizations, or sell things, or influence and persuade people.

6. Conventional People-Environment: filled with people who prefer activities involving "the explicit, ordered, systematic manipulation of data, such as keeping records, filing materials, reproducing materials, organizing written and numerical data according to a prescribed plan, operating business and data-processing machines." "Conventional," incidentally, refers to the "values" that people in this environment usually hold—representing the central mainstream of our culture.

   I summarize this as: C = people who like detailed work, and like to complete tasks or projects.

According to John's theory every one of us has three preferred people-environments, from among these six. The letters, above, for your three preferred people-environments gives you what is called your "Holland Code." The question is, Which three?

Back in 1975 I invented a quick and easy way for you to find out, based on John's system. It's turned out it corresponds to the results you would get from the SDS, 92% of the time.[6] So if you want a much more certain answer, you should take the SDS. But when you're in a hurry, this is close. I call it "The Party Exercise." Here is how the exercise goes (*do it, please*):

On the next page is an aerial view of a room in which a party is taking place. At this party, people with the same interests have (for some reason) all gathered in the same corner of the room. And that's true for all six corners.

1. Which corner of the room would you instinctively be drawn to, as the group of people you would most enjoy being with for the longest time? (Leave aside any question of shyness, or whether you would have to actually talk to them; you could just listen.)

   Write the letter for that corner here: ☐

---

6. Amusing anecdote: John was a good friend of mine, and when I first showed him this Party Exercise I had invented, I asked him what he thought of it. With a twinkle in his eye he snorted, "Huh! Probably put me out of business!" Nope, it didn't. His SDS has sold more than thirty million copies, and is the basis for many other career tests or instruments.

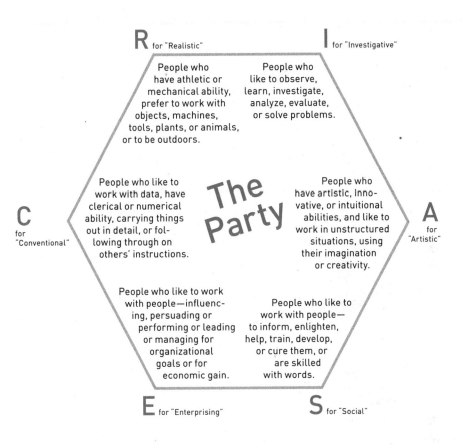

2. After fifteen minutes, everyone in the corner you chose leaves for another party crosstown, except you. Of the groups that still remain now, which corner or group would you be drawn to the most, as the people you would most enjoy being with for the longest time?

Write the letter for that corner here: ☐

3. After fifteen minutes, this group too leaves for another party, except you. Of the corners, and groups, which remain now, which one would you most enjoy being with for the longest time?

Write the letter for that corner here: ☐

The three letters you just chose are called your "Holland Code."[7]

Put that code here: ☐ ☐ ☐

Now, copy that code on to the petal, My Preferred Kinds of People to Work With, found on pages 184–85. And we are done (with that petal). Time now to move on to another side of Who You Are.

---

7. Incidentally, John always encouraged people to write down somewhere all six versions (technically called *permutations*) of your code. Thus, if your code were, say, SIA, its permutations would be: SIA, SAI, IAS, ISA, ASI, AIS. This is especially useful if you are ever going to look up careers that correspond to your code. Put "Holland codes for careers" into your favorite search engine, and you will find such sites as www.vista-cards.com/occupations.

Further, he and I worked together on this application of his system to daydreams: list all the things you've ever dreamed of doing. Then, to the right of each, try to *guess*—guess!—at what you think the three-letter Holland code would be for each. When done, look at each code and assign a value of 3 to any letter in the first position; assign a value of 2 to any letter in the second position; and assign a value of 1 to any letter in the third position (e.g., in the case of IAS, you'd give 3 points to "I," 2 points to "A," and 1 point to "S"). Do this for every code you've written down, then total up all the points for each letter. How many points did "R" get, how many points did "I" get, etc. Choose the top three with the most points, in order, when you're done, and you have the Holland Code of your daydreams. As John said to me, "This is the most reliable way of determining someone's code, but who would believe it, except you and me?"

I Am a Person Who . . .
Can Do These Particular Things

And *loves* having these transferable skills. Or gifts. Or talents. Or abilities. (Or whatever you want to call them.)

There is a trend these days toward speaking of your gifts in terms of categories like "action verbs," or "communication or people skills," "technical skills," "research and analytical skills," "management, supervision, and leadership skills," "clerical and administrative skills," "problem-solving and development skills," "financial skills," etc. I prefer breaking transferable skills down into simpler categories: are they skills with information, data, and the like, or are they skills with people, or are they skills with things?" And now, to the Petal:

Third Petal

WHAT I CAN DO AND LOVE TO DO
(MY FAVORITE TRANSFERABLE SKILLS)

My Favorite Transferable Skills Petal

Goal in Filling Out This Petal: To discover what your transferable skills are, that can be used in any field or interest. These are your skills with people, or your skills with data, or your skills with things. They are things you probably were born knowing how to do, or at least you began with a natural gift and have honed and sharpened it since.

What You Are Looking For: Not just what you *can* do, but which of those skills you most *love* to use.

Form of the Entries on Your Petal: Verbs, usually in pure verb form (e.g. *analyze*) though they may sometimes be in *gerund* form (ending in -ing, e.g., *analyzing*).

Example of a Good Petal: (These stories show that I can) *innovate, manipulate, analyze, classify, coach, negotiate;* OR (These stories show that I am good at) *innovating, manipulating, analyzing, classifying, coaching, negotiating.*

Example of a Bad Petal: *Adaptable, charismatic, reliable, perceptive, discreet, dynamic, persistent, versatile.*

   Why Bad: These are all *traits*, that is, they are the style with which you do your best, favorite, transferable skills. They are important, but they are not transferable skills. Incidentally, there is a new category floating around in the past ten years, called "soft skills." These are really just another way of speaking about traits, because examples typically given are things like "a good work ethic," "a positive attitude," "acting as a team player," "flexibility," "working well under pressure," and "ability to learn from criticism."

Here, you are looking for what you may think of as the basic building-blocks of your work. So, if you're going to identify your dream job, and/or attempt a thorough career-change, you must, above all else, identify your functional, transferable skills. And while you may think you know what your best and favorite skills are, in most cases your self-knowledge could probably use a little work.

A weekend should do it! In a weekend, you can inventory your *past* sufficiently so that you have a good picture of the *kind* of work you would love to be doing *in the future.* (*You can, of course, stretch the inventory over a number of weeks, maybe doing an hour or two one night a week, if you prefer. It's up to you as to how fast you do it.*)

A Crash Course on "Transferable Skills"

Many people just "freeze" when they hear the word "skills."

It begins with high school job-hunters: "I haven't really got any skills," they say.

It continues with college students: "I've spent four years in college. I haven't had time to pick up any skills."

And it lasts through the middle years, especially when a person is thinking of changing his or her career: "I'll have to go back to college, and get retrained, because otherwise I won't have any skills in my new field." Or: "Well, if I claim any skills, I'll start at a very entry kind of level."

All of this fright about the word "skills" is very common, and stems from a total misunderstanding of what the word means. A misunderstanding that is shared, we might add, by altogether too many employers, or human resources departments, and other so-called "vocational experts."

By understanding the word, you will automatically put yourself way ahead of most job-hunters. And, especially if you are weighing a change of career, you can save yourself much waste of time on the adult folly called, "I must go back to school." I've said it before, and I'll say it again: *maybe* you need some further schooling, but very often it is possible to make a dramatic career-change without any retraining. It all depends. And you won't really *know* whether or not you need further schooling, until you have finished all the exercises in this section of the book.

All right, then, if transferable skills are the heart of your vision and your destiny, let's see just exactly what transferable skills *are*.

Here are the most important truths you need to keep in mind about transferable, functional skills:

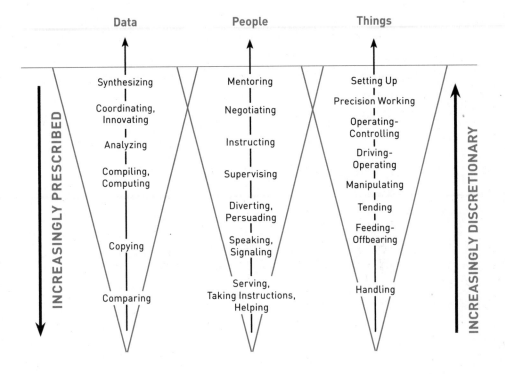

1. Your transferable (functional) skills are the most basic unit—the atoms—of whatever career you may choose.

   Above is a famous diagram of them, invented by the late Sidney A. Fine (reprinted by his permission).

2. You should always claim the highest skills you legitimately can, on the basis of your past performance.

   As we see in the functional/transferable skills diagram above, your transferable skills break down into three *families*, according to whether you use them with Data/Information, People, or Things. And again, as this diagram makes clear, within each family there are *simple* skills, and there are higher, or *more complex* skills, so that these all can be diagrammed as inverted pyramids, with the simpler skills at the bottom, and the more complex ones in order above it.

Incidentally, as a general rule—to which there are exceptions—
each *higher* skill requires you to be able also to do all those skills
listed below it. So of course you can claim *those*, as well. But you
want to especially claim the highest skill you legitimately can,
on each pyramid, based on what you have already proven you
can do, in the past.

3. The higher your transferable skills, the more freedom you
   will have on the job.

   Simpler skills can be, and usually are, heavily *prescribed* (by the
   employer), so if you claim *only* the simpler skills, you will have to
   "fit in"—following the instructions of your supervisor, and doing
   exactly what you are told to do. The *higher* the skills you can
   legitimately claim, the more you will be given discretion to carve
   out the job the way you want to—so that it truly fits *you*.

4. The higher your transferable skills, the less competition you will
   face for whatever job you are seeking, because jobs that use such
   skills will rarely be advertised through normal channels.

   Not for you the way of classified ads, resumes, and agencies. No,
   if you can legitimately claim higher skills, then to find such jobs
   you *must* follow the step-by-step process I am describing here.

   The essence of our approach to job-hunting or career-changing
   is that once you have identified your favorite transferable skills,
   and your favorite special knowledges, you may then approach
   *any organization that interests you, whether they have a known
   vacancy or not*. Naturally, whatever places you visit—and
   particularly those that have not advertised any vacancy—you
   will find far fewer job-hunters that you have to compete with.

   In fact, if the employers you visit happen to like you well
   enough, they may be willing to create for you a job that does not
   presently exist. *In which case, you will be competing with no one,
   since you will be the sole applicant for that newly created job.* While
   this doesn't happen all the time, it is astounding to me how
   many times it *does* happen. The *reason* it does is that the employers often have been *thinking* about creating a new job within their
   organization, for quite some time—but with this and that, they
   just have never gotten around to *doing* it. Until you walked in.

Then they decided they didn't want to let you get away, since *good employees are as hard to find as good employers.* And they suddenly remember that job they have been thinking about creating for many weeks or months, now. So they dust off their *intention,* create the job on the spot, and offer it to you! And if that new job is not only what *they* need, but is exactly what *you* were looking for, then you have a dream job. Match-match. Win-win.

From our country's perspective, it is also interesting to note this: by this job-hunting initiative of yours, you have helped accelerate the creation of more jobs in your country, which is so much on everybody's mind here in the new millennium. How nice to help your country, as well as yourself!

5. Don't confuse transferable skills with traits.

Functional/transferable skills are often confused with traits, temperaments, or type. People think transferable skills are such things as: *has lots of energy, gives attention to details, gets along well with people, shows determination, works well under pressure, is sympathetic, intuitive, persistent, dynamic, dependable,* etc. As mentioned earlier, these are not functional/transferable skills, but traits, or the *style* with which you do your transferable skills. For example, take *"gives attention to details."* If one of your *transferable skills* is *"conducting research"* then *"gives attention to details"* describes the manner or style with which you do the transferable skill called *conducting research.* If you want to know what your traits are, popular tests such as the *Myers-Briggs Type Indicator* measure that sort of thing.[8]

---

8. The Myers-Briggs Type Indicator, or "MBTI®," measures what is called *psychological type.* For further reading about this, see:

Paul D. Tieger and Barbara Barron-Tieger, *Do What You Are: Discover the Perfect Career for You Through the Secrets of Personality Type,* Fourth Edition, Little, Brown & Company, 2007. For those who cannot obtain the MBTI®, this book includes a method for readers to identify their personality types. This is one of the most popular career books in the world. It's easy to see why. Many have found great help from the concept of personality type, and the Tiegers are masters in explaining this approach to career-choice. Highly recommended.

Donna Dunning, *What's Your Type of Career? Unlock the Secrets of Your Personality to Find Your Perfect Career Path,* Nicholas Brealey Publishing, 2010. This is a dynamite book on personality type. Donna Dunning's knowledge of "Type" is encyclopedic!

David Keirsey and Marilyn Bates, *Please Understand Me: Character & Temperament Types,* B&D Books, 1984. Includes the Keirsey Temperament Sorter—again, for those who cannot obtain the MBTI®.

If you have access to the Internet, there are clues, at least, about your traits or "type":

Working Out Your Myers-Briggs Type
www.teamtechnology.co.uk/mb-intro/mb-intro.htm
An informative article about the Myers-Briggs

The 16 Personality Types
www.personalitypage.com/high-level.html
A helpful site about Myers types

What Is Your Myers-Briggs Personality Type?
www.personalitypathways.com/type_inventory.html
www.personalitypathways.com
Another article about personality types; also, there's a Myers-Briggs Applications page, with links to test resources

Myers-Briggs Foundation home page
www.myersbriggs.org
The official website of the Foundation; lots of testing resources

Human Metrics Test (Jung Typology)
www.humanmetrics.com/cgi-win/JTypes2.asp
Free test, loosely based on the Myers-Briggs

Myers-Briggs Type Indicator Online
www.discoveryourpersonality.com/MBTI.html
On this site you can find the official Myers-Briggs test, $60

The Keirsey Temperament Sorter
http://keirsey.com
Free test, similar to the Myers-Briggs

"I WOULDN'T RECOGNIZE MY SKILLS IF THEY CAME UP AND SHOOK HANDS WITH ME"

Now that you know what transferable skills technically *are*, the problem that awaits you now, is figuring out your own. If you are one of the few lucky people who already know what your transferable skills are, blessed are you. Write them down, and put them in the order of preference, for you, on the Flower Diagram (pages 184–85).

If, however, you don't know what your skills are (and 95% of all workers *don't*), then you will need some help. Fortunately, there is an exercise to help.

It involves the following steps:

1. Write a Story (The First of Seven)

Yes, I know, I know. You can't do this exercise because you don't like to write. *Writers are a very rare breed.* That's what thousands of job-hunters have told me, over the years. And for years I kind of believed them— until "texting" came along. Let's face it: we human beings are "a writing people," and we only need a topic we have a real passion for, or interest in, for the writing genie to spring forth from within each of us, pen or keyboard in hand.

So, call the *Seven Stories* you're about to write your personal *offline blog*, if you prefer. But start writing. Please.

Here is a specific example:

> *A number of years ago, I wanted to be able to take a summer trip with my wife and four children. I had a very limited budget, and could not afford to put my family up in motels. I decided to rig our station wagon as a camper.*
>
> *First I went to the library to get some books on campers. I read those books. Next I designed a plan of what I had to build, so that I could outfit the inside of the station wagon, as well as topside. Then I went and purchased the necessary wood. On weekends, over a period of six weeks, I first constructed, in my driveway, the shell for the "second story" on my station wagon. Then I cut doors, windows, and placed a six-drawer bureau within that shell. I mounted it on top of the wagon, and pinioned it in place by driving two-by-fours under the station wagon's rack on top. I then outfitted the inside of the station wagon, back in the wheel-well, with a table and a bench on either side, that I made.*
>
> *The result was a complete homemade camper, which I put together when we were about to start our trip, and then disassembled after we got back home. When we went on our summer trip, we*

were able to be on the road for four weeks, yet stayed within our budget, since we didn't have to stay at motels. I estimate I saved $1,900 on motel bills, during that summer's vacation.

Ideally, each story you write should have the following parts, as illustrated above:

1. Your goal: what you wanted to accomplish: *"I wanted to be able to take a summer trip with my wife and four children."*

2. Some kind of hurdle, obstacle, or constraint that you faced (self-imposed or otherwise): *"I had a very limited budget, and could not afford to put my family up in motels."*

3. A description of what you did, step by step (how you set about to ultimately achieve your goal, above, in spite of this hurdle or constraint): *"I decided to rig our station wagon as a camper. First I went to the library to get some books on campers. I read those books. Next I designed a plan of what I had to build, so that I could outfit the inside of the station wagon, as well as topside. Then I went and purchased the necessary wood. On weekends, over a period of six weeks, I . . ." etc., etc.*

4. A description of the outcome or result: *"When we went on our summer trip, we were able to be on the road for four weeks, yet stayed within our budget, since we didn't have to stay at motels."*

5. Any measurable/quantifiable statement of that outcome, that you can think of: *"I estimate I saved $1,900 on motel bills, during that summer's vacation."*

Now write *your* story, using the sample as a guide.

Don't pick a story where you achieved something *big*. At least to begin with, write a story about a time when you had fun!

Do not try to be too brief. This isn't Twitter.

If you absolutely can't think of any experiences you've had where you enjoyed yourself, and accomplished something, then try this: describe the seven most enjoyable jobs that you've had; or seven roles you've had so far in your life, such as: wife, mother, cook, homemaker, volunteer in the community, citizen, dressmaker, student, etc. Tell us something you did or accomplished, in each role.

2. Analyze Your Story, to See What Transferable Skills You Used

On the next page, write the title of your first story *above* the number 1. Then work your way down the column *below* that number 1, asking yourself in each case: "Did I use this skill in *this story*?"

If the answer is "Yes," color the little square in, with a red pen or whatever you choose.

Work your way through the entire *Parachute* Skills Grid that way, with your first story.

Voilà! You are done with Story #1. However, "one swallow doth not a summer make," so the fact that you used certain skills in this first story doesn't tell you much. What you are looking for is patterns— transferable skills that keep reappearing in story after story. They keep reappearing because they are your favorites (assuming you chose stories where you were *really* enjoying yourself).

THE PARACHUTE SKILLS GRID

Your Seven Stories

In the space to the left, write above each number, in turn, the name you give to each story. Begin with Story #1. After you have written it, give it a name. Enter that name here (turn page on its side) above #1.

1	2	3	4	5	6	7	Skills with People; as my story shows, I can . . .
							Initiate, lead, be a pioneer
							Supervise, manage
							Follow through, get things done
							Motivate
							Persuade, sell, recruit
							Consult
							Advise
							Coordinate
							Negotiate, resolve conflicts
							Help people link up or connect
							Heal, cure
							Assess, evaluate, treat
							Convey warmth and empathy
							Interview, draw out
							Raise people's self-esteem
							Instruct
							Teach, tutor, or train (individuals, groups, animals)

1	2	3	4	5	6	7	Skills with People; as my story shows, I can . . . *(continued)*
							Speak
							Listen
							Counsel, guide, mentor
							Communicate well, in person
							Communicate well, in writing
							Divert, amuse, entertain, perform, act
							Play an instrument
							Interpret, speak, or read a foreign language
							Serve, care for, follow instructions faithfully
							Skills with Data, Ideas; as my story shows, I can . . .
							Use my intuition
							Create, innovate, invent
							Design, use artistic abilities, be original
							Visualize, including in three dimensions
							Imagine
							Use my brain
							Synthesize, combine parts into a whole
							Systematize, prioritize
							Organize, classify
							Perceive patterns
							Analyze, break down into its parts
							Work with numbers, compute
							Remember people, or data, to unusual degree
							Develop, improve
							Solve problems

1	2	3	4	5	6	7	Skills with Data, Ideas; as my story shows, I can ... (continued)
							Plan
							Program
							Research
							Examine, inspect, compare, see similarities and differences
							Pay attention to details
							Use acute senses (hearing, smell, taste, sight)
							Study, observe
							Compile, keep records, file, retrieve
							Copy
							Skills with Things; as my story shows, I can ...
							Control, expedite things
							Make, produce, manufacture
							Repair
							Finish, restore, preserve
							Construct
							Shape, model, sculpt
							Cut, carve, chisel
							Set up, assemble
							Handle, tend, feed
							Operate, drive
							Manipulate
							Use my body, hands, fingers, with unusual dexterity or strength

3. Write Six Other Stories, and Analyze Them for Transferable Skills

Now, write Story #2, from any period in your life, analyze it using the grid, etc., etc. And keep this process up, until you have written, and analyzed, seven stories.

If you are finding it difficult to come up with seven stories, it may help you to know how others chose one or more of their stories:[9]

"As I look back, I realize I chose a story that:

- Is somehow abnormal or inconsistent with the rest of my life

- Reveals my skills in a public way

- Is in a field (such as leisure, learning, etc.) far removed from my work

- I remembered through or because of its outcome

- Represented a challenge/gave me pride because it was something:
  - I previously could not do
  - My friends could not do
  - I was not supposed to be able to do
  - Only my father/mother could do, I thought
  - Only authorized/trained/experts were supposed to be able to do
  - Somebody told me I could not do
  - My peers did not do/could not do
  - The best/brilliant/famous could or could not do
  - I did not have the right degree/training to do
  - People of the opposite sex usually do

- I would like to do again:
  - In a similar/different setting
  - With similar/different people
  - For free for a change/for money for a change

---

9. This list copyright © 1994 Daniel Porot.

- Excited me because:
  - I never did it before
  - It was forbidden
  - I took a physical risk
  - I was taking a financial risk
  - No one had ever done it before
  - It demanded a long and persistent (physical/mental) effort
  - It made me even with someone
- I loved doing it because:
  - I kind of like this sort of thing
  - The people involved were extremely nice
  - It did not cost me anything
- It will support/justify the professional goals I have already chosen"

4. Patterns and Priorities

When you've finished this whole inventory, for all seven of your accomplishments/achievements/jobs/roles or whatever, you want to look for PATTERNS and PRIORITIES.

a. For Patterns, because it isn't a matter of whether you used a skill once only, but rather whether you used it again and again. "Once" proves nothing; "again and again" is very convincing.

b. For Priorities (that is, which skills are most important to you), because the job you eventually choose may not be able to use all of your skills. You need to know *what you are willing to trade off, and what you are not.* This requires that you know which skills, or family of skills, are most important to you.

So, after finishing your seven stories (or if you're in a hurry, at least five), look through that Skills Grid, and now *guess* which *might* be your top ten favorite or your top twenty-four favorite skills. These should be your best *guesses,* and they should be about *your favorite* skills: not the ones you think the job-market will like the best, but the ones *you* enjoy using the most.

At this point you want to be able to prioritize those ten or those twenty-four *in exact order of priority.* We need something a little more scientific than *guesses.* Time for the Prioritizing Grid again, either the ten-item one, or the twenty-four (or fewer) one (pages 158–59). Your choice. Run your *guesses* through the grid you choose, and when you're done with that grid's Section D, copy the top ten (from either grid) on to the building blocks diagram below, as well as onto your Favorite Transferable Skills petal, on pages 184–85.

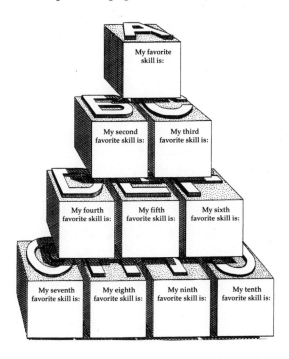

A word of explanation about this building blocks diagram. Its purpose is to show, as the Skills Petal cannot, how rearranging your skills can define a new career. Suppose for example I end up with these top ten favorite skills: analyze, teach, research, write, diagnose, synthesize, entertain, classify, convey warmth, lead, motivate. *(I might prefer to put them in their gerund form: analyzing, teaching, researching, writing, diagnosing, synthesizing, entertaining, classifying, conveying warmth, leading, motivating.)* Either way, if I enter these terms onto those building blocks, the top one helps to define the kind of job or career I'm looking for. Put "analyzing" in the top block, I might seek a job as an analyst. But,

PRIORITIZING GRID FOR 10 ITEMS OR LESS

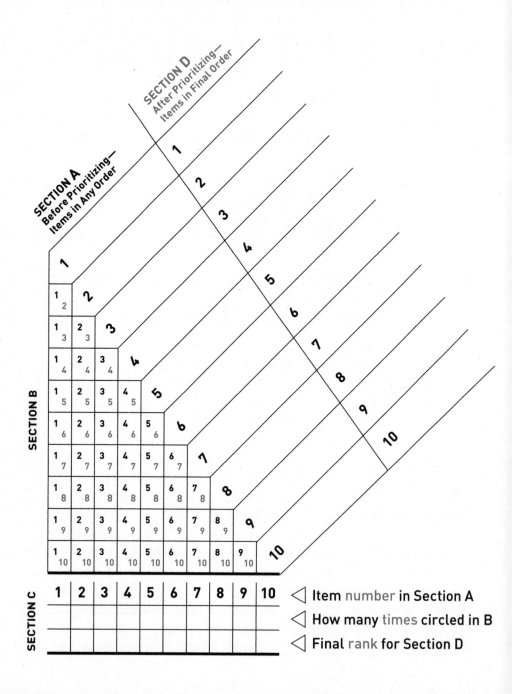

SECTION D—
After Prioritizing—
Items in Final Order

SECTION A
Before Prioritizing—
Items in Any Order

SECTION B

SECTION C

◁ Item number in Section A
◁ How many times circled in B
◁ Final rank for Section D

1 1 1 1 1 1 1 1 1 1 1 1 1 1 1 1 1 1 1 1 1 1 1
2 3 4 5 6 7 8 9 10 11 12 13 14 15 16 17 18 19 20 21 22 23 24

2 2 2 2 2 2 2 2 2 2 2 2 2 2 2 2 2 2 2 2 2 2
3 4 5 6 7 8 9 10 11 12 13 14 15 16 17 18 19 20 21 22 23 24

3 3 3 3 3 3 3 3 3 3 3 3 3 3 3 3 3 3 3 3 3
4 5 6 7 8 9 10 11 12 13 14 15 16 17 18 19 20 21 22 23 24

4 4 4 4 4 4 4 4 4 4 4 4 4 4 4 4 4 4 4 4
5 6 7 8 9 10 11 12 13 14 15 16 17 18 19 20 21 22 23 24

5 5 5 5 5 5 5 5 5 5 5 5 5 5 5 5 5 5 5
6 7 8 9 10 11 12 13 14 15 16 17 18 19 20 21 22 23 24

6 6 6 6 6 6 6 6 6 6 6 6 6 6 6 6 6 6
7 8 9 10 11 12 13 14 15 16 17 18 19 20 21 22 23 24

7 7 7 7 7 7 7 7 7 7 7 7 7 7 7 7 7
8 9 10 11 12 13 14 15 16 17 18 19 20 21 22 23 24

8 8 8 8 8 8 8 8 8 8 8 8 8 8 8 8
9 10 11 12 13 14 15 16 17 18 19 20 21 22 23 24

9 9 9 9 9 9 9 9 9 9 9 9 9 9 9
10 11 12 13 14 15 16 17 18 19 20 21 22 23 24

10 10 10 10 10 10 10 10 10 10 10 10 10 10
11 12 13 14 15 16 17 18 19 20 21 22 23 24

11 11 11 11 11 11 11 11 11 11 11 11
12 13 14 15 16 17 18 19 20 21 22 23 24

12 12 12 12 12 12 12 12 12 12 12 12
13 14 15 16 17 18 19 20 21 22 23 24

13 13 13 13 13 13 13 13 13 13 13
14 15 16 17 18 19 20 21 22 23 24

14 14 14 14 14 14 14 14 14 14
15 16 17 18 19 20 21 22 23 24

15 15 15 15 15 15 15 15 15
16 17 18 19 20 21 22 23 24

16 16 16 16 16 16 16 16
17 18 19 20 21 22 23 24

17 17 17 17 17 17 17
18 19 20 21 22 23 24

18 18 18 18 18 18
19 20 21 22 23 24

19 19 19 19 19
20 21 22 23 24

20 20 20 20
21 22 23 24

21 21 21
22 23 24

22 22
23 24

23
24

PRIORITIZING GRID FOR 24 ITEMS

Total times each number got circled

1	2	3	4	5	6
7	8	9	10	11	12
13	14	15	16	17	18
19	20	21	22	23	24

if instead I move "teaching" to the top block, then I might seek a job as a teacher. And so on, with "researching," "writing," "diagnosing," etc.

Here we see the folly of most training programs for the unemployed. They deal with roles when they should be dealing with skills. An unemployed construction worker, for example, is typically *retrained* for just one role: say, *computer repair person*. But if we see ourselves not as one role, but as ten different skills, then after retraining, there are several careers (or roles) we can pursue.

5. "Flesh Out" Your Favorite Transferable Skills with Your Traits

We discussed traits earlier (pages 147–48). In general, traits describe: How you deal with time, and promptness.

How you deal with people and emotions.

How you deal with authority, and being told what to do at your job.

How you deal with supervision, and being told how to do your job.

How you deal with impulse vs. self-discipline, within yourself.

How you deal with initiative vs. response, within yourself.

How you deal with crises or problems.

You need to flesh out your skill-description for each of your favorite skills so that you are able to describe each of your talents or skills with more than just a one-word verb or gerund, like *organizing*.

Let's take *organizing* as our example. You tell us proudly: "I'm good at organizing." That's a fine start at defining your skills, but unfortunately it doesn't yet tell us much. Organizing WHAT? People, as at a party? Nuts and bolts, as on a workbench? Or lots of information, as on a computer? These are three entirely different skills. The one word *organizing* doesn't tell us which one is yours.

So, please look at your top ten favorite transferable skills, and ask yourself if you want to flesh out any of them with an object—some kind of Data/Information, or some kind of People, or some kind of Thing—or with a Trait (adverb or adjective).

Why adjectives here? Well, "I'm good at organizing information painstakingly and logically" and "I'm good at organizing information in a flash, by intuition," are two entirely different skills. The difference between them is spelled out not in the verb, nor in the object, but in the

A CHECKLIST OF MY STRONGEST TRAITS

I am very . . .

- ❑ Accurate
- ❑ Achievement-oriented
- ❑ Adaptable
- ❑ Adept
- ❑ Adept at having fun
- ❑ Adventuresome
- ❑ Alert
- ❑ Appreciative
- ❑ Assertive
- ❑ Astute
- ❑ Authoritative
- ❑ Calm
- ❑ Cautious
- ❑ Charismatic
- ❑ Competent
- ❑ Consistent
- ❑ Contagious in my enthusiasm
- ❑ Cooperative
- ❑ Courageous
- ❑ Creative
- ❑ Decisive
- ❑ Deliberate
- ❑ Dependable/have dependability
- ❑ Diligent
- ❑ Diplomatic
- ❑ Discreet
- ❑ Driving
- ❑ Dynamic
- ❑ Effective
- ❑ Energetic
- ❑ Enthusiastic
- ❑ Exceptional
- ❑ Exhaustive
- ❑ Experienced
- ❑ Expert
- ❑ Extremely economical
- ❑ Firm
- ❑ Flexible
- ❑ Humanly oriented
- ❑ Impulsive
- ❑ Independent
- ❑ Innovative
- ❑ Knowledgeable
- ❑ Loyal
- ❑ Methodical
- ❑ Objective
- ❑ Open-minded
- ❑ Outgoing
- ❑ Outstanding
- ❑ Patient
- ❑ Penetrating
- ❑ Perceptive
- ❑ Persevering
- ❑ Persistent
- ❑ Pioneering
- ❑ Practical
- ❑ Professional
- ❑ Protective
- ❑ Punctual
- ❑ Quick/work quickly
- ❑ Rational
- ❑ Realistic
- ❑ Reliable
- ❑ Resourceful
- ❑ Responsible
- ❑ Responsive
- ❑ Safeguarding
- ❑ Self-motivated
- ❑ Self-reliant
- ❑ Sensitive
- ❑ Sophisticated, very sophisticated
- ❑ Strong
- ❑ Supportive
- ❑ Tactful
- ❑ Thorough
- ❑ Unique
- ❑ Unusual
- ❑ Versatile
- ❑ Vigorous

adjectival or adverbial phrase there at the end. So, expand the definition of any of your ten favorite skills that you choose, in the fashion I have just described.

When you are face-to-face with a person-who-has-the-power-to-hire-you, you want to be able to explain what makes you different from nineteen other people who can basically do the same thing that you can do. It is often the adjective or adverb that will save your life, during that explanation.

Now, on to another side of Who You Are.

I Am a Person Who . . .
Has Favorite Working Conditions

Fourth Petal

MY FAVORITE WORKING CONDITIONS

My Favorite Working Conditions Petal

Goal in Filling Out This Petal: To state the working conditions and surroundings, that would make you happiest, and therefore enable you to do your most effective work.

What You Are Looking For: Avoiding past bad experiences.

Form of the Entries on Your Petal: Descriptors of physical surroundings.

Example of a Good Petal: *A workspace with lots of windows, nice view of greenery, relatively quiet, decent lunch period, flexibility about clocking in and clocking out, lots of shops nearby.*

Example of a Bad Petal: *Understanding boss, good colleagues, fun clients, etc.*

> **Why Bad:** These all belong on the petal called Preferred Kinds of People to Work With, not this one, which is just about the physical surroundings at your work. Of course, since this is your Flower Diagram, you can put any info you like on any petal you like. It's just that if you want your thinking to be clear, it's useful to preserve the difference between "what is my physical setting going to be like?" and "who will I be working with?"

Your physical setting where you work can cheer you up or drag your spirits down. It's important to know this before you weigh whether to take a particular job offer, or not. So, let's start with working conditions that made you unhappy in the past, and then flip them over into positives, by filling out the chart on the opposite page.

Plants that grow beautifully at sea level, often perish if they're taken ten thousand feet up the mountain. Likewise, we do our best work under certain conditions, but not under others. Thus, the question: "What are your favorite working conditions?" actually is a question about "Under what circumstances do you do your most effective work?"

As I just mentioned, the best way to approach this is by starting with the things you *disliked* about all your previous jobs, using the chart to list these. Copy this chart onto a larger piece of notebook paper if you wish, before you begin filling it out. *Column A may begin with such factors as: "too noisy," "too much supervision," "no windows in my workplace," "having to be at work by 6 a.m.," etc.*

If you are baffled as to how to prioritize the Column A list in the space provided for that ranking (Column B), I recommend you use the ten-item Prioritizing Grid on the next page. (For a refresher on how to use it, turn to "Instructions for Using the Prioritizing Grid," pages 130–33.) This time, when you compare each two items, the

DISTASTEFUL WORKING CONDITIONS

	Column A — Distasteful Working Conditions	Column B — Distasteful Working Conditions Ranked	Column C + The Keys to My Effectiveness at Work
Places I Have Worked Thus Far in My Life	I Have Learned from the Past That My Effectiveness at Work Is Decreased When I Have to Work Under These Conditions	Among the Factors or Qualities Listed in Column A, These Are the Ones I Dislike Absolutely the Most (in Order of Decreasing Dislike)	I Believe My Effect- iveness Would Be at an Absolute Maximum, If I Could Work Under These Conditions (The Opposite of the Qualities in Column B, in Order):
		1a.	1b.
		2a.	2b.
		3a.	3b.
		4a.	4b.
		5a.	5b.
		6a.	6b.
		7a.	7b.
		8a.	8b.
		9a.	9b.
		10a.	10b.

PRIORITIZING GRID FOR 10 ITEMS OR LESS

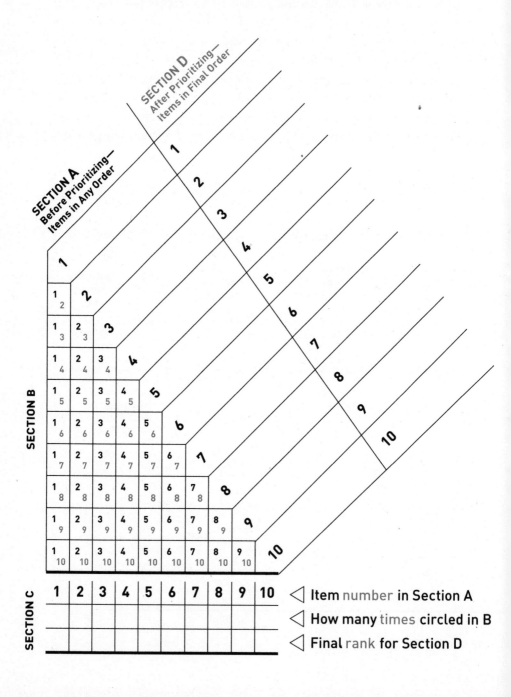

◁ Item number in Section A

◁ How many times circled in B

◁ Final rank for Section D

question you must ask yourself is, "If I were offered two jobs, and in the first job offer I would be rid of my first distasteful working condition (1) but not the second (2), while in the second job offer I would be rid of my second distasteful working condition (2), but not the first (1), which job offer would I take?"

After you've finished prioritizing, what have you ended up with, in Section D? The exact list you copy into Column B of your Distasteful Working Conditions chart, page 163.

Now that you have that list in Column B, ranked in terms of most distasteful down to least distasteful working conditions, turn to Column C in that chart and write *the opposite*, or something near *the opposite*, directly opposite each item in Column B.

Copy the top five items in Column C, onto the Favorite Working Conditions petal of your Flower Diagram, pages 184–85.

Now, on to another side of Who You Are.

"THE VALUE OF MY HOUSE IS WAY DOWN, THE VALUE OF MY CAR IS PRACTICALLY NOTHING, AND I FOUND OUT THIS SUIT IS ONLY WORTH $23."

I Am a Person Who . . .
Prefers a Certain Level of Responsibility and Salary

Fifth Petal

MY PREFERRED SALARY AND LEVEL OF RESPONSIBILITY

My Preferred Salary Petal

Goal in Filling Out This Petal: To gain a realistic picture of how much money you will need to earn, or want to earn, at whatever job you find.

What You Are Looking For: A range, because most employers are thinking in terms of a range, too. When you negotiate salary, as you will almost certainly have to, you want the bottom of your range to be near the top of theirs.

Form of the Entries on Your Petal: Total dollars needed, weekly, monthly, or annually. Stated in thousands (symbol: K).

Example of a Good Petal: $75K to $85K

Example of a Bad Petal: $300K
> **Why Bad:** Well, it's not a range, which it needs to be; and it's too high unless you put on the petal the reason why such a high income is expected, and justified.

Money is important. Or else we've got to barter for our food, clothing, and shelter. So, when we're out of work, unless we have huge amounts of money in our savings account or investments, we are inevitably thinking: "What am I going to do, so that I have enough money to put food on the table, clothes on my back, and a roof over our heads for myself—and for my family or partner (*if I have one*)?"

Happiness is important, too. So, we may find ourselves thinking: "How much do I really need to be earning, for me to be truly happy with my life?"

Are these two worries—money and happiness—related? Can money buy happiness?

Partly, it turns out. Partly. A study, published in 2010, of the responses of 450,000 people in the U.S. to a daily survey, found that the less money they made, the more unhappy they tended to be, day after day.[10] No surprise, there. And, obviously, the more money they made, measured in terms of percentage improvement, the happier they tended to be, *as measured by the frequency and intensity of moments of smiling, laughter, affection, and joy all day long, vs. moments of sadness, worry, and stress.*

So, money does buy happiness. But only up to a point. That point was found to be around $75,000 annual income (*at the end of 2011, median household income was $51,413*[11]). If people made more money than $75,000, it of course further improved their *satisfaction* with how their life was going, but it did not increase their happiness. Above $75,000, they started to report reduced ability to spend time with people they liked, to enjoy leisure, and to savor small pleasures. Happiness depends on things like that, and on other factors too: good health, a loving relationship, loving friends, a feeling of competence, gaining mastery, respect, praise, or even love, because we are really good at what we do.

So, this petal cannot be filled out all by itself. It is inextricably tied to the other petals—most particularly, to what you love to do, and where you love to do it.

Still, salary is something you must think out ahead of time, when you're contemplating your ideal job or career. Level goes hand in hand with salary, of course.

---

10. Daniel Kahneman and Angus Deaton, *Proceedings of the National Academy of Sciences*, Early Edition, September 6, 2010.
11. According to Sentier Research, reported by Paul Davidson, "U.S. Median Household Income Up 4% at End of 2011," *USA Today*, February 9, 2012.

1. The first question here is at what level would you like to work, in your ideal job?

Level is a matter of how much responsibility you want, in an organization:

- ❑ Boss or CEO (this may mean you'll have to form your own business)
- ❑ Manager or someone under the boss who carries out orders
- ❑ The head of a team
- ❑ A member of a team of equals
- ❑ One who works in tandem with one other partner
- ❑ One who works alone, either as an employee or as a consultant to an organization, or as a one-person business

Enter a two- or three-word summary of your answer, on the Preferred Salary and Level of Responsibility petal of your Flower Diagram, pages 184–85.

2. The second question here is what salary would you like to be aiming for?

Here you have to think in terms of minimum or maximum. Minimum is what you would need to make, if you were just barely "getting by." And you need to know this *before* you go in for a job interview with anyone (*or before you form your own business, and need to know how much profit you must make, just to survive*).

Maximum could be any astronomical figure you can think of, but it is more useful here to put down the salary you realistically think you could make, with your present competency and experience, were you working for a real, *but generous,* boss. (If this maximum figure is still depressingly low, then put down the salary you would like to be making five years from now.)

Make out a detailed list of what you will need monthly, in each category:[12]

---

12. If this kind of budget planning is just not *you*, there is help available. Online, you will find that MoneySavingExpert.com has a free budget-planner (click on Banking at the top, then under Current Accounts you will see BudgetPlanner; click on that). Other online tools are listed at http://tinyurl.com/cuq2bdy. Offline, think of some buddy, friend, relative, family member, or other, who is a whiz at this type of thing and can volunteer to help you. If you come up empty, consider any groups you belong to in the community: local religious center, church, synagogue, mosque, gym, social club, and ask the manager there if they can suggest anybody who is wise and generous with their time. Ask them, gently, for help. Thank them afterward.

Housing

    Rent or mortgage payments . . . . $_____

    Electricity/gas. . . . . $_____

    Water . . . . $_____

    Phone/Internet. . . . . $_____

    Garbage removal . . . . $_____

    Cleaning, maintenance, repairs[13]. . . . . $_____

Food

    What you spend at the supermarket

    and/or farmer's market, etc. . . . . $_____

    Eating out . . . . $_____

Clothing

    Purchase of new or used clothing. . . . . $_____

    Cleaning, dry cleaning, laundry . . . . $_____

Automobile/transportation

    Car payments . . . . $_____

    Gas (*who knows?*[14]) . . . . $_____

    Repairs. . . . . $_____

    Public transportation (*bus, train, plane*) . . . . $_____

Insurance

    Car . . . . $_____

    Medical or health care. . . . . $_____

    House and personal possessions. . . . . $_____

    Life . . . . $_____

Medical expenses

    Doctors' visits. . . . . $_____

    Prescriptions. . . . . $_____

    Fitness costs . . . . $_____

---

13. If you have extra household expenses, such as a security system, be sure to include the quarterly (or whatever) expenses here, divided by three.

14. Your checkbook stubs and/or online banking records will tell you a lot of this stuff. But you may be vague about your cash or credit card expenditures. For example, you may not know how much you spend at the supermarket, or how much you spend on gas, etc. But there is a simple way to find out. Keep notes on your Smartphone or iPad for two weeks (there are apps for that), jotting down everything you pay cash (or use credit cards) for—on the spot, right after you pay it. At the end of those two weeks, you'll be able to take that notepad and make a realistic guess of what should be put down in these categories that now puzzle you. (Multiply the two-week figure by two, and you'll have the monthly figure.)

Support for other family members
> Child-care costs (*if you have children*)............ $_____
> Child-support (*if you're paying that*)............. $_____
> Support for your parents (*if you're helping out*)..... $_____

Charity giving/tithe (*to help others*)................ $_____

School/learning
> Children's costs (*if you have children in school*) ..... $_____
> Your learning costs (*adult education,*
> *job-hunting classes, etc.*)...................... $_____

Pet care (*if you have pets*) .... $_____

Bills and debts (*usual monthly payments*)
> Credit cards........................... $_____
> Local stores .... $_____
> Other obligations you pay off monthly.......... $_____

Taxes
> Federal[15] (*next April's due, divided by*
> *months remaining until then*).................... $_____
> State (*likewise*) .... $_____
> Local/property (*next amount due, divided by*
> *months remaining until then*).................... $_____
> Tax-help (*if you ever use an accountant,*
> *pay a friend to help you with taxes, etc.*) .... $_____

Savings.. $_____

Retirement (*Keogh, IRA, SEP, etc.*) .... $_____

Amusement/discretionary spending
> Movies, Netflix, etc............................ $_____
> Other kinds of entertainment .... $_____
> Reading, newspapers, magazines, books......... $_____
> Gifts (*birthday, Christmas, etc.*).................. $_____
> Vacations .... $_____

Total Amount You Need Each Month.............. $_____

15. Incidentally, for U.S. citizens, looking ahead to next April 15, be sure to check with your local IRS office or a reputable accountant to find out if you can deduct the expenses of your job-hunt on your federal (and state) income tax returns. At this writing, some job-hunters can, if—big IF—this is not your first job that you're looking for, if you haven't been unemployed too long, and if you aren't making a career-change. Do go find out what the latest "ifs" are. If the IRS says you are eligible, keep careful receipts of everything related to your job-hunt, as you go along: telephone calls, stationery, printing, postage, travel, etc.

Multiply the total amount you need each month by 12, to get the yearly figure. Divide the yearly figure by 2,000, and you will be reasonably near the *minimum* hourly wage that you need. Thus, if you need $3,333 per month, multiplied by 12 that's $40,000 a year, and then divided by 2,000, that's $20 an hour.

Parenthetically, you may want to prepare another version of this budget: one with the expenses you'd ideally *like* to make.

Now, enter the salary figure and any notes you want to add, about the level of responsibility you want to take on, to justify this salary, plus any "non-monetary" rewards you seek (from the Optional Exercise below), on the Preferred Salary and Level of Responsibility petal, found on pages 184–85.

Optional Exercise

You may wish to put down other rewards, besides money, that you would hope for, from your next job or career. These might be:

❏ Adventure

❏ Challenge

❏ Respect

❏ Influence

❏ Popularity

❏ Fame

❏ Power

❏ Intellectual stimulation from the other workers there

❏ A chance to be creative

❏ A chance to help others

❏ A chance to exercise leadership

❏ A chance to make decisions

❏ A chance to use your expertise

❏ A chance to bring others closer to God

❏ Other:

If you do check off things on this list, arrange your answers in order of importance to you, and then add them to the petal.

I Am a Person Who . . .
Prefers Certain Places to Live

Sixth Petal

MY PREFERRED PLACE TO LIVE

My Preferred Place to Live Petal

Goal in Filling Out This Petal: To define where you would most like to work and live, and be happiest, if you ever have a choice. Or, to resolve a conflict between you and your partner as to where you want to move to, when you retire.

What You Are Looking For: Having a clearer picture about what you hope for, in life. Now or later. Now, if you're able to move and want to make a wise decision as to *where*. Later, If you're currently tied down to a particular place because "I need to be near my kids or my ailing parents, or whatever," in which case this becomes a planning for the future: retirement, or earlier. It's important to think about the future *now*, because an opportunity may come along when you least expect it, and you might pass right by it, unless you've given it some thought, and instantly recognize it.

Form of the Entries on Your Petal: You can stay general (*city, suburbs, rural, up in the mountains, on the coast,* or *overseas*); or you can get very specific if you're really ready to move, naming names and places—as this exercise will teach you to do.

Example of a Good Petal: *First preference: Jackson, Wyoming; Second preference: Honolulu; Third preference: New York City.*

Example of a Bad Petal: *The West; a suburb; snow.*

> **Why Bad:** Too broad. Doesn't really offer any help in making a decision. And it isn't prioritized, as the good petal is.

DIRECTIONS FOR DOING THIS EXERCISE

1. Copy the chart that is on the next two pages, onto a larger (11 x 17-inch) piece of paper or cardboard, which you can obtain from any arts and crafts store or supermarket, in your town or city. If you are doing this exercise with a partner, make a copy for them too, so that each of you is working on a clean copy of your own, and can follow these instructions independently.

2. In *Column 1,* each of you should list all the places where you have ever lived.

3. In *Column 2,* each of you should list all the factors you disliked (and still dislike) about each place. The factors do not have to be put exactly opposite the name in *Column 1.* The names in *Column 1* exist simply to jog your memory.

   If, as you go, you remember some good things about any place, put those factors at the bottom of the next column, *Column 3.*

   If the same factors keep repeating, just put a checkmark after the first listing of that factor, every time it repeats.

   Keep going until you have listed all the factors you disliked or hated about each and every place you named in *Column 1.* Now, in effect, throw away *Column 1;* discard it from your thoughts. The negative factors were what you were after. *Column 1* has served its purpose.

4. Look at *Column 2,* now, your list of negative factors, and in *Column 3* try to list each one's opposite (or near opposite). For example, "the sun never shone, there" would, in *Column 3,* be turned into "mostly sunny, all year 'round." It will not always be *the exact opposite.* For example, the negative factor "rains all the time" does not necessarily translate into the positive "sunny all the time." It might be something like "sunny at least 200 days a year." It's your call. Keep going, until every negative factor in *Column 2* is turned into its opposite, a positive factor, in *Column 3.* At the bottom, note the positive factors you already listed there, when you were working on *Column 2.*

My Geographical Preferences
DECISION MAKING FOR JUST YOU

Column 1	Column 2	Column 3	Column 4
Names of Places I Have Lived	From the Past: Negatives	Translating the Negatives into Positives	Ranking of My Positives
	Factors I Disliked and Still Dislike about Any Place		1.
			2.
			3.
			4.
			5.
			6.
			7.
			8.
		Factors I Liked and Still Like About Any Place	9.
			10.

Our Geographical Preferences
DECISION MAKING FOR YOU AND A PARTNER

Column 5	Column 6	Column 7	Column 8
Places That Fit These Criteria	Ranking of His/Her Preferences	Combining Our Two Lists (Columns 4 & 6)	Places That Fit These Criteria
	a.	a.	
		1.	
	b.	b.	
		2.	
	c.	c.	
		3.	
	d.	d.	
		4.	
	e.	e.	
		5.	
	f.	f.	
		6.	
	g.	g.	
		7.	
	h.	h.	
		8.	
	i.	i.	
		9.	
	j.	j.	
		10.	

5. In *Column 4*, now, list the positive factors in *Column 3*, in the
    order of most important (to you), down to least important (to
    you). For example, if you were looking at, and trying to name a
    new town, city, or place where you could be happy and flourish,
    what is the first thing you would look for? Would it be, good
    weather? or lack of crime? or good schools? or access to cultural
    opportunities, such as music, art, museums, or whatever? or
    would it be inexpensive housing? etc., etc. Rank all the factors in
    Column 4. Use the ten-item Prioritizing Grid on page 178 if you
    need to.

6. If you are doing this by yourself, list on a *scribble sheet* the top ten
    factors, in order of importance to you, and show it to everyone
    you meet for the next ten days, with the ultimate question: "Can
    you think of places that have these ten factors, or at least the top
    five?" Jot down their suggestions on the back of the *scribble
    sheet*. When the ten days are up, look at the back of your sheet
    and circle the three places that seem the most interesting to you.
    If there is only a partial overlap between your dream factors and
    the places your friends and acquaintances suggested, *make sure
    the overlap is in the factors that count the most*. Now you have some
    names that you will want to find out more about, until you are
    sure which is your absolute favorite place to live, and then your
    second, and third, as backups. Enter in *Column 5*.

    Put the names of the three places, and/or your top five
    geographical factors, on the Flower Diagram, on the Preferred
    Place(s) to Live petal, pages 184–85.

7. If you are doing this with a partner, skip *Column 5*. Instead,
    when you have finished your *Column 4*, look at your partner's
    Column 4, and copy it into *Column 6*. The numbering of *your* list
    in *Column 4* was 1, 2, 3, 4, etc. Number your partner's list, as you
    copy it into *Column 6*, as a, b, c, d, etc.

8. Now, in *Column 7*, combine your *Column 4* with *Column 6* (your partner's old *Column 4*). Both of you can work now from just one person's chart. Combine the two lists as illustrated on the chart. First your partner's top favorite geographical factor ("a"), then *your* top favorite geographical factor ("1"), then your partner's second most important favorite geographical factor ("b"), then yours ("2"), etc., until you have twenty favorite geographical factors (*yours and your partner's*) listed, in order, in *Column 7*.

9. List on a *scribble sheet* the top ten factors, and both of you should show it to everyone you meet, for the next ten days, with the same question as above: "Can you think of any places that have these ten factors, or at least the top five?" Jot down their suggestions on the back of the *scribble sheet*. When the ten days are up, you and your partner should look at the back of your sheet and circle the three places that look the most interesting to the two of you. If there is only a partial overlap between your dream factors and the places your friends and acquaintances suggested, make sure the overlap is in the factors that matter the most to the two of you, i.e., the ones that are at the top of your list in *Column 7*. Now you have some names of places that you will want to find out more about, until you are sure which is the absolute favorite place to live for both of you, and then your second, and third, as backups. Enter in *Column 8*.

Put the names of the top three places, and/or your top five geographical factors, on the Flower Diagram, on the Preferred Place(s) to Live petal, pages 184–85.

Conclusion: Was all of this too much work? Then do what one family did: they put a map of the U.S. up on a corkboard, and then they each threw a dart at the map from across the room, and when they were done they asked themselves where the most darts landed. It turned out to be around "Denver." So, *Denver* it was!

And now we turn to the last side of Who You Are.

PRIORITIZING GRID FOR 10 ITEMS OR LESS

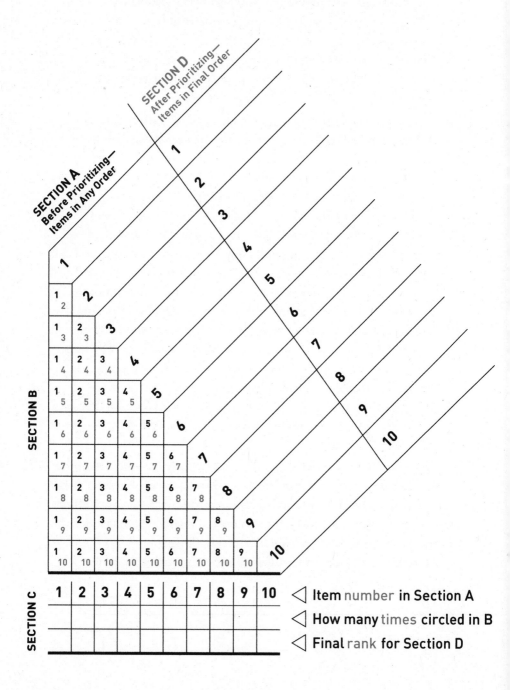

I Am a Person Who . . .
Has a Certain Goal, Purpose, or Mission in Life

Seventh Petal

MY GOAL, PURPOSE, OR MISSION IN LIFE

My Purpose in Life Petal

Goal in Filling Out This Petal: To know the moral compass or spiritual values by which you want to guide your life. The most victorious life is one that is dedicated to some larger cause or mission.

What You Are Looking For: Some definition of the purpose and mission of your life. This may help you pick out the kinds of organizations or companies you'd like to work for, if you find ones that are serving the same mission as yours.

Form of the Entries on Your Petal: A description of what kingdom of life you want to make better, with some attending details.

Example of a Good Petal: *My purpose in life is to help the human spirit. I want there to be more faith, more compassion, more forgiveness, in families, because I have lived.*

Example of a Bad Petal: *More justice in the world.*
   Why Bad: An admirable goal, but it is too vague. Doesn't give you any guidance as to what kind of work to look for.

As John L. Holland famously said, "We need to look further down the road than just headlight range at night." The road is the road of Life. You need to dream about the broad outcome of your life, and not just this year's job-search. What kind of footprint do you want to leave on this Earth, after your journey here is done? Figure that out, and you're well on your way to defining your life as having purpose and a mission.

The Nine Kingdoms of Mission and Purpose

Generally speaking, mission breaks down into nine kingdoms—corresponding to our nature. As you look these over, the question is, which one appeals to *you* the most? Time for some hard thinking (ouch!). So, read on, *slowly*. Take time to ponder and think.

1. The Mind. The question is: *When you have finished your life here on Earth, do you want there to be more knowledge, truth, or clarity in the world, because you were here? Knowledge, truth, or clarity concerning* what *in particular?* If this is You, then your sense of purpose is pointing you toward the kingdom of the mind.

2. The Body. The question is: *When you have finished your life here on Earth, do you want there to be more wholeness, fitness, or health in the world, more binding up of the body's wounds and strength, more feeding of the hungry, and clothing of the poor, because you were here? What issue in particular?* If this is You, then your sense of purpose is pointing you toward the kingdom of the body.

3. The Eyes and Other Senses. The question is: *When you have finished your life here on Earth, do you want there to be more beauty in the world, because you were here? If so, what kind of beauty entrances you? Is it art, music, flowers, photography, painting, staging, crafts, clothing, jewelry, or what?* If this is You, then your sense of purpose is pointing you toward the kingdom of the eyes and senses.

4. The Heart. The question is: *When you have finished your life here on Earth, do you want there to be more love and compassion in the world, because you were here? Love or compassion for whom? Or for what?* If this is You, then your sense of purpose is pointing you toward the kingdom of the heart.

5. The Will or Conscience. The question is: *When you have finished your life here on Earth, do you want there to be more morality, more justice, more righteousness, more honesty in the world, because you were here? In what areas of human life or history, in particular? And in what geographical area?* If this is You, then your sense of purpose is pointing you toward the kingdom of the conscience.

6. The Spirit. The question is: *When you have finished your life here on Earth, do you want there to be more spirituality in the world, more faith, more compassion, more forgiveness, more love for God and the human family in all its diversity, because you were here? If so, with what ages, people, or with what parts of human life?* If this is You, then your sense of purpose is pointing you toward the kingdom of the spirit, or (if you prefer) *The Kingdom of God*.

7. Entertainment. The question is: *When you have finished your life here on Earth, do you want there to be more lightening of people's loads, more giving them perspective, more helping them to forget their cares for a spell, do you want there to be more laughter in the world, and joy, because you were here? If so, what particular kind of entertainment do you want to contribute to the world?* If this is You, then your sense of purpose is pointing you toward the kingdom of entertainment.

8. Our Possessions. The question is: *Is your major concern the often false love of possessions in this world? When you have finished your life here on Earth, do you want there to be better stewardship of what we possess—as individuals, as a community, as a nation—in the world, because you were here? Do you want to see simplicity, quality (rather than quantity), and a broader emphasis on the word "enough," rather than on the word "more, more"? If so, in what areas of human life in particular?* If this is You, then your sense of purpose is pointing you toward the kingdom of possessions.

9. The Earth. The question is: *Is the planet on which we stand, your major concern? When you have finished your life here on Earth, do you want there to be better protection of this fragile planet, more exploration of the world or the universe—exploration, not exploitation—more dealing with its problems and its energy, because you were here? If so, which problems or challenges in particular, draw your heart and soul?* If this is You, then your sense of purpose is pointing you toward the kingdom of the Earth.

In sum, remember that all of these are worthwhile purposes and missions, all of these are necessary and needed, in this world. The question is, which one in particular draws you to it, *the most?* Which one do you most want to lend your brain, your energies, your skills and gifts, your life, to serve, while you are here on this Earth?[16]

When you are done, enter a summary paragraph of what you have decided your purpose or mission is, on the Goal, Purpose, or Mission in Life petal, on pages 184–85.

P.S. There are two challenges you may run into, in doing this particular exercise. First Challenge: you just come up empty on this exercise, despite hard thinking. No harm done. If you want an answer, just keep the question on the back-burner of your mind; eventually some insight is going to break through. Tomorrow, next week, next month, or a year from now. Be patient with yourself.

Second Challenge: This subject doesn't grab you at all. Okay. Then instead of writing a statement of purpose or mission for your life, you can write instead a statement outlining what you think about *life*: why are we here, why are *You* here, and so on. This is often called "Your Philosophy of Life":

In writing a philosophy of life, it should be no more than two pages, single spaced, and can be less; it should address whichever of these elements you think are most important; pick and choose. You do not have to write about all of them. In most cases, you will only need two or three sentences about each element you choose to comment on.

Beauty: what kind of beauty stirs us, what the function of beauty is in the world

Behavior: how we should behave in this world

Beliefs: what our strongest beliefs are

Celebration: how we like to play or celebrate, in life

Choice: what its nature and importance is

Community: what our concept is about belonging to each other; what we think our responsibility is to each other

Compassion: what we think about its importance and use

Confusion: how we live with it, and deal with it

Death: what we think about it and what we think happens after it

---

16. And by the way, if you want to have fun, if you have a computer go to the Internet, choose a browser like Google or Bing, and type your kingdom (*the Mind, etc.*) into the search line, and see if anything pops up that intrigues you.

Events: what we think makes things happen, how we explain why they happen

Free will: whether we are "predetermined" or have free will

God: see Supreme Being

Happiness: what makes for the truest human happiness

Heroes and heroines: who ours are, and why

Human: what we think is important about being human, what we think is our function

Love: what we think about its nature and importance, along with all its related words: compassion, forgiveness, grace

Moral issues: which ones we believe are the most important for us to pay attention to, wrestle with, help solve

Paradox: what our attitude is toward its presence in life

Purpose: why we are here, what life is all about

Reality: what we think is its nature, and components

Self: deciding whether physical self is the limit of your being, deciding what trust in self means

Spirituality: what its place is in human life, how we should treat it

Stewardship: what we should do with God's gifts to us

Supreme Being: our concept of, and what we think holds the universe together

Truth: what we think about it, which truths are most important

Uniqueness: what we think makes each of us unique

Values: what we think about ourselves, what we think about the world, prioritized as to what matters most (to us)

When you are done writing, put a summary paragraph on your Goal, Purpose, or Mission in Life petal, on pages 184–85.

And, finally:

I Am a Person Who . . .
Has Completed My Flower

The Flower

"That One Piece of Paper"

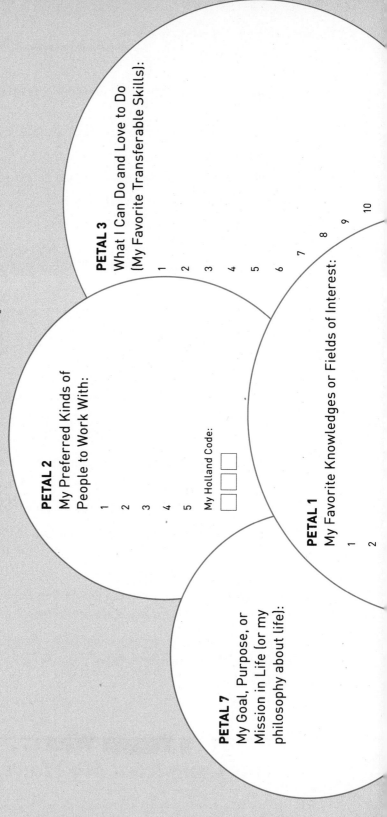

PETAL 3
What I Can Do and Love to Do
(My Favorite Transferable Skills):

1

2

3

4

5

6

7

8

9

10

PETAL 2
My Preferred Kinds of
People to Work With:

1

2

3

4

5

My Holland Code:

PETAL 1
My Favorite Knowledges or Fields of Interest:

1

2

PETAL 7
My Goal, Purpose, or
Mission in Life (or my
philosophy about life):

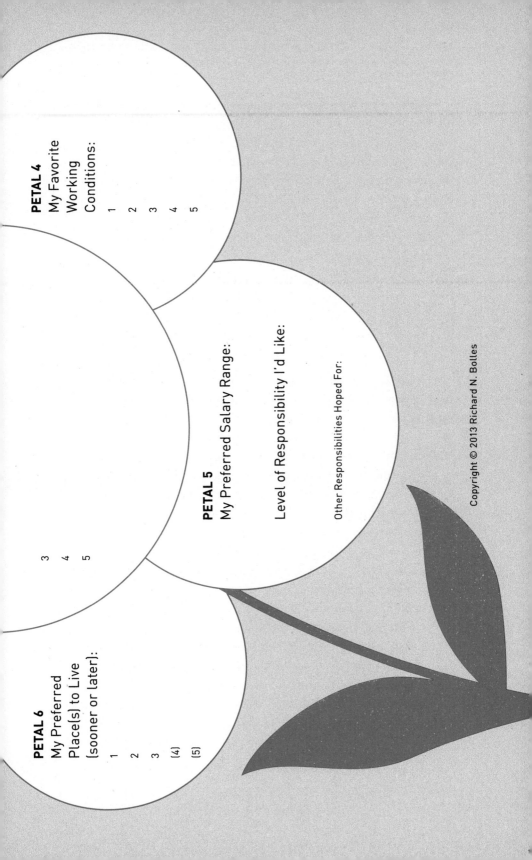

PETAL 4
My Favorite
Working
Conditions:

1

2

3

4

5

PETAL 5
My Preferred Salary Range:

Level of Responsibility I'd Like:

Other Responsibilities Hoped For:

PETAL 6
My Preferred
Place(s) to Live
(sooner or later):

1

2

3

(4)

(5)

3

4

5

Readers have asked to see an example of "That One Piece of Paper" all filled out. Rich W. Feller—a student of mine back in 1982, now a world-famous professor and the 2012–2013 President of the National Career Development Association—filled out his flower as you see, on the facing page. He said "That One Piece of Paper" has been his life-long companion ever since, and his guiding star. (The petals then were slightly different.)

Rich Feller first put his personal "picture" together over thirty years ago. Here are his comments about its usefulness since, and how "That One Piece of Paper" helped him, how he's used it, and how it's changed.

WHAT THE PARACHUTE FLOWER HAS MEANT TO ME

More than anything I've gained from an academic life, my Flower has given me hope, direction, and a lens to satisfaction. Using it to assess my life direction during crisis, career moves, and stretch assignments, it helps me define and hold to personal commitments. In many ways it's my "guiding light." Data within my Flower became and remain the core of any success and satisfaction I have achieved.

After I first filled out my own Flower Diagram in a two-week workshop with Dick Bolles back in 1982, I decided to teach the Flower to others. My academic position has allowed me to do this, abundantly. Having now taught the Flower to thousands of counselors and career development and human resource specialists, I continually use it with clients, and in my own transitional retirement planning.

I'm overwhelmed with how little has changed within my Flower, over the years. My Flower is the best of what I am. Its petals are my compass, and using my "favorite skills" are the mirror to a joyful day. I trust the wisdom within "That One Piece of Paper." It has guided my work and my life, ever since 1982, and it has helped my wife and I define our hopes for our son.

Example
(Rich Feller's Flower)

Favorite People-Environment

1. Strong social, perceptual skills 2. Emotionally and physically healthy 3. Enthusiastically include others 4. Heterogeneous in interests and skills 5. Social changers, innovators 6. Politically, economically astute 7. Confident enough to confront/cry and be foolish 8. Sensitive to non-traditional issues 9. I and R (see page 137) 10. Non-materialistic

Favorite Values

1. Improve the human condition 2. Promote interdependence and futuristic principles 3. Maximize productive use of human/material resources 4. Teach people to be self-directed/self-responsible 5. Free people from self-defeating controls (thoughts, rules, barriers) 6. Promote capitalistic principles 7. Reduce exploitation 8. Promote political participation 9. Acknowledge those who give to the community 10. Give away ideas

Favorite Interests

1. Large conference planning 2. Regional geography & culture 3. Traveling on $20/day 4. Career planning seminars 5. Counseling techniques/theories 6. American policies 7. Fundamentals of sports 8. Fighting sexism 9. NASCAR auto racing 10. Interior design

Favorite Skills

1. Observational/learning skills • continually expose self to new experiences • perceptive in identifying and assessing potential of others 2. Leadership skills • continually searches for more resonsibility • sees a problem/acts to solve it 3. Instructing/interpreting/guiding • committed to learning as a life-long process • create atmosphere of acceptance 4. Serving/helping/human relations skills • shapes atmosphere of particular place • relates well in dealing with public 5. Detail/follow-through skills • handle great variety of tasks • resource broker 6. Influencing/persuading skills • recruiting talent/leadership • inspiring trust 7. Performing skills • getting up in front of a group (if I'm in control) • addressing small and large groups 8. Intuitional/innovative skills • continually develop/generate new ideas 9. Develop/plan/organize/execute • designing projects • utilizing skills of others 10. Language/read/write • communicate effectively • can think quickly on my feet

Favorite Working Conditions

1. Receive clinical supervision 2. Mentor relationship 3. Excellent secretary 4. Part of larger, highly respected organization with clear direction 5. Near gourmet and health food specialty shops 6. Heterogeneous colleagues (race, sex, age) 7. Flexible dress code 8. Merit system 9. Can bike/bus/walk to work 10. Private office with window

Geography

1. Close to major city 2. Mild winters/low humidity 3. Change in seasons 4. Clean and green 5. 100,000 people 6. Nice shopping malls 7. Wide range of athletic options 8. Diverse economic base 9. Ample local culture 10. Sense of community (pride)

Salary and Level of Responsibility

1. Can determine 9/12 month contract 2. Can determine own projects 3. Considerable clout in organization's direction without administrative responsibilities 4. Able to select colleagues 5. 3 to 5 assistants 6. $35K to $50K 7. Serve on various important boards 8. Can defer clerical and budget decisions and tasks 9. Speak before large groups 10. Can run for elected office

The process of filling out and acting on "That One Piece of Paper" taught me a lot. Specifically, it taught me **the importance of the following ten things, often running contrary to what my studies and doctoral work had taught me previously.**

I learned from my Flower the importance of:

1. Chasing after passions, honoring strengths, and respecting skill identification

2. Challenging societal definitions of balance and success

3. Committing to something bigger than oneself

4. Living authentically and with joy

5. Being good at what matters to oneself and its relationship to opportunity

6. Finding pleasure in all that one does

7. Staying focused on well-being and life satisfaction

8. Personal clarity and responsibility for designing "possible selves"

9. Letting the world know, humbly but clearly, what we want

10. "Coaching" people amidst a world of abundance where individuals yearn for individual meaning and purpose more than they hunger for possessions, abject compliance with society's expectations, or simply fitting in

This technologically enhanced, global workplace we now face in the twenty-first century certainly challenges all we thought we knew about our life roles. Maintaining clarity, learning agility, and identifying development plans have become elevated to new and critical importance, if we are to maintain choice. As a result I've added the following four emphases to "Rich's Flower": Have, do, learn, and give. That is to say, I try to keep a running list (constantly updated) of ten things that I want to:

1. Have
2. Do
3. Learn
4. Give

Through the practice of answering the four questions listed above, I can measure change in my growth and development.

I feel so fortunate to have the opportunity to share with others how much I gained from the wisdom and hope embedded within "Rich's Flower."

I humbly offer my resume, home location and design, and family commitments on my website at www.mycahs.colostate.edu/Rich.Feller. I'd be honored to share my journey, and encourage others to nurture and shine light on their garden as well. I believe you'll find about 90% of the Flower's items influence our daily experience.

Rich Feller
Professor of Counseling and Career Development
University Distinguished Teaching Scholar
Colorado State University
Fort Collins, CO

Okay, like Rich, you've now got your completed Flower. Nice diagram. What do you do with it?

Well, that's the subject of our next chapter.

You've got to be careful
If you don't know where you're going,
Because you might not get there.

—*Yogi Berra (1925–)*

Chapter 8

You Need to Do Some Informational Interviewing

Okay, you've got your completed Flower done. That was the previous chapter. Now what? Your Flower pictorial is beautiful, but what does it mean? What's the next step? These are natural questions.

The Five Different Kinds of Informational Interviewing

What will help you the most, here? You guessed it: *people*. You've got to do some *networking*. I'll bet that sounds familiar!

If someone out of work knows only three words about their job-hunt, those three words will be: *resumes, interviews,* and *networking.* And if there's one really overworked word in that crowd, it's *networking.*

It's used by more job-hunters, and with the least understanding of it, than any other word that I can think of. Job-hunters will go endlessly to group meetings—job support groups, business presentations, college reunions, even beer parties or cocktail parties—and when you ask them what they're doing, they will say, "I'm unemployed. I'm networking. Isn't that what I'm supposed to do?"

Job-hunters will collect people's business cards day after day, week after week, convinced that this will somehow pay off down the line. They approach networking as something magical, based on the unproved belief: *"He or she who ends up with the most business cards, wins at the job-hunt."*

Job-hunters will "friend" reflexively on Facebook and "link" with everyone they can on LinkedIn, trying to collect as many names as possible. Then there's always Google+.

And if you ask them *why* they are doing this, they will reply, "I dunno. I'm just networking!" And networking, and networking.

Well, now you need to network and at last we have a reason. You *network* in order to find out what career, job, or work your Flower Diagram points to.

There are five different kinds of information you need to find out. Hence, there are five kinds of Informational Interviewing—*call them five kinds of networking, if you prefer.* We will look at them in a certain logical order as you seek the meaning of your Flower pictorial. Here are the five, in order:

Informational Interviewing Step One

HOW TO FIND OUT THE NAME OF YOUR FLOWER: WHAT CAREERS OR JOBS YOUR FLOWER POINTS TO

1. First, look at your completed Flower Diagram, and from the center of the Flower choose the top *three* of your favorite Knowledges (or fields of interest, favorite fields, or fields of fascination— whatever you want to call them). All nouns. On one piece of blank paper, say $8^1/_2$ x 11, or on your mobile device, copy these in the top half of that page, in their order of importance to you (most important at the top). Beneath them all, midway down the page, draw a line, straight across.

2. Then, look at the Skills petal on your completed Flower Diagram and choose your top *five* favorite Transferable Skills. All verbs. Copy them down, in order, below the line.

3. Now, take this page and show it to at least five friends, family members, or professionals whom you know. Ask them what jobs or work this page suggests to them. Tell them you just want them to take some wild guesses, combining as many of the eight factors on that page, as possible. *Plan B:* If they absolutely draw a blank, tell them interests or special knowledges (in the top half of the page) usually point toward a career field, while

transferable skills (in the bottom half) usually point toward a job-title or job-level, in that field. So, ask them, in the case of your favorite special knowledges, "What career fields do these suggest to you?" And in the case of your transferable skills, "What job-title or jobs do these skills suggest to you?"

4. Jot down *everything* these people suggest to you, on your computer, iPad, smartphone, or small pad of paper. Whether you like their suggestions, or not. This is just brainstorming, for the moment.

5. After you have done this for a week or so, with everyone you meet, sit down and look at all these notes. Anything helpful or valuable here? If you see some useful suggestions, circle them and determine to explore them. If nothing looks interesting, go talk to five more of your friends, acquaintances, or people you know in the business world or nonprofit sector. Repeat, as necessary.

6. As you ponder any suggestions that look worth exploring, consider the fact we saw in chapter 7, that all jobs can be described as working primarily with *people* or working primarily with *information/data* or working primarily with *things.* Most jobs involve all three, but which is your *primary* preference? It is often your *favorite* skill that will give you the clue. If it *doesn't,* then go back and look at the *whole* Transferable Skills petal, on your Flower Diagram. What do you think? Are your favorite skills weighted more toward working with *people,* or toward working with *information/data,* or toward working with *things*?

7. Just remember what you are trying to do here: find a name for your flower. What you call it—name of Flower, name of a field based on your favorite subjects, the name of your new career, or whatever—doesn't matter. You are trying to find the names of careers or jobs that would give you a chance to use your skills in the most effective way. You want competence, and therefore happiness, in the job-market.

8. If you would be unique, you must combine, as much as you can, two or three fields: that's what can make you unique, with very little competition from others.

Here is how to go about doing that: let us say your three favorite knowledges are gardening and carpentry and a limited knowledge of psychiatry. What you want to do is use all three expertises, not just one of them—if you possibly can. So, put those three favorite knowledges on a series of overlapping circles, as seen above. Now, to figure out how to combine these three, imagine that each circle is a person; that is, in this case, Psychiatrist, Carpenter, and Gardener. You ask yourself which person took the longest to get trained in their specialty. The answer, here, is the psychiatrist. The reason you ask yourself this question, is that the person with the longest training is most likely to have the broadest overview of things. So, you go to see a psychiatrist, either at a private clinic or at a university or hospital. You ask for fifteen minutes of his or her time, and pay them if necessary. Then you ask the psychiatrist if he or she knows how to combine psychiatry with *one*— just one, initially—of your other two favorite knowledges. Let's say you choose gardening, here. "Doctor, do you know anyone who combines a knowledge of psychiatry with a knowledge of gardening or plants?"

Since I'm talking about a true story here, I can tell you what the psychiatrist said: "*Yes, in working with catatonic patients, we often give them a plant to take care of, so they know there is something that is depending on them for its future, and its survival.*"

"And how would I also employ a knowledge of carpentry?"

"*Well, in building the planters, that's a start, isn't it?*"

This is the way you learn how to combine your three favorite knowledges, all at once, no matter what those three may be. The Internet can also be useful, sometimes, with this research.

During this stage of your information gathering, don't ever think to yourself: "Well, I see what it is that I would die to be able to do, but I know there is no job in the world like that." Dear friend, you don't know any such thing. You haven't completed your informational interviewing, yet. Now I grant you that after you have completed it, and conducted your job-search, you still may not be able to find all that you want—down to the last detail. But you'd be surprised at how much of your dream you may be able to find. Sometimes it will be found in stages. One retired man I know, who had been a senior executive with a publishing company, found himself bored to death in retirement, after he turned sixty-five. He decided he didn't care what field he worked in, at that point, so he contacted his favorite business acquaintance, who told him apologetically, "Times are tough. We just don't have anything open that matches or requires your abilities; right now all we need is someone in our mail room." The sixty-five-year-old executive said, "I'll take that job!" He did, and over the ensuing years steadily advanced once again, to just the job he wanted: as a senior executive in that organization, where he utilized all his prized skills, for a number of years. Finally, he retired for the second time, at the age of eighty-five.

Always keep in mind your dream. Get as close to it as you can. Then be patient. You never know what doors will open up.

Informational Interviewing Step Two

HOW TO TRY ON CAREERS BEFORE YOU DECIDE WHICH ONES TO PURSUE

Maybe you're looking for the same kind of work you've previously done; you know that industry or field, and you know it well. Okay, then *you* can skip this step.

But what if you just can't find any jobs in your old field or industry (think: *record stores*). Suppose you just have to go for a career change. Or maybe you really *want* to do a career change. You've found one, or ones, that sound attractive. But before you go and get all the training or education it requires, or before you go job-hunting for that career, you need to *try it on.*

This is exactly analogous to shopping at a clothing store and trying on different suits (or dresses) that you see in their window or on their racks. Why do you try them on? Well, the suits or dresses that look *terrific* in the window don't always look so hot when you see them on *you*. The clothes don't hang quite right, etc.

It's the same with careers. Ones that *sound* terrific in books or in your imagination don't always look so great when you actually see them up close and personal.

What you want of course is a career that looks terrific—in the window, *and* also on you. So this is where you need to go talk to people who are already doing the kind of job or career that you're thinking about. The website LinkedIn should be invaluable to you, in locating the names of such people.

Once you find them, if they live nearby ask for twenty minutes of their time face to face—Starbucks?—and keep to your word, unless during the chat they *insist* they want to go on talking. *Some* workers— not all—are desperate to find someone who will actually listen to them; you may come as an answer to their prayers.

Here are some questions that will help when you're talking *with workers who are actually doing the career or job you think you might like to do*:

- "How did you get into this work?"
- "What do you like the most about it?"
- "What do you like the least about it?"
- And, "Where else could I find people who do this kind of work?" (*You should always ask them for more than one name, here, so that if you run into a dead end at any point, you can easily go visit the other name[s] they suggested.*)

If at any point in these informational interviews with workers, it becomes more and more clear to you that this career, occupation, or job you are exploring definitely doesn't fit you, then the last question (above) gets turned into a different kind of inquiry:

- "Do you have any ideas as to who else I could talk to—*about my skills and special knowledges or interests*—who might know what other careers use the same skills and knowledge?" If they come up with names, go visit the people they suggest. If they can't think of anyone, ask them, "If you don't know of anyone, who do you think might know?"

Sooner or later, as you do this informational interviewing with workers, you'll find a career that fits you just fine. It uses your favorite skills. It employs your favorite special knowledges or fields of interest. Okay, now you must ask how much training, etc., it takes, to get into that field or career. You ask the same people you have been talking to, previously.

More times than not, you will hear *bad news*. They will tell you something like: "In order to be hired for this job, you have to have a master's degree and ten years' experience at it."

Is that so? Keep in mind that no matter how many people tell you that such-and-such are the rules about getting into a particular occupation, and there are no exceptions—believe me there *are* exceptions to almost *every* rule, except for those few professions that have rigid entrance examinations as, say, medicine or law. Otherwise, *somebody* has figured out a way around the rules. You want to find out who these people are, and go talk to them, to find out *how they did it*.

So, in your informational interviewing, you press deeper; you search for *exceptions:*

"Yes, but do you know of anyone in this field who got into it without that master's degree, and ten years' experience?

"And where might I find him or her?

"And if you don't know of any such person, who do you think might know?"

In the end, maybe—just maybe—you can't find any exceptions. It's not that they aren't out there; it's just that you don't know how to find them. So, what do you do when everyone tells you that such and such a career takes *years* to prepare for, and you can't find *anyone* who took a shortcut? What then?

Good news. Every professional specialty has one or more *shadow* professions, which require much less training. For example, instead of becoming a doctor, you can go into paramedical work; instead of becoming a lawyer, you can go into paralegal work; instead of becoming a licensed career counselor, you can become a career coach. There is always a way to get *close*, at least, to what you dream of.

Informational Interviewing Step Three

HOW TO FIND OUT WHAT KINDS OF ORGANIZATIONS HAVE SUCH JOBS

Before you think of individual places where you might like to work, it is helpful to stop and think of all the *kinds* of places where one might get hired, so you can be sure you're casting the widest net possible. *(A fisherman's metaphor, of course.)*

Let's take an example. Suppose in your new career you want to be a teacher. You must then ask yourself: *"What kinds of places hire teachers?"* You might answer, *"Just schools"*—and finding that schools in your geographical area have no openings, you might say, *"Well, there are no jobs for people in this career."*

But wait a minute! There are countless other *kinds* of organizations and agencies out there, besides schools, that employ *teachers.* For example, corporate training and educational departments, workshop sponsors, foundations, private research firms, educational consultants, teachers' associations, professional and trade societies, military bases, state and local councils on higher education, fire and police training academies, and so on and so forth.

"Kinds of places" also means places with different *hiring options,* besides full-time, such as:

- places that would employ you part-time (maybe you'll end up deciding, or having, to hold down two or even three part-time jobs, which together add up to one full-time job);
- places that take temporary workers, on assignment for one project at a time;
- places that take consultants, one project at a time;
- places that operate primarily with volunteers, etc.;
- places that are nonprofit;
- places that are for-profit;
- and, don't forget, places that you yourself could start up, should you decide to be your own boss (see chapter 11).

During this interviewing for information, you should not only talk to people who can give you a broad overview of the career that you are considering. You should also talk with actual workers in those kinds of organizations, who can tell you in more detail what the tasks are in the kinds of organizations that interest you.

Informational Interviewing Step Four

HOW TO FIND OUT THE NAMES OF PARTICULAR PLACES THAT INTEREST YOU

As you interview workers about their jobs or careers, somebody will probably innocently mention, somewhere along the way, actual names of organizations that have such kind of workers—plus what's good or bad about the place. This is important information for you. Jot it all down. Keep notes religiously!

But you will want to supplement what they have told you, by seeking out other people to whom you can simply say: "I'm interested in this kind of organization, because I want to do this kind of work; do you know of particular places like that, that I might investigate? And if so, where they are located?" Use face-to-face interviews, use LinkedIn, use the Yellow Pages, use search engines, to try to find the answer(s) to that question. Incidentally, you must not care, at this point, if they have *known* vacancies or not. The only question that should concern you for the moment is whether or not the place looks interesting, or even intriguing to you. *(The only caveat is that if times are still tough, you will probably want to modify your search to the extent that you investigate smaller places—100 or fewer employees—rather than larger; and newer places, rather than older.)* But for a successful job-hunt you should choose places based on *your interest in them,* and not wait to choose places until you've heard they have a vacancy. Vacancies can suddenly open up in a moment, and without warning.

Moreover, companies approached after you've done thorough homework on yourself and on them, will sometimes create a job just for you. I got the following letter from Dale Stanway, former City Manager, Calgary, Canada, just last week:

I nudged my son, Reid, on to most of your great advice contained in your books. He did the homework you recommend and in about nine weeks he has managed to have two companies create new positions just for him. He found the people with the power to hire him and found out their most important need and presented them with a solution . . . him.

That's down the line. For now, you're still collecting names. What will you end up with, when this step is done? Well, you'll likely have either *too few names* or *too many* to go investigate. There are ways of dealing with either of these eventualities.

TOO MANY NAMES

You will want to cut the territory down, to a manageable number of *targets*.

Let's take an example. Suppose you discover that the career that interests you the most is *welding*. You want to be a welder. Well, that's a beginning. You've cut the 23 million U.S. job-markets down to:

• I want to work in a place that hires welders.

But the territory is still too large. There might be thousands of places in the country, that use welders. You can't go visit them all. So, you've got to cut down the territory, further. Suppose that on your Preferred Place to Live petal you said that you really want to live and work in the San Jose area of California. That's helpful: that cuts down the territory further. Now your goal is:

• I want to work in a place that hires welders, within the San Jose area.

But, the territory is still too large. There could be 100, 200, 300 organizations that fit that description. So you look at your Flower Diagram for further help, and you notice that under *working conditions* you said you wanted to work for an organization with fifty or fewer employees. Good, now your goal is:

- **I want to work in a place that hires welders, within the San Jose area, that has fifty or fewer employees.**

This territory may still be too large. So you look again at your Flower Diagram for further guidance, and you see that you said you wanted to work for an organization that works with, or produces, wheels. So now your statement of what you're looking for, becomes:

- **I want to work in a place that hires welders, within the San Jose area, has fifty or fewer employees, and makes wheels.**

Using your Flower Diagram, you can thus keep cutting down the territory, until the *"targets"* of your job-hunt are no more than ten places. That's a manageable number of places for you to *start with*. You can always expand the list later, if none of these ten turns out to be promising or interesting.

TOO FEW NAMES

In this case, you want to expand the territory. Your salvation here is probably not going to be informational interviewing face-to-face, but print or digital directories. There is, first of all, the Yellow Pages of your local phone book, either in print or online. Look under every heading that is of any interest to you. Also, see if the local chamber of commerce publishes a business directory; often it will list not only small companies but also local divisions of larger companies, with names of department heads; sometimes they will even include the North American Industry Classification System (NAICS) codes, which is useful if you want to search by the code of your chosen field. Thirdly, see if your town or city publishes a business newsletter, directory, or even a Book of Lists on its own. It will, of course, cost you, but it may be worth it.

Some metropolitan areas (San Francisco comes to mind) have particularly helpful ones. Forty of them are listed at www.bizjournals.com.

If you are diligent here, you won't lack for names, believe me—unless it's a very small town you live in, in which case you'll just have to cast your net a little wider, to include other towns, villages, or cities that are within commuting distance from you.

Informational Interviewing Step Five

HOW TO LEARN ALL ABOUT A PLACE
BEFORE YOU WALK IN

At some point you will be happy. You've found a career that you would die to do. You've interviewed people *actually doing that work*, and you like it even more. You've found names of places that hire people in that career.

Okay, now what? Do you rush right over there? No, you research those places first. This is an absolute *must*. Remember, companies and organizations love to be loved. You demonstrate you love them when you have taken the trouble to find out all about them, before you walk in. That's called *research*.

What is it you should research about places before you approach them for a hiring-interview? Well, first of all, you want to know something about the organization from the inside: what kind of work they do there. Their style of working. Their so-called *corporate culture*. And what kinds of goals they are trying to achieve, what obstacles or challenges they are running into, and how your skills and knowledges can help them. In the interview you must be prepared to demonstrate that you have something they need. That begins with finding out *what* they need.

Secondly, you want to find out if you would enjoy working there. You want to take the measure of those organizations. As I mentioned earlier, everybody takes the measure of a workplace, but most job-hunters or career-changers only do it *after* they are hired there. In the U.S., for example, a survey of the federal/state employment service once found that 57% of those who found a job through that service were not working at that job just thirty days later, and this was *because* they used the first ten or twenty days *on the job* to find out they didn't really like it there at all.

You, by doing this research ahead of time, are choosing a better path by far. Yes, even in tough times, you do want to be picky. Otherwise, you'll take the job in desperation, thinking, "Oh, I could put up with anything," and then finding out after you take the job that you were kidding yourself. So you have to quit, and start your job-hunt all over again. By doing this research now, you are saving yourself a lot of grief. So, you need to know, ahead of time, if this place just doesn't fit. Now, how do you find that out? There are several ways, some face to face, some not:

- **Friends and Neighbors.** Ask *everyone* you know, if they know anyone who works at the places that interest you. And, if they do, ask them if they could arrange for you and that person to get together, for lunch, coffee, or tea. At that time, tell them why the place interests you, and indicate you'd like to know more about it. (*It helps a lot if your mutual friend is sitting there with the two of you, so the purpose of this little chat won't be misconstrued.*) This is the vastly preferred way to find out about a place. However, obviously you need a couple of additional alternatives up your sleeve, in case you run into a dead end here.

- **People at the Organizations in Question, or at Similar Organizations.** LinkedIn has an extensive menu where you can find a company's name. They will tell you who works there, or used to work there. An e-mail will sometimes produce an interesting contact; but in this increasingly busy busy life, even the best-hearted people may sometimes say they just cannot give you any time, due to overload. If so, respect that.

  You can go in person to organizations and ask questions about the place. This is not recommended with large organizations that have security guards and so on. But with small organizations (in this case, 50 employees or fewer) you sometimes can find out a great deal by just showing up. Here, however, I must caution you about several *dangers*.

First, make sure you're not asking them questions that are in print somewhere, which you could easily have read for yourself instead of bothering *them*. This irritates people.

Second, make sure that you approach the gateway people—front desk, receptionists, customer service, etc.—*before* you ever approach people higher up in that organization.

Third, make sure that you approach subordinates rather than the top person in the place, if the subordinates would know the answer to your questions. Bothering the boss there with some simple questions that someone else could have answered is committing job-hunting suicide.

Fourth, make sure you're not using this approach simply as a sneaky way to get in to see the boss, and make a pitch for them to hire you. You said this was just information gathering. Don't lie. Don't ever lie. They will remember you, but not in any way you want to be remembered.

- **What's on the Internet.** Many job-hunters or career-changers think that every organization, company, or nonprofit, has its own website, these days. Not true. Sometimes they do, sometimes they don't. It often has to do with the size of the place, its access to a good Web designer, its desperation for customers, etc. Easy way to find out: if you have access to the Internet, type the name of the place into your favorite search engine (*Google, Bing, or whatever*) and see what that turns up. Try more than one search engine. Sometimes one knows things the others don't.

- **What's in Print.** Not books; their time lag is too great. But often the organization has timely stuff—in print, or on its website—about its business, purpose, etc. Also, the CEO or head of the organization may have given talks, and the front desk there may have copies of those talks. In addition, there may be brochures, annual reports, etc., that the organization has put out, about itself. How can you get copies? The person who answers the phone there, if you call, will know the answer, or at least know who to refer you to. Also, if it's a decent-size organization, public libraries in that town or city may have files on that organization—newspaper clippings, articles, etc. You never know; and it never hurts to ask your friendly neighborhood research librarian.

- Temporary Agencies. Many job-hunters and career-changers have found that a useful way to explore organizations is to go and work at a temporary agency. To find these, put into Google the name of your town or city and (on the same search line) the words "Temp Agencies" or "Employment Agencies." A directory of 8,000 such agencies, and people's ratings of some of them, can be found at the website Rate-A-Temp: www.rateatemp.com/temp-agency-list.

  Employers turn to such agencies in order to find (a) job-hunters who can work part-time for a limited number of days; and (b) job-hunters who can work full-time for a limited number of days. The advantage to you of temporary work is that if there is an agency that loans out people with your particular skills and expertise, you get a chance to be sent to a number of different employers over a period of several weeks, and see each one from the inside. Maybe the temp agency won't send you to exactly the place you hoped for, but sometimes you can develop contacts in the place you love, even while you're temporarily working somewhere else—if both organizations are in the same field. At the very least you'll pick up experience that you can later cite on your resume.

- Volunteering. If you're okay financially for a while, but can't find work, you volunteer to work for nothing, short-term, at a place which has a "cause" or mission that interests you. You can find a directory of places that are known to do this, in what are called "internships" (www.internships.com) or "volunteer opportunies" (listed at www.globalvolunteernetwork.org or www.volunteermatch.org). Also, you can put into your search engine the name of the city or town where you live, together with the phrase "volunteer opportunities," and see what that turns up. Or you can just walk into an organization or company of your choice, and ask if they would let you volunteer your time, there.

Your goal is, first of all, to research the place.

Secondly, if you've been out of work a lengthy period of time, your goal is to feel useful. You're making your life count for something.

Thirdly, your distant hope is that maybe somewhere down the line they'll actually want to hire you to stay on, for pay. The odds of that happening in these hard times are pretty remote, so don't count on it and don't push it; but *sometimes* they may ask you to stay. For pay. The success rate of this as a method for finding jobs isn't terrific. But it does happen.

Send a Thank-You Note, Please, *Please*, Pleeze

After anyone has done you a favor, anytime during your job-hunt, you must be sure to send them a thank-you note by the very next day, at the latest. Such a note goes to anyone who helps you, or who talks with you. That means friends, people at the organization in question, temporary agency people, secretaries, receptionists, librarians, workers, or whomever.

Ask them, at the time you are face-to-face with them, for their business card (if they have one), or ask them to write out their name and work address, on a piece of paper, for you. You don't want to misspell their name. It is difficult to figure out how to spell people's names, these days, simply from the sound of it. What sounds like "Laura" may actually be "Lara." What sounds like "Smith" may actually be "Smythe," and so on. Get that name and address, but get it right, please.

And let me reiterate: thank-you notes must be prompt. E-mail the thank-you note that same night, or the very next day at the latest. Follow it with a lovely copy, handwritten or printed, nicely formatted, and sent through the mail. Most employers these days prefer a printed letter to a handwritten one, but if your handwriting is beautiful, then go for it.

Don't ramble on and on. Your mailed thank-you note can be just two or three sentences. Something like: *"I wanted to thank you for talking with me yesterday. It was very helpful to me. I much appreciated your taking the time out of your busy schedule to do this. Best wishes to you,"* and then sign it. Of course, if there's any additional thought you want to add, then add it. And when you're done, remember to sign it.

What If I Get Offered a Job Along the Way, While I'm Just Gathering Information?

Not likely. Let me remind you that during this part of your networking, you are talking to *workers*, not employers.

Nonetheless, an occasional employer *may* stray across your path during all this Informational Interviewing. And that employer *may* be so impressed with You, that they want to hire you, on the spot. So, it's *possible* that you'd get offered a job while you're still doing your information gathering. Not very *likely*, but *possible*. And if that happens, what should you say?

Well, if you're desperate, you will probably have to say *yes*. I remember one wintertime when I was in my thirties, with a family of five, when I had just gone through the knee of my last pair of pants, we were burning pieces of old furniture in our fireplace to stay warm, the legs on our bed had just broken, and we were eating spaghetti until it was coming out our ears. In such a situation, you can't afford to be picky. You've got to put food on the table, and stave off the debt-collectors. Now.

But if you're not *desperate,* if you have time to be more careful, then you respond to the job-offer in a way that will buy you some time. You tell them what you're doing: that the average job-hunter tries to screen a job *after* they take it. But you are examining careers, fields, industries, jobs, and particular organizations *before* you decide where you would do your best and most effective work. And you're sure this employer would do the same, if they were in your shoes. (If they're not impressed with your thoroughness and professionalism, at this point, than I assure you this is not a place where you want to work.)

Add that your informational interviewing isn't finished yet, so it would be premature for you to accept their job offer, until you're *sure* that this is the place where you could be most effective, and do your best work.

Then, you add: "Of course, I'm tickled pink that you would want me to be working here. And when I've finished my personal survey, I'll be glad to get back to you about this, as my preliminary impression is that this is the kind of place I'd like to work in, and the kind of people I'd like to work for, and the kind of people I'd like to work with."

In other words, *if you're not desperate yet,* you don't walk immediately through any opened doors, but neither should you allow them to shut.

As I said, this scenario is highly unlikely. You're networking with *workers*. But it's nice to be prepared ahead of time, in your mind, just in case it does ever happen.

A Final Word: Bridge-People
(*Formerly Called Contacts, Links, or Friends*)

When you've found a place that interests you and you want to get an interview there, what will save your neck is this kind of person, whom I call "Bridge-People."

When you're trying to get information about a place, the informants who will be most useful to you will, again, turn out to be bridge-people. They know you; and they know them. They thus bridge the gap between you and a job. Bingo! You learn about the job. You end up getting the job. That is how most jobs get filled. Thanks to that *bridge-person*.

You can't identify a bridge-person until you have a target company or organization in mind. But when that time comes, here's how you go about identifying *bridge-people:*[1]

1. The website, LinkedIn, is your best friend here. Each employer you want to pursue should have a Company Profile page. (Unless the company is just *too small*.) Identify what place you want to approach, and look up its Company Profile page; go there.

2. Start with the company. Ask LinkedIn to tell you the people in your network who work for the company you are targeting. Then sort that list. You can sort it by *employees* there, who share:

   a. A LinkedIn group with You

   b. A former employer with You

   c. A school with You

   d. An industry with You

   e. A language with You

   f. A specific location with You

---

1. I am indebted to my dear friend Susan Joyce for these ideas. She is at job-hunt.org ("put the dash in your job-hunt").

3. Then go to your school. On that same Company Profile page, look for your school—if you ever attended vo-tech school, community college, college, university, or grad school, ask LinkedIn to tell you who among your fellow alumni work for the company or organization you are targeting.

4. Then go to the company activity. On that same Company Profile page, ask LinkedIn to tell you new hires (who), departures (who), job-title changes, job postings, number of employees who use LinkedIn, where current employees work, where current employees worked before they worked for *this* company, where former employees went after they worked for this company, etc. Insightful statistics!

5. As for connecting with the bridge-people whose names you discover, currently LinkedIn requires you to have one of their *paid* memberships, rather than the *free* one, to send a note to someone who's not a direct connection. But if they're still working at the company, you can phone the company and ask for them. Or you can search for their contact information through a larger search engine (Google their name!).

6. If you come up blank, both on LinkedIn and all the other places you search for names, such as family, friends, Facebook, etc., (no bridge-person can be found who knows *you* and also knows *them*) you can advertise on LinkedIn, for such connections. They have "ads by LinkedIn Members" available to you, for modest cost (so far!). You can also browse LinkedIn groups, and join those (ten at the most) that seem most likely to be seen by the kinds of companies you are trying to reach. However, don't just join them! Post intelligent questions, respond to intelligent "post-ers" that you think make sense. In other words, attain as high visibility there as you can; maybe *employers* will then come after *you*.

Bridge-people or not, never forget that people are crucial to your job-hunt. Fish swim in water, humans swim in a social context. We are social animals. Social in our work. Social during our job-hunt. Never job-hunt alone, if you can help it.

Do not pray for tasks equal to your powers.
Pray for powers equal to your tasks.
   —*Phillips Brooks (1835–1893)*

Chapter 9

How to Deal with Any Handicaps You Have

I know what you're thinking. If you got a job-interview (or interviews), and got turned down, you're thinking that there is some handicap (*hidden or obvious*) that is keeping you from getting hired.

Maybe you were thinking this, even before you went in for an interview. (*You turned to this chapter straightaway, didn't you?*)

You're thinking, I'm getting turned down (or *I will be turned down*) because:

I have a physical handicap *or*

I have a mental handicap *or*

I never graduated from high school *or*

I never graduated from college *or*

I am just graduating *or*

I just graduated two years ago and am still unemployed *or*

I graduated way too long ago *or*

I am too beautiful or handsome *or*

I am too ugly *or*

I am too fat *or*

I am too thin *or*

I am too old *or*

I am too young *or*

I am too near retirement *or*

I have only had one employer in life *or*

I have hopped from job to job all my life *or*

I have been out of the job-market too long *or*

I have been in the job-market far too long *or*

I am too inexperienced *or*

I have a prison record *or*

I have a psychiatric history *or*

I have not had enough education and am underqualified *or*

I have too much education and am overqualified *or*

I am Hispanic *or*

I am Black *or*

I am Asian *or*

My English is not very good *or*

I speak heavily accented English *or*

I am too much of a specialist *or*

I am too much of a generalist *or*

I am ex-clergy *or*

I am ex-military *or*

I am too assertive *or*

I am too shy *or*

I have only worked for volunteer organizations *or*

I have only worked for small organizations *or*

I have only worked for a large organization *or*

I have only worked for the government *or*

I come from a very different culture or background *or*

I come from another industry *or*

I come from another planet.

If all of this were true, there would be only three weeks in our life when we are employable!

Okay, but let's get one thing straight, from the beginning here: you can't possibly have a handicap that will keep employers from hiring you. You can only have a handicap will keep *some* employers from hiring you. No matter what handicap you have, or think you have, it cannot possibly keep you from getting hired anywhere in the world. It can only keep you from getting hired *at some places.*

As I said in chapter 4, "There are millions of separate, distinct, unrelated employers out there with very different requirements for hiring. Unless you look dirty, wild, and disreputable, and smell really bad, if you know what your *talent* is, I guarantee some employer is looking for *you.* Even if you're crazy, there's some employer crazier than you. You have to keep going. Some employers out there *do* want you, no matter what the others think. Your job is to find *them.*"

You Cannot Generalize About Employers

As far as your handicap is concerned, all employers divide into just two tribes: employers who are interested in hiring you for *what you can do*; vs. employers who are bothered by *what you can't do.*

No matter how many times you run into the latter kind, once you discover their attitude, you should just courteously thank them for their time, and ask if they know of any other employers who might be interested in someone with your skills. Then, gently take your leave.

And speaking of courtesy, always remember to write and mail them a thank-you note that very night, no matter how mad or frustrated they may have made you feel.

And then keep going, day after day, week after week, month after month, if necessary, until you find the other kind of employer: the one who only looks at what you *can* do, not at what you can't.

Everyone Is Handicapped

You may wonder how many job-hunters are handicapped. Well, the answer is: *everyone*. Or, you may wonder how many people in the entire workforce are handicapped. Again, the answer is: *everyone*.

What! Well, sure. A real handicap means *dis-ability*: there are some things a person does not have the ability to do. The reason doesn't matter.

Now, consider how many skills there are, in the whole world. Nobody knows the number, so let's make one up. Let's say there are 4,341 transferable skills in the world.

How many of those 4,341 do you think the average person has? Nobody knows that number either, so let's again make one up. Let's guess *big* here. Let's guess the average person has 1,341 skills. That's 1,341 things the average worker can do. You know, things like *dig, analyze, communicate, sell, design, cook, repair*—those sorts of things.

But if there are 4,341 skills in all the world, and the average person only has 1,341 of them, then that leaves 3,000 things the average person can't do.

Of course, what those 3,000 are, will vary from person to person. But, in the end, *everybody* is handicapped. Everybody.

So when you go job-hunting, if you have a real handicap, but it doesn't keep you from performing the particular job or career that you are going after, then what's so special about *your* handicap, compared with other people's? The answer is *Nothing*.

Unless—*unless*—you are so focused on the idea that you are handicapped, and so obsessed with what you *can't* do, that you have forgotten all the things you *can* do.

Unless you're thinking of all the reasons why an employer might not hire you, instead of all the reasons why an employer would be lucky to get you.

Unless you're going about your job-hunt feeling like *a job-beggar*, rather than standing tall to offer yourself as *a helpful resource* for this employer.

What You Can Do, What You Can't

To get your mind off what you *can't* do, and on to what you *can*, take a piece of paper, online or off, and divide it into two columns, viz,

I have this skill:	I don't have this skill:

Then, get a list of transferable skills from somewhere.

You could use the Skills Grid in chapter 7.

Or, you could use the famous *List of 246 Skills as Verbs,* that you will find on the next page.

Or if you want a much longer list for any reason, Canadian career-expert Martin Buckland has a free mega list of 2,010 "Resume Action Verbs" at his site, Elite Résumés (http://aneliteresume.com).

Whichever list you use, copy as many of the skills as you choose, onto that piece of paper, putting each skill in the proper column, depending on whether you *can* do the skill, or *cannot.* (*Or not yet, anyway.*) Use additional sheets, if needed.

When you are done with these two columns, *can, can't,* pick out your favorite five things that you *can* do, and *love* to do; and write out some examples of how you actually did *that,* sometime in your past. Your *recent* past, if possible.

A LIST OF 246 SKILLS AS VERBS

achieving	acting	adapting	addressing	administering
advising	analyzing	anticipating	arbitrating	arranging
ascertaining	assembling	assessing	attaining	auditing
budgeting	building	calculating	charting	checking
classifying	coaching	collecting	communicating	compiling
completing	composing	computing	conceptualizing	conducting
conserving	consolidating	constructing	controlling	coordinating
coping	counseling	creating	deciding	defining
delivering	designing	detailing	detecting	determining
developing	devising	diagnosing	digging	directing
discovering	dispensing	displaying	disproving	dissecting
distributing	diverting	dramatizing	drawing	driving
editing	eliminating	empathizing	enforcing	establishing
estimating	evaluating	examining	expanding	experimenting
explaining	expressing	extracting	filing	financing
fixing	following	formulating	founding	gathering
generating	getting	giving	guiding	handling
having responsibility	heading	helping	hypothesizing	identifying
illustrating	imagining	implementing	improving	improvising
increasing	influencing	informing	initiating	innovating
inspecting	inspiring	installing	instituting	instructing
integrating	interpreting	interviewing	intuiting	inventing
inventorying	investigating	judging	keeping	leading
learning	lecturing	lifting	listening	logging
maintaining	making	managing	manipulating	mediating
meeting	memorizing	mentoring	modeling	monitoring
motivating	navigating	negotiating	observing	obtaining
offering	operating	ordering	organizing	originating
overseeing	painting	perceiving	performing	persuading
photographing	piloting	planning	playing	predicting
preparing	prescribing	presenting	printing	problem solving
processing	producing	programming	projecting	promoting
proofreading	protecting	providing	publicizing	purchasing
questioning	raising	reading	realizing	reasoning
receiving	recommending	reconciling	recording	recruiting
reducing	referring	rehabilitating	relating	remembering
rendering	repairing	reporting	representing	researching
resolving	responding	restoring	retrieving	reviewing
risking	scheduling	selecting	selling	sensing
separating	serving	setting	setting-up	sewing
shaping	sharing	showing	singing	sketching
solving	sorting	speaking	studying	summarizing
supervising	supplying	symbolizing	synergizing	synthesizing
systematizing	taking instructions	talking	teaching	team building
telling	tending	testing & proving	training	transcribing
translating	traveling	treating	trouble-shooting	tutoring
typing	umpiring	understanding	understudying	undertaking
unifying	uniting	upgrading	using	utilizing
verbalizing	washing	weighing	winning	working
writing				

Dream Killers

What about a *disability* that seems to negate all your dreams: there is something you've always dreamed of doing, but your handicap makes it impossible.

Well, first of all, someone may have invented a technology or simple strategy that gets around that disability. You never know. There are some very clever people in the world. How to find them? If your particular disability has a name, look it up on the Internet. Put its name into a search engine like Google, and see what turns up. Look particularly on the list it gives you, for any professional association that deals with your disability. Contact them, and ask them what information they have.

An alternative way of dealing with a dream killer is to search for jobs *similar* to the one you hunger to do, but can't.

Example: one career counselor in Europe was working with a young adult who was dying to be a commercial airplane pilot. The killer: his eyesight was too poor.

So the counselor sent him out to the large airport nearby, with a pad of yellow paper and a pen, and told him to spend the day listening to anyone who worked out there, in whatever capacity. He was told to try to list every kind of occupation that he saw or heard about, there at the airport—besides pilot. The next day he showed his list to his counselor. It was very long. When asked if he'd come across any occupation that interested him, he said, "Yes. I love the idea of making the seats that they put inside new airplanes." So, that's the job he pursued. He ended up in the airline industry, even though he couldn't be a pilot.

Disability or Prejudice?

It is important to keep in mind, that "handicap" is a broad term, which can refer either to job-hunters' *disabilities* or employers' *prejudices*. There is a difference, and you need to remember that.

Suppose you cannot hear. If you are considering a job that requires acute hearing, then that is a disability: it means there are certain skills you don't have that are essential, at least for *that* job.

But now let us suppose you can hear perfectly, but you are way overweight. If you are applying for that same job, overweight is not a disability unless it interferes with your ability to do that work. Nonetheless a particular employer may be prejudiced against overweight people, and simply won't hire you, even though this has nothing to do with your ability to do the job. So, there you have the difference: a **disability** is something within *you*. A **prejudice** is something within *the employer*.

Both may technically be handicaps, because both may keep you from getting hired, but it is important to understand that *a real handicap* is a disability you have—you cannot do some important task required in that particular job. On the other hand, a prejudice is *a phantom handicap*. It may raise its ugly head in one particular interview or more, but if you keep on going, find the right employer, then poof! the so-called handicap vanishes.

You must just be sure you don't share those prejudices. That is, don't look at yourself through *their* eyes. Look at yourself through your own eyes.

The Key Employer Prejudices

1. The employer prejudice that is getting all the attention currently, relates to how long you've been out of work. We saw this in chapter 1. It is a prejudice that some employers have, and some employers don't. If you've been out of work a year or more, you will find employers who won't hire you because of it. Too bad! Just keep going until you find employers who don't have that prejudice.

2. The next employer prejudice that you may run into is age. Reason? Millions of baby boomers (*the 76 million people born 1946–1964*) are beginning to enter the so-called "retirement years." A lot of *them*—no, make that a lot of *us*—are not going to find generous pensions waiting, when we hit sixty or sixty-five, but are going to have to keep working long after we ever thought

we would have to. And how easy will it be to get hired at that age? Guess! But again, your comfort lies in the fact that this is a prejudice, not a handicap: some employers won't be prejudiced that you are as old as you are, if they see you are still on fire with passion about what you do, not merely marking time between now and then.

The related employer prejudice that is rearing its ugly head these days concerns money. Given all our years of experience, many of us who are job-hunting over fifty, will expect a salary befitting all our years of experience and wisdom, only to discover that some employers are prejudiced against paying us that much—since they could hire two less-experienced workers in their twenties for what it would cost them to hire just us.

And yet, despite this prejudice, there are still employers out there who *will* hire you, regardless of how old you are, if . . . (and here we have a lot of *"if"s*—all of which lie within your control, thank heaven):

They will hire you IF you choose to approach a small company and they don't have to put you late into a pension plan; and

They will hire you IF you come with a positive attitude toward your aging. For example, thinking of your current age not in terms of work but in terms of music—particularly a symphony. A symphony, traditionally, has four movements, as they're called. So does Life. There is the first movement, infancy; then the second movement, the time of learning; the long third movement follows, the time of working; and finally, a fourth movement. It is traditionally spoken of, in terms of work: hence, we call it *retirement*. It is much better to think of it as the Fourth Movement, a triumphant, powerful ending to the symphony of our life here on Earth. Go listen to Beethoven's Third Symphony, the Eroica; and

They will hire you IF you convey energy, even in this period of your life. Ask any employer what they are looking for, when they interview a job candidate who is fifty years or older, and they will tell you: *energy*. Okay, but where shall we find energy, after fifty? When we were younger, energy came from the *physical* side of our nature. We were "feeling our oats," as they say. We

could go all day, and all night. "My, where do you get all your
energy?" our grandmother would ask us. We were a dynamo . . .
of *physical* energy. But after fifty, physical energy may be harder
to come by, despite workouts, exercise, and marathons. Increasingly, our energy must spring not from our muscles but from our
excitement about Life; there are inevitably *some* employers dying
to have that excitement in their organization; and

They will hire you IF you have done some life/work planning, and you know alternative ways to describe who you are
and what you can do, because you did the homework on Who
You Are, in chapter 7; and

They will hire you IF you *keep going* on interviews until you
encounter an employer or two who isn't prejudiced about
your age.

What do I mean by *keep going*? Well, here is one successful
job-hunter's actual records (the "process" she is referring to, is
Daniel Porot's PIE method, described at the end of this chapter):

> *Here are the figures you wanted: In the course of my surveying,*
> *September through November, I was referred to 120+ people.*
> *Of these I contacted 84 and actually met with 50. I met most*
> *people at their offices, a few for lunch, a couple for dinner, and*
> *one for breakfast! The process worked so well for me, I am really*
> *excited about my new prospects.*

Job-hunting success, regardless of your age, often requires this
kind of persistence, keeping at it, working at your job-hunt far
longer and far harder than the average job-hunter would ever
dream of doing, because you know you will be valuable to any
organization that is able to see you clearly, without prejudice.

3. Next employer *prejudice:* ex-offenders. When you run into any
employer prejudice, what you should do is *Google* it by name on
the Internet, and see what you turn up. You may discover some
very useful advice, strategies, or resources. This is the case if
you are (*or you work with*) an ex-offender. The most detailed help
I know of, is found on the website run by a man named Dick
Gaither. Let me tell you about him. He is head of Job Search
Training Systems in Indiana, and has worked with ex-offenders

a lot, over many years. E-mail Dick at workwizard@aol.com and he will send you 126 pages of useful information and guidance that you can print out. Incredibly helpful, and . . . it's free. A great public service, from a tremendous human being.

4. Next employer prejudice: ex–mental patients. The same comments that I made above, apply here.

5. Others. There is hardly a group you can name who do not face *some* prejudice from *some* employers.

There are employers good and kind, and employers who aren't. Personally, I draw comfort from all the employers I run into who are a credit to the human race. Here is a letter I got from a successful job-hunter[1] just last week:

> *As we went along in the interview, some of the things the employer told me were, "I'm very flexible with schedules. I want to put people in activities that I know they'll be the best in, but that means that some weeks you're scheduled for three evening shifts. If that's ever a problem, I really want you to tell me, because I can fix it. I'm also a firm believer that you need to be at your absolute best before you can pour into people here. That means, if you get really stressed out, I want you to tell me. Just yesterday one of our employees came to me and said, 'I'm so overwhelmed right now!' So I sat down with her and we moved some stuff around. Now, that also means that we are extremely team-oriented. If someone cannot take a shift because something is going on at home, everyone needs to be willing to take that up sometimes. But, you always know that everyone here is willing to do the same for you. Also, when we're stressed we seem to resort to silliness." I knew immediately that this was the place for me. . . .*

1. Kayla DeVitto.

The Last Handicap: Shyness

During the whole job hunt, what's going to torpedo you most? What handicap is king? Well, shyness is at the top of the list. Call it anything else if you want to—low self-esteem, fear, anxiety, nervousness, sweating—but shyness it is, and shyness it remains. Often, we, the unemployed, who may be absolute experts at connecting and communicating with faceless people on the Internet—through computer games, apps, Facebook, LinkedIn, Twitter, Instagram, and other social media—suddenly turn to jelly when we have to go face-to-face with people.

Shy. A lot of us would never think to use that word to describe ourselves. But surveys have found that as many as 75% of us have been painfully shy at some point in our lives. Many of us still are. *(This always comes as a great surprise to my European friends, because they picture Americans as assertive, aggressive, and similar words. And sure, some of us are; but that's not who most of us are, especially when we're out of work, and have go sit across the desk from employers, face-to-face. I myself have been painfully shy, much of my life. No one would ever guess.)*

So, what to do if we are shy and feel utterly unequipped to deal with all the social interaction we're going to have to do during our job-hunt? There is an answer, and a method that works. First, a bit of history.

The late John Crystal often ran into this problem. So John suggested that the way anyone cures themselves of shyness is through enthusiasm. If you're talking with someone, for example, and you are enthusiastic about the topic under discussion, you will forget that you are shy, in your excitement. Everything depends on what you're talking about, and how you feel about that topic.

So, he said, if you're shy, only go after a job you feel really enthusiastic about. Seek information only about a curiosity that you feel enthusiastic about the prospect of learning the answer to. And so on. And so forth.

John followed this up by inventing a practical three-stage plan of action, to cure job-hunters of shyness. Those who have followed John's advice in this regard have had a success rate of 86% in overcoming their shyness and fears, and finding a job.

Daniel Porot and I subsequently took John's system, and organized it. We observed that John was really recommending three types of interviews, as I noted in chapter 4:

Interviews for employment.

But preceded, necessarily, by interviewing just for information, which—among other things—is a warm-up for employment interviews.

And this was preceded by practice interviewing, which—among other things—is a warm-up for information interviews.

Each type of interview prepares for the next; and there you have it: a three-stage plan, for overcoming shyness.

Daniel, who has been Europe's premiere job-hunting expert for decades, organized this into an attractive and well-thought-out chart; and gave it its now famous name: "The PIE Method," which has helped thousands of job-hunters and career-changers in Europe, Asia, and the U.S. with their shyness and with their job-hunt.[2]

Why is it called "PIE"?

P   is for the warm-up phase. John Crystal named this warm-up "The Practice Field Survey."[3] Daniel Porot calls it P for pleasure.

I   is for "Informational Interviewing."

E   is for the employment interview with the-person-who-has-the-power-to-hire-you.

---

2. Daniel has summarized his system in a book published here in the U.S. in 1996: it is called *The PIE Method for Career Success: A Unique Way to Find Your Ideal Job*, published by JIST Works, Inc. It is now basically out of print but can be found used on Amazon.com, BarnesandNoble.com, or Alibris.com. Daniel has a wonderful website of "career games" at www.careergames.com.

3. If you want further instructions about this whole process, I refer you to "The Practice Field Survey," pages 187–96 of *Where Do I Go from Here with My Life?* by John Crystal and me, published by Ten Speed Press.

How do you use this P for practice to get comfortable about going out and talking to people one-on-one?

This is achieved by choosing a topic—any topic, however silly or trivial—that is a pleasure for you to talk about with your friends, or family. To avoid anxiety, it should not be connected to any present or future careers that you are considering. Rather, the kinds of topics that work best, for this exercise, are:

- a hobby you love, such as skiing, bridge playing, exercise, computers, etc.

- any leisure-time enthusiasm of yours, such as a movie you just saw, that you liked a lot

- a longtime curiosity, such as how do they predict the weather, or what policemen do

- an aspect of the town or city you live in, such as a new shopping mall that just opened

- an issue you feel strongly about, such as the homeless, AIDS sufferers, ecology, peace, health, returning veterans, etc.

There is only one condition about choosing a topic: it should be something you love to talk about with other people; a subject you know nothing about, but you feel a great deal of enthusiasm for, is far preferable to something you know an awful lot about, but it puts you to sleep.

Having identified your enthusiasm, you then need to go talk to someone who is as enthusiastic about this thing, as you are. For best results with your later job-hunt, this should be someone you don't already know. Use the Yellow Pages, ask around among your friends and family, *Who do you know that loves to talk about this?* It's relatively easy to find the kind of person you're looking for.

You love to talk about skiing? Try a ski-clothes store, or a skiing instructor. You love to talk about writing? Try a professor on a nearby college campus, who teaches English. You love to talk about physical exercise? Try a trainer, or someone who does physical therapy.

Once you've identified someone you think shares your enthusiasm, you then go talk with them.

When you are face-to-face with your fellow enthusiast, the first thing you must do is relieve their understandable anxiety. Everyone has had someone visit them who has stayed too long, who has worn out their welcome. If your fellow enthusiast is worried about you staying too long, they'll be so preoccupied with this fear that they won't hear a word you are saying.

So, when you first meet them, ask for ten minutes of their time, only. Period. Stop. Exclamation point. And watch your time like a hawk, using your watch or smartphone timer, as I explained in chapter 4.

Okay, you're there. Now what? Well, a topic may have its own unique set of questions. For example, I love movies, so if I met someone who shared this interest, my first question would be, "What movies have you seen lately?" Or, "What did you think of *Django*?" Or, "Who's your favorite actress?" And so on.

If it's a topic you love, and often talk about, you'll know what kinds of questions you begin with. But, if no questions come to mind, your fall-back position is the following ones, which have proved to be good conversation starters for thousands of job-hunters and career-changers before you, no matter what their topic or interest.

Addressed to the person you're doing the Practice Interviewing with:

- How did you get involved with/become interested in this? (*"This"* is the hobby, curiosity, aspect, issue, or enthusiasm, that you are so interested in.)
- What do you like the most about it?
- What do you like the least about it?
- Who else would you suggest I go talk to who shares this interest?
- Can I use your name?
- May I tell them it was you who recommended that I talk with them?
- *Then, choosing one person from the list of several names they may have given you, you say,* "Well, I think I will begin by going to talk to this person. Would you be willing to call ahead for me, so they will know who I am, when I go over there?"

Incidentally, it's perfectly okay for you to take someone with you during this Practice Interviewing—preferably someone who is more

Initial:	Pleasure **P**	Information **I**	Employment **E**
Kind of Interview	Practice Field Survey	Informational Interviewing or Research	Employment Interview or Hiring Interview
Purpose	To Get Used to Talking with People to Enjoy It; to "Penetrate Networks"	To Find Out If You'd Like a Job, Before You Go Trying to Get It	To Get Hired for the Work You Have Decided You Would Most Like to Do
How You Go to the Interview	You Can Take Somebody with You	By Yourself or You Can Take Somebody with You	By Yourself
Who You Talk To	Anyone Who Shares Your Enthusiasm About a (for You) Non-Job-Related Subject	A Worker Who Is Doing the Actual Work You Are Thinking About Doing	An Employer Who Has the Power to Hire You for the Job You Have Decided You Most Would Like to Do
How Long a Time You Ask For	10 Minutes (and DON'T run over—asking to see them at 11:45 a.m. may help keep you honest, since most employers have lunch appointments at noon)	Ditto	Ditto (or 19 minutes; but notice the time, and keep your word)
What You Ask Them	Any Curiosity You Have about Your Shared Interest or Enthusiasm	Any Questions You Have about This Job or This Kind of Work	You Tell Them What It Is You Like about Their Organization and What Kind of Work You Are Looking For

Initial:	Pleasure **P**	Information **I**	Employment **E**
What You Ask Them (continued)	If Nothing Occurs to You, Ask: **1.** How did you start, with this hobby, interest, etc.? **2.** What excites or interests you the most about it? **3.** What do you find is the thing you like least about it? **4.** Who else do you know who shares this interest, hobby, or enthusiasm, or could tell me more about my curiousity? **a.** Can I go and see them? **b.** May I mention that it was you who suggested I see them? **c.** May I say that you recommended them? Get their name and address.	If Nothing Occurs to You, Ask: **1.** How did you get interested in this work and how did you get hired? **2.** What excites or interests you the most about it? **3.** What do you find is the thing you like the least about it? **4.** What kinds of challenges or problems do you have to deal with in this job? **5.** What skills do you need in order to meet those challenges or problems? **6.** Who else do you know of who does this kind of work, or similar work but with this difference_____? Get their name and address.	You tell them: **1.** The kinds of challenges you like to deal with. **2.** What skills you have to deal with those challenges. **3.** What experience you have had in dealing with those challenges in the past.
Afterward: That Same Night	SEND A THANK-YOU NOTE.	SEND A THANK-YOU NOTE.	SEND A THANK-YOU NOTE.

outgoing than you feel you are. And on the first few interviews, let them take the lead in the conversation, while you watch to see how they do it.

Once it is *your turn* to conduct these Practice Interviews, it will usually be easy for you to figure out what to talk about.

Alone or with someone, keep at this Practice Interviewing until you feel very much at ease in talking with people and asking them questions about things you are curious about.

In all of this, as you're trying to conquer shyness, *fun* is the key. If you're having fun, you're doing it right. That depends, of course, on how enthusiastic you are, about what you're exploring.

If you're not having fun, you need to keep at it, until you are. It may take seeing four people. It may take ten. Or twenty. You'll know. Once you're comfortable with Practice Interviewing, you'll be ready to try your hand at Informational Interviewing, which I discussed in chapter 8.

In Conclusion:
Self-Esteem Versus Egotism

As most of us know, the proper attitude toward ourselves is called "good self-esteem." But self-esteem is an art. An art of *balance*. A balance between thinking too little of ourselves, and thinking too much of ourselves.

The name for thinking too much of ourselves is "egotism." We have all run into that, at some point in our lives, so we know what it looks like. Some of us have even caught a passing glimpse of it in the mirror.

In our culture and others, we are taught to recoil from this in horror. We even have mythologies warning us against it; the story of Narcissus comes to mind. Poor guy! *(See http://tinyurl.com/a3a33 if you are unfamiliar with the myth.)*

In order to avoid egotism, a lot of us go way overboard in the other direction. We shrink from ever declaring that we have any virtue, any excellency, any special gifts, lest we be accused of boasting. And so we fall into that opposite pit from egotism, namely, ingratitude. We appear ungrateful for the gifts that life, the universe, God—you name it—has already given us.

So, how do we adopt the proper attitude toward our gifts—speaking of them honestly, humbly, gratefully—without sounding egotistical?

Just this: the more you see your own gifts clearly, the more you must pay attention to the gifts that others have.

The more sensitive you become to how unusual you are, the more you must become sensitive to how unusual those around you are.

The more you pay attention to yourself, the more you must pay attention to others.

The more you ponder the mystery of You, the more you must ponder the mystery of all those you encounter, every loved one, every friend, every acquaintance, every stranger.

People from other cultures will tell you about *"the tall poppy" theory of life*, with its implication that you shouldn't stand taller than others in your field. That has a lot of truth to it. But you make yourself equal to others not by lowering yourself but by raising them.

Pay attention to others. What are the favorite skills of your best friend or mate? Do you know? Are you sure? Have you asked them what they think they are? Have you complimented them on these skills, during the past week? Start now!

Just remember, it's no sin to praise yourself as long as that heightens your awareness of what there is to praise in them.

What is success?
To laugh often and much;
To win the respect of intelligent people
and the affection of children;
To earn the appreciation of honest critics
and endure the betrayal of false friends;
To appreciate beauty;
To find the best in others;
To leave the world a bit better, whether by
a healthy child, a garden patch
or a redeemed social condition;
To know even one life has breathed
easier because you have lived;
This is to have succeeded.

—*Bessie Anderson Stanley (1879–1952)*
Traditionally attributed to Ralph Waldo Emerson
(1803–1882)

Chapter 10

Five Ways to Change Careers

The First Way to Change Careers:
The Internet

The first idea that occurs to people seeking guidance on how to change careers, these days, is the Internet. Naturally, there is lots of advice there, but more specifically there is O*Net Online, which I mentioned in chapter 2. It is a digital, online treasure house of information, and up-to-date information at that, about careers.

Go to the site (www.onetonline.org/find or www.onetonline.org/search) and you will see. Suggested careers (or occupations) are grouped or classified by any or all of the following: by industries in great demand; green economies; largest number of openings anticipated; STEM disciplines (that would be Science, Technology, Engineering, and Math); amount of preparation or training required;

O*NET-SOC codes; Military Occupation Classification (equivalencies); abilities required; occupational knowledge required; interests, skill sets, work values, and work activities required; values you want at work; tasks and duties involved; tools, technology, machines, equipment, and software used; and so on.

Once you find an occupation you want to know more about, they have a specially developed Content Model (www.onetcenter.org/content.html), which can run ten to twelve pages of print-outs for each occupation. Maintained by the U.S. government's Department of Labor, it is very thorough, but at the same time (*hate so say it*), limited. Chief among its limitations is the fact that while its predecessor, *The Dictionary of Occupational Titles*, Fourth Edition, covered 12,741 occupations, O*Net covers only 900 or so.[1] Their claim is that the D.O.T. (as it's called) was for *a manufacturing age*, while O*NET is for *an information age*.

Anyway, this decision to just cover 900 or so, leaves a lot of careers, occupations, and jobs *uncovered and unmentioned*.[2] Still, you may find a lot of very helpful stuff, there. Especially if you're a returning veteran (www.mynextmove.org/vets).

The Second Way to Change Careers: ## Tests

They're technically not "tests." Their real name is instruments, or assessments. But we'll use the popular name for them, here.

I'm not sure how well they'll help you choose a new career, but you will find them everywhere: in books, on the Internet, in the offices of guidance counselors, or vocational psychologists, career coaches, etc. And *sometimes* this turns out to be exactly the kind of guidance, the kind of insight, the kind of direction, that career choosers or changers are looking for.

---

1. In case you care, a scholarly analysis of the limitations of O*NET by Robert J. Harvey at Virginia Tech may be found by putting "Robert J. Harvey Construct Validity" into your favorite search engine, and clicking on the first entry. To keep up-to-date on what O*NET is doing, or has to offer, you can go to www.onetonline.org/help/new.
2. Limited funds are cited by O*NET as a large part of the reason for this decision.

But why only *sometimes*? Why doesn't this search for *a magic bullet* always work? Aha! Good question! Since I've watched these tests literally for decades, I can share with you my:

Six Learnings About Testing

1. **You are absolutely unique. There is no person in the world like you. It follows from this that no test can measure YOU; it can only describe the family to which you belong.**

   Tests tend to divide the population into what we might call groups, tribes, or families—made up of all those people who answered the test the same way. After you've taken any test, don't ever say to yourself, "This must be who I am." (No, no, this must be who your family am.)

   I grew up in the Bolles family (surprise!) and they were all very "left-brained." I was a maverick in that family. I was right-brained. Fortunately, my father was an immensely loving man, who found this endearing. When I told him the convoluted way by which I went about figuring out something, he would respond with a hearty affectionate laugh, and a big hug, as he said: "Dick, I will never understand you." Tests are about families, not individuals. The results of any test are descriptors—not of you, but of your family—i.e., all those who answered the test the same way you did. The SAI family. Or the blue family. Or the INTJ family. Or whatever. The results are an accurate description of that family of people, in general; but are they descriptors also of you? Depends on whether or not you are a maverick in that family, the same way I was in mine. These family characteristics may or may not be true in every respect to you. You may be exactly like that group, or you may be different in important ways.

2. **Don't try to figure out ahead of time how you want the test to come out. Stay loose and open to new ideas.**

   It's easy to develop an emotional investment that the test should come out a certain way. I remember a job-hunting workshop where I asked everyone to list the factors they liked about any place where they had ever lived, and then prioritize those factors, to get the name of a new place to live. We had this immensely lovable woman from Texas in the workshop, and when we all got back together after a "break" I asked her how she was doing. With a glint in her eye she said, "I'm prioritizing, and I'm gonna keep on prioritizin', until it comes out: Texas!" That was amusing, as she intended it to be; it's not so amusing when you try to make the test results come out a certain way. If you're gonna take tests, you need to be open to new ideas. If you find yourself always trying to outguess the test, so it will confirm you on a path you've already decided upon, then testing is not for you.

3. **In taking a test, you should just be looking for clues, hunches, or suggestions, rather than for a definitive answer that says "this is what you must choose to do with your life."**

   And bear in mind that an online test isn't likely to be as insightful as one administered by an experienced psychologist or counselor, who may see things that you can't. But keep saying this mantra to yourself, as you read or hear the test results: "Clues. Clues, I'm only looking for clues."

4. **Take several tests and not just one. One can easily send you down the wrong path.**

   People who do a masters or doctorate program in "Testing and Measurement" know that tests are notoriously flawed, unscientific, and inaccurate. Sometimes tests are more like parlor games than anything else. Basing your future on tests' outcomes is like putting your trust in the man behind the curtain in *The Wizard of Oz.*

5. **In good career planning, you're trying, in the first instance, to broaden your horizons, and only later narrow your options down; you are *not* trying to narrow them down from the outset.**
   Bad career planning looks like this:

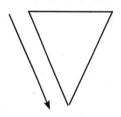 Most computerized tests embody the idea of starting with a wide range of options, and narrowing them down. So, each time you answer a question, you narrow down the number of options. For example, if you say, "I don't like to work outdoors," immediately all outdoor jobs are eliminated from your consideration, etc., etc.

A model of good career planning looks like this, instead:

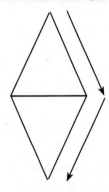 Good career-choice or career planning postpones the "narrowing down," until it has first broadened your horizons, and expanded the number of options you are thinking about. For example, you're in the newspaper business; but have you ever thought of teaching, or drawing, or doing fashion? You first expand your mental horizons, to see all the possibilities, and only then do you start to narrow them down to the particular two or three that interest you the most.

So, what's a good test? All together now: a test that broadens to show you new possibilities for your life.

And, what's a bad test? Again, all together: a test that narrows the possibilities for your life. Often this is the result of a counselor's interpretation of a test, or rather misinterpretation.

I'll give you an example: I met a man who, many years before, had taken the Strong Inventory.[3] He was told, by his counselor, that this inventory measured that man's native gifts or aptitudes. And, in his particular case, the counselor said, the inventory revealed he had no mechanical aptitude whatsoever. For years thereafter, this man told me, "I was afraid to even pick up a hammer, for fear of maiming myself. But there finally came a time in my life when my house needed aluminum siding, desperately, and I was too poor to hire anyone else to do it for me. So I decided I had to do it myself, regardless of what the test said. I climbed the ladder, and expected to fail. Instead, it was a glorious experience! I had never enjoyed myself so much in my whole life. I later found out that the counselor was wrong. The inventory didn't measure aptitudes; it only measured current interests. Now, today, if I could find that counselor, I would wring his neck with my own bare hands, as I think of how much of my life he ruined with his misinterpretation of that test."

---

3. See www.personalitydesk.com.

6. **Testing will always have "mixed reviews."**

On the one hand, you can run into successful men and women who will tell you they took this or that test twenty years ago, and it made all the difference in their career direction and ultimate success. On the other hand, there are the horror stories.

If you want to explore testing in any depth, there is an excellent course online, from S. Mark Pancer, at Wilfred Laurier University in Waterloo, Ontario, Canada, which can be found at http:// tinyurl.com/coc3ftg. Pay special attention to Lectures 1 and 19.

If you like tests, help yourself. There are lots of them on the Internet. Counselors can also give them to you, for a fee; if you want one, shop around.

If you want to know where to start, you might try these tests, which are the ones I personally like the best:

- *Dr. John Holland's Self-Directed Search.* We saw this already in chapter 7 with the People petal (page 135) but in case you don't recall, this is at www.self-directed-search.com and costs $4.95 to take online.

- *The University of Missouri's Career Interests Game,* at http://tinyurl .com/yeu4zvv. This is based on a shortened version of the Self-Directed Search, namely my "Party Exercise." Well designed.

If you want further suggestions, you can type "career tests" or "personality tests" into Google, and see what turns up. You'll find lots and lots of stuff.

The Third Way to Change Careers:
Using the Flower Exercise

This pathway to changing your career is not very popular—compared, say, to the Internet, because it requires a lot more time of you, and a lot more work. I described it back in chapters 6, 7, and 8 (*in case you're skipping around in this book, and haven't been there* yet). It is a careful, thorough, step-by-step process, for ensuring that you are choosing a career that fits you like a glove: a dream career, or dream job, your mission in life, as it is often called. It is not for the faint-hearted or the lazy. But if the other ways to change careers don't turn up any careers that look interesting to you, you may end up being very grateful that there is this way. I get letters like this all the time:

> *I have already benefited greatly from The Flower exercise. I found hope in having a second alternative after doing the homework. . . . The series of life-changing activities in this book has definitely helped me to better understand who I am, to further appreciate my talents, and to utilize the resources I have readily available.*

So, just in case you haven't looked at chapters 6, 7, and 8 yet, let me quickly rehearse here the steps involved in this way of choosing a new career:

1. You do the Flower Exercise (chapter 7), which gives you the basic building blocks of Who You Are, so you can match a career to You.

2. Then you put together on one piece of paper your five favorite transferable skills, and your three favorite fields of knowledge, and start informational interviewing (chapter 8) so as to find the names of careers that fit those building blocks (*or "petals"*).

3. Along the way, you see if you can figure out how to combine your three favorite fields into one career, so as to make yourself unique.

4. Then you "try on" the jobs to see if they fit *You*, by talking to actual workers in the kind of career or careers you have tentatively picked out.

5. Then you find out what *kinds* of organizations in the geographical area that interests you (*where you are already?*) have such jobs.

6. Then you find out the *names* of actual organizations that interest you, where you could do your most effective work.

7. And, finally, you learn about those places before you walk in, or secure an appointment to talk to them about working there, whether or not they have a known vacancy at that moment.

The essence of what you're doing here is: look at your past, break that experience down into its most basic "atoms" (namely, skills), then build a new career for the future from your *favorite* "atoms," retracing your steps from the bottom up, in the exact opposite direction. This is illustrated in the following model:

THE SYSTEMATIC BREAKDOWN AND BUILDING UP TO DEFINE A CAREER THAT FITS YOU

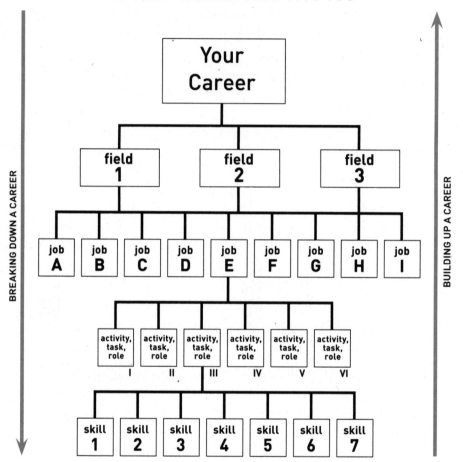

The Fourth Way to Change Careers:
Changing a Career in Two Steps

This is not so much a way to identify a new career, as a way to move into that career, once you have figured out where you want to go next. This is a plan that has worked very well for many career-changers: changing careers in two steps, not one.

And how exactly do you do that?

Well, let's start with a definition: a job is *a job-title* in a *field*.

That means, a job has two parts: *title* and *field*. *Title* is really a symbol for *what you do*. *Field* is *where you do it*, or *what you do it with*.

A dramatic career-change typically involves trying to change both at the same time. It's what's called *Difficult Path* in the diagram below. Problem with trying to take this difficult path is that you can't claim any prior experience. But if you do it in two steps, ah! That's different.

THREE TYPES OF CAREER-CHANGE, VISUALIZED

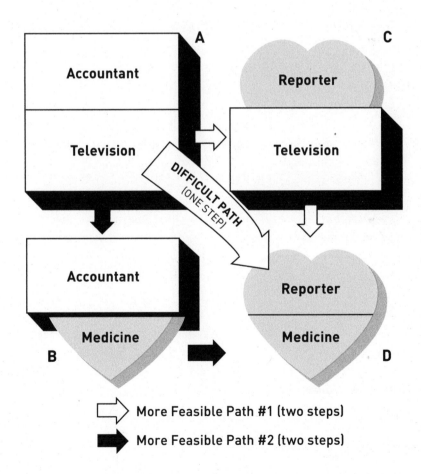

Let's say you are presently an accountant working for a television network, and you want to make a career change. You want to become a reporter on new medical developments.

If you try the Difficult Path above, if you go out into the job-market as the first—accountant in the television industry—and you try to jump to a new career as the second—reporter in medicine—well, that's a pretty large jump. Of course, sometimes you can pull that off, with a bit of luck and a huge number of links on LinkedIn, friends on Facebook, or followers on Twitter.

But what if?

What if that doesn't work? Then you're likely to run into the following scenario:

Interviewer: *"So, I see you want to be a reporter. Were you ever a reporter before?"* Your answer: *No.*

Interviewer: *"And I see you want to be in the medical field. Were you ever in the medical field before?"* Your answer: *No.*

End of story. You are toast.

On the other hand, if you were to change only one of these *at a time*—field or job-title—you could always claim prior experience.

In the diagram above, let's say you move from A to B to D, over a period of three years, and in two steps.

Interviewer during your first move (a change just in your field): *"Were you ever in this kind of work before?"* Your answer: *"Yes, I've been an accountant for x number of years."*

Interviewer during your second move (a change now in your job-title): *"Were you ever in this kind of work before?"* Your answer: *"Yes, I've been in medicine for x number of years."*

Another example: let's say in that diagram, you make a different set of two moves over a period of three years: you move from A to C to D.

Interviewer during your first move (a change just in your job-title): *"Were you ever in this kind of work before?"* Your answer: *"Yes, I've been in television for x number of years."*

Interviewer during your second move (a change just in your field): *"Have you ever done this kind of work before?"* Your answer: *"Yes, I've been a reporter for x number of years."*

By doing career-change in two steps, each time you make a move you are able to legitimately claim that you've had prior *experience*.

Needless to say, your likelihood of getting hired each time has just increased tremendously.

The Fifth Way to Change Careers: Finding Out What the Job-Market Will Need

With a run of just plain bad luck, you may have used all four previous ways of changing careers, but nothing worked. You're stuck. Your needs or wishes are dying on the vine.

Well, then be glad there is this fifth way of changing careers. It is not based on your needs or wishes, but on projections about the coming needs and wishes of the job-market, during the present decade, 2010–2020. It starts at the opposite end: not what you want, but what the market wants.

These are typically called *Hot Jobs*, though I'd take that with a grain of salt, if I were you. There are dozens of these lists online and off (just Google *Hot Jobs*). Just remember: take what you read, wherever you read it, not with just a grain of salt, but with *a barrel*. "Projections" is just a nice word for "guesses." The way that *some* of these guys and gals decide what constitutes a "hot job" would make your hair stand on end. I know; I've talked with them. *(Think dart boards.)*

The U.S. government gets into this projections game with their *Occupational Outlook Handbook 2012–2013*, which you can find at your local library, or better yet, online at www.bls.gov/ooh (it may be 2013–2014 by the time you read this). Here you can browse careers/occupations by occupational group, number of new jobs projected to be available, faster-than-average job growth projected, level of education or training required, median pay, etc. Oh, and it has a lovely feature called "similar occupations." That's great if for any reason you don't qualify for some job that otherwise really fascinates you.

"I WANT TO EXPERIENCE A WARM CLIMATE, FLY THROUGH THE AIR, SEE SOME COLOR, EAT A PEACH — I WANT TO LIVE!"

Conclusion: **Eight Cautions About Changing Careers**

Whenever you have to choose or change a career, here are eight cautions to keep in mind. Many of them you've already thought of; this is just a reminder:

1. Go for *any* career that seems interesting or even fascinating to you. But *first* talk to people who are already doing that work, to find out if the career or job is as great as it seems at first impression. Ask them: *What do you like best about this work? What do you like least about this work? And, how did you get into this work?* This last question, which sounds like mere cheeky curiosity, actually can give you important clues about how you could get into this line of work or career.

2. In moving from one career to another, make sure that you preserve constancy in your life as well as change, during the transition. In other words, don't change *everything*. Remember

the words of Archimedes about his mythical long lever: *Give me a fulcrum and a place to stand, and with a lever I will move the Earth.*[4] You need a place to stand, when you move your life around, and that place is provided by the things that stay constant about you: your character, your relationships, your faith, your values, your transferable skills.

3. If you can, you'll do better to start with yourself and what *you* want, rather than with the job-market, and what's "hot." The difference is "enthusiasm" and "passion." Yours. You're much more attractive to employers when you're *on fire.* Maybe times are just too tough where you are, to start with your vision of what you want to do with your life, for now, anyway; but *try.*

4. The best *work*, the best career, for you, the one that makes you happiest and most fulfilled, is going to be one that uses: your *favorite* transferable skills, in your *favorite* subjects, fields, or special knowledges, in a job that offers you your *preferred* people-environments, your *preferred* working conditions, with your *preferred* salary or other rewards, working toward your *preferred* goals and values. This requires thorough self-inventory. Detailed instructions are to be found back in chapter 7.

5. The more time and thought you can give to the choosing of a new career, the better your choice is going to be. There is a penalty for seeking "quick and dirty" fixes.

6. If you are young, or relatively young, you don't have to get it right, the first time. It's okay to make a mistake, in your choice. Bucky Fuller used to always say that *Man* was the only creature that learns primarily from making mistakes. You'll have time to correct a bad decision. Most of us will have at least three *careers* during our lifetime, and eight or more *jobs.*

7. Choosing and then finding employment in a new career that you really fancy, should feel like a fun task, as much as possible. The more fun you're having, the more this points to the likelihood that you're doing it right. To make it more fun, take a

---

4. Archimedes (ca. 235 BCE), Greek inventor, mathematician, and physicist. His saying here is loosely paraphrased.

large piece of white paper, and then with some colored pencils or pens draw a picture of your ideal life: where you live, who's with you, what you do, what your dwelling looks like, what your ideal vacation looks like, etc. Don't let *reality* get in the way. Pretend a magic wand has been waved over your life, and it gives you everything you think your ideal life would be. Now, *of course* you're going to tell me you can't draw. Okay, then make symbols for things, or create little "doodads," with labels— anything so that you can *see* all together on one page your vision of your ideal life—however haltingly expressed.

The power of this exercise sometimes amazes me. Reason? By avoiding words and using pictures or symbols as much as possible, it bypasses the left side of the brain ("the safekeeping self," as George Prince calls it) and speaks directly to the right side of your brain ("the experimental self"), whose job is to engineer change. Do fun things like this, as you're exploring a new life for yourself.

8. One final word of caution here: if you're just graduating from high school, don't go get a college degree in some career field just because you think that this will guarantee you a job! It will not.

I wish you could see my e-mails, filled with bitter letters from people who believed this myth, went and got a degree in a field that looked just great, thought it would be a snap to find a job, but are still unemployed two years later. Good times or bad. They are bitter (often), angry (always), and disappointed in a society that they feel lied to them. Now that they have that worthless degree, and still can't find a job, they find a certain irony in the phrase, *"Our country believes in getting a job by degrees."* To avoid this costly mistake, what you must do is take the choosing of a career into your own hands, with the help of this book, and then explore the career you've chosen down to the last inch, find out if you love it, and *then* go get your degree. Not because it guarantees a job, but because you feel passion, enthusiasm, and energy with this choice. You feel you have found the kind of life that other people only dream of.

I do not think there is any thrill
That can go through the human heart
Like that felt by the inventor
As he sees some creation of the brain
Unfolding to success. . . .
Such emotions make a man forget
Food, sleep, friends, love, everything.
—*Nikola Tesla (1856–1943)*

Chapter 11

How to Start Your Own Business

If you're unemployed, and just can't find any job-openings, no matter how hard you try, you're probably going to think about starting your own business. According to some surveys, up to 80% of all workers toy with this idea at some point in their lives. According to official statistics, only 10% actually do it, in any given year. But if you're seriously considering it, you should do your research carefully beforehand; and, you should try to find a business that really fits You.

Creating Your Own Business

It may be that, in thinking about creating your own job, you know exactly *what* business you'd like to start, because you've been thinking about it for *years*, and may even have been *doing* it for years—but in the employ of someone else.

But now, you're thinking about doing this kind of work for yourself, whether it be business services, consultancy, or repair work, or some kind of craft, or some kind of product, or service. Maybe your dream is: *I want to run a bed-and-breakfast place.* Or *I want a horse ranch, where I can raise and sell horses.* Or *I want to grow lavender and sell soap and perfume made from it.* Stuff like that.

The first thing you should do is read up on all the virtues and perils of running your own business. The Internet has tons of stuff about this. For example:

World Wide Web Tax

www.wwwebtax.com/miscellaneous/self_employment_tax.htm

Wow. If you're going to be self-employed, you really really want this site. One of the banes of being self-employed is dealing with taxes; this site has more than 1,300 pages to help you handle all of that: articles, resources, links, downloadable tax forms (going back ten years!), in PDF format, of course. The site is selling something (e-filing tax returns), but it has a lot of free information about what self-employed people have to do vis-à-vis taxes, in the United States at least.

Business Owner's Toolkit

www.toolkit.com/small_business_guide/index.aspx

Yikes, there is a lot of information here for the small business owner. Everything about your business: starting, planning, financing, marketing, hiring, managing, getting government contracts, taxes—all that stuff.

Small Business Administration

www.sba.gov

The SBA has endured some bad press in the face of the multiple natural catastrophes that have been striking the U.S. in the past five years, from hurricanes to tornadoes to floods. But keep in mind that it was established to help start, manage, and grow small businesses. Lots of useful articles and advice are online, here. Also, check out its *Starting a Business* resources at http://tinyurl.com/24h59yy.

The Business Owners' Idea Café

www.businessownersideacafe.com

Great, fun site for the small business owner.

A Small Business Expert

http://asmallbusinessexpert.com

Scott Steinberg, a hugely popular analyst and industry insider for all the major TV networks, has just produced a free—yes I said free—*Business Experts Guidebook,* for those considering starting their own business. You can download it from his website (above). Unbelievably comprehensive! He will also allow you to download a free 2012 Online Marketing Guide.

Free Agent Nation

www.fastcompany.com/online/12/freeagent.html

Daniel Pink, before he became famous for such books as *Drive* and *A Whole New Mind,* was the first to call attention to how many people were refusing to work for any employer. "Free Agent Nation" is his classic work, written in 1997, on the site of the popular magazine *Fast Company.* It's still regarded as timeless, though of course its statistics *are* outdated. His basic thesis: self-employment has become a broader concept than it was in another age. The concept now includes not only those who own their own business but also free agents: independent contractors who work for several clients; temps and contract employees who work each day through temporary agencies; limited-timeframe workers who work only for a set time, as on a project, then move on to another company; consultants; and so on. This is a fascinating article to help you decide if you want to be a "free agent."

Working Solo

www.workingsolo.com/faqstarting.html

www.workingsolo.com/resources/resources.html

Working Solo is a good site for the small business worker. The first URL, above, is a series of questions to help you determine if you have it in you to be an entrepreneur. The second URL gives you a whole bunch of resources if you decide *Yes.*

Nolo's Business, LLCs & Corporations

www.nolo.com/legal-encyclopedia/business-llcs-corporations

Lots of helpful legal stuff here, about how to form an LLC, and other stuff you'll really need to know.

Entrepreneur

www.entrepreneurmag.com

Entrepreneur magazine's website. It has lists of home-based businesses, start-up ideas, how to raise money, shoestring start-ups, small business myths, a franchise and business opportunity site-seeing guide, how to research a business opportunity—and more.

How to Avoid Going "Belly-Up"

You have a great idea for starting your own business. But you know that a lot of start-ups, online and off, don't make it. You want to avoid this happening to you. You want to interview others who have started the same kind of business, so you don't make the same mistakes they did. Your interviewing, then, should have three steps to it. Those steps can be summarized in a simple formula:

$$A - B = C$$

To explain:

1. You must find out what skills, knowledge, or experience it takes to make this kind of business idea work, by interviewing several business owners. *This is "A."*

2. Then you need to make a list of the skills, knowledge, or experience that you have. *This is "B."*

3. Then by subtracting "B" from "A," you will arrive at a list of skills, etc., that are required for success in such a business, *that you don't have.* And you must then go out and hire or co-opt a friend or mate or volunteer who has those skills you are lacking (at the moment, anyway). *This is "C."*

I will explain these three steps in a little more detail:

a. You first write out *in as much detail as you can* just exactly what kind of business you are thinking about starting. Do you want to be a freelance writer, or a craftsperson, or a consultant, independent screenwriter, copywriter, digital artist, songwriter, photographer, illustrator, interior designer, video person, videographer, film person, filmmaker, counselor, therapist, plumber, electrician, agent, soap maker, bicycle repairer, public speaker, or *what*?

b. You then identify towns or cities that are at least fifty to seventy-five miles away (so they won't feel you are in competition with them directly down the block, as it were) and by using the Yellow Pages, the chamber of commerce, or some smartphone apps, try to identify at least three businesses in those towns, that are identical or at least similar to the business you are thinking of starting. You drive to that town or city, and talk to the founder or owner of each such business.

c. When you talk to them, you explain that you're exploring the possibility of starting your own business, similar to theirs, but seventy-five miles away. You ask them if they would mind sharing something of their own history, so you can better understand what pitfalls or obstacles one runs into, when starting this kind of business. You ask them what skills, knowledge, or experience they think are necessary to making this kind of business successful.

Will the business owners you interview give you this information? Well, that depends. Some may be afraid of you as a potential competitor, some are just clinging on their business in the current economy by their fingernails, and have no time to help others. So, *maybe not*. But if that happens, thank them politely for their time, and go on to the next name on your list.

On the other hand, there are loads of people in this world who love to help others get started and they have very generous hearts. Generous with their time, generous with their stories, generous with their advice.

Your goal is to find three such people, who are willing to help you by relating their own history, because when you're done you should know enough to make a list of the necessary skills, knowledge, and experience they all agree are essential. These days, everyone's preference is to do such interviewing by e-mail. I think this is a big mistake. Face to face is to be preferred, in every case. Try business people in a city that's an hour's drive away. They are not as likely to see you as a potential competitor, unless you're both going to compete with each other head to head on the Internet. When you have a list you're satisfied with, give this list a name. Call it "A" of course.

d. Back home you sit down and inventory your own skills, knowledge, and experience, by doing the self-inventory described in chapter 7, the Flower Exercise. Give this list a name, also. Call it "B."

e. Having done this, subtract "B" from "A." This gives you another new list, which you should name "C." "C" is by definition a list of the skills or knowledge that you *don't* have, but *must* find— either by taking courses yourself, or by hiring someone with those skills, or by getting a friend or family member (who has those skills) to volunteer to help you for a while.

f. For example, if your investigation revealed that it takes good accounting practices in order to turn a profit, and you don't know a thing about accounting, you now know enough to go out and hire a part-time accountant *immediately*—or, if you absolutely have no money, maybe you can talk an accountant friend of yours into giving you some volunteer time, for a while.

I can illustrate this whole process with a case history. Our job-hunter is a woman who has been making harps for some employer, but now is thinking about going into business for herself, not only *making* harps at home, but also *designing* harps, with the aid of a computer. After interviewing several home-based harp makers and harp designers, and finishing her own self-assessment, her chart of $A - B = C$ came out looking like the opposite page.

If she decides she does indeed want to try her hand at becoming an independent harp maker and harp designer, she now knows what she needs *but lacks*: computer programming, knowledge of the principles

A − B = C

Skills and Knowledge Needed to Run This Kind of Business Successfully	Skills and Knowledge That I Have	Skills and Knowledge Needed, Which I Don't Have, So I'm Going to Go Out and Hire Someone Who Has Them
Precision-working with tools and instruments	Precision-working with tools and instruments	
Planning and directing an entire project	Planning and directing an entire project	
Programming computers, inventing programs that solve physical problems		Programming computers, inventing programs that solve physical problems
Problem solving: evaluating why a particular design or process isn't working	Problem solving: evaluating why a particular design or process isn't working	
Being self-motivated, resourceful, patient, persevering, accurate, methodical, and thorough	Being self-motivated, resourceful, patient, persevering, accurate, methodical, and thorough	
Thorough knowledge of: Principles of electronics		*Thorough knowledge of:* Principles of electronics
Physics of strings	Physics of strings	
Principles of vibration	Principles of vibration	
Properties of woods	Properties of woods	
Accounting		Accounting

of electronics, and accounting. In other words, List C. These she must either go to school to acquire for herself, OR enlist from some friends of hers in those fields, on a volunteer basis, OR go out and hire, part-time.

It should be *always* possible—with a little blood, sweat, and imagination—to find out what A − B = C is, for any business you're dreaming of doing.

But let's say you've come up with a business idea that you're just sure no one else has ever thought of. Who do you go interview, then? *Parallel businesses.* Let's take a ridiculous example. You want to start a business of using computers to monitor the growth of plants in the Antarctic(!). A parallel business, in this case, would be:

someone who's *used computers with plants here in the States,*

or someone who's *used computers in the Antarctic,*

or someone who has *worked with plants in the Antarctic,* etc.

You would get names of these people, go talk to them, and along the way you might even discover that there *is* actually someone who has used computers to monitor the growth of plants at the South Pole. Then again, you might not.

But what you *would* get, for certain, is an awareness of most of the pitfalls that wait for you, by learning from the experience of those who are in these *parallel* businesses or careers.

There is always the danger of a new start-up, online or off, going belly-up. *Your* startup. But with wise preparation you can minimize that possibility.

Are you cut out for this sort of thing? Only you can answer that, in your innermost thoughts. Just remember, it takes a lot of guts to try ANYTHING new (to you) in today's brutal economy. It's easier, however, if you keep these things in mind:

1. There is always some risk, in trying something new. Your goal, I hope, is not to avoid risk—there is no way to do that—but to make sure ahead of time that the risks are *manageable.*

2. As we have seen, you find this out before you start, by first talking to others who have already done what you are thinking of doing; then you evaluate whether or not you still want to go ahead and try it.

3. Have a plan B, laid out, *before you start*, as to what you will do if it doesn't work out; i.e., know where you are going to go, next. Don't wait, *puh-leaze!* Write it out, now. *This is what I'm going to do, if this doesn't work out.*

4. If you're sharing your life with someone, be sure to sit down with that partner or spouse and ask what the implications are *for them* if you try this new thing. Will they have to give up things? If so, what? Are they willing to make those sacrifices? And so on. You have a responsibility to make them full partners in any decision you're facing. Love demands it!

Starting up your own business outside the home without first listening to the experience of those who have gone before you, and profiting from their mistakes, is just nuts. Yet millions of people do just that, every year. And then they wonder why it didn't work out. As one woman said to me, "Yes, I knew I was being foolish, but I thought I'd get lucky." P.S. She didn't.

But you are wiser.

It is up to you to do your research thoroughly, weigh the risks, decide if they're *manageable* risks, count the costs, get counsel from those intimately involved with you, and then if you decide you still want to create your own job by starting this kind of business, go ahead and try—no matter what your well-meaning but cautious friends or family may say. They love you, they're concerned for you, and you should thank them for that; but come on, you only have one life here on this Earth, and that life is *yours* (under God) to say how it will be spent, or not spent. Parents, well-meaning friends, etc., can give loving advice, but in the end they get no vote. Just you . . . and God.

Starting a Home Business

A home seems like an excellent place to create your own job. Low rent (ha!). Short commute! Low overhead. That's the vision. Sound like it might be a fit, for you?

Well, let's start out with a dose of reality. It *can* be a great idea (I have a home business myself). But be aware that there are three major problems with home businesses:

1. The first major problem of home businesses is that this is a rich playground for scams, that can cost you lots of money but never give any back. A lot of people like the idea of a home business, so vultures have taken advantage of that. You will run into ads on TV and on the Web and in your e-mail, offering you a home business "buy-in." They sound enticing. But, as AARP's Bulletin of March 23, 2009, pointed out: of the more than three million Web entries that surface from a Google search on the terms "work at home," more than 95% of the results are scams, links to scams, or other dead ends. Even the sites that claim to be scam-free often feature ads that link to scams. The statistic is: a 48-to-1 scam ratio among ads offering you a nice home business. That's forty-eight scams for every one true ad. *This swamp is filled with alligators!* For further details and warnings, see http://tinyurl.com/2d6xkc3.

2. The second major problem of home businesses is that even if you start a legitimate one, be it as writer, artist, business expert, lawyer, accountant (doing people's taxes), consultant, childcare, or the like, out of your home, it's often difficult to maintain a balance between business and family time. Sometimes the *family* time gets shortchanged, while in other cases the demands of family (particularly with small children) may become so interruptive, that the *business* gets shortchanged. So, do think out thoroughly ahead of time *how* you would go about doing this *well*.

3. The third major problem of home businesses is that it puts you into a perpetual job-hunt. Yes, I know. You like the idea of a home business because you *hate* job-hunting. You are attracted to the idea of a home business because this seems like an ideal way to cut short your job-hunt, by creating your own job.

   The irony is, that a home business makes you in a very real sense a *perpetual* job-hunter—because you have to be *always* seeking new clients or customers—which is to say, new *employers*. Yes, they are *employers* because they *pay* you for the work you are doing. The only difference between this and a full-time job is that here *the contract is limited.* But if you are running your own business, you will have to *continually* beat the bushes for new clients or customers. Some of us have absolutely no appetite for that aspect of home businesses. *Forewarned is forearmed.*

Of course, the dream of most budding home business people is that you will become so well known, and so in demand, that clients or customers will be literally beating down your doors, and you will be able to stop this endless job-hunt. But that only happens to a relative minority, sorry to report. The greater likelihood is that you will *always* have to beat the bushes for employers/clients. It may get easier as you get better at it, or it may get harder, if the economy goes further south. But you must learn to make your peace with it—however grudgingly. Otherwise, you're probably going to find *a home business* is just a glamorous synonym for *"starving."* I know *many* home business people to whom this has happened, and it happened precisely because they couldn't stomach going out to beat the bushes for clients or customers. If that's true for you, but you're still determined to start a home business, then for heaven's sake start out by *hiring* someone part-time, who is willing to do this for you—one who, in fact, "eats it up."

Anyway, there are a bunch of resources on the Web, to help you make a home business succeed, such as www.ahbbo.com. This is a great site, with lots of information for you if you want to learn more about a home-based business. There are more than a hundred articles at www.ahbbo.com/articles.html.

Buying a Branch of a Business That Already Exists

Franchises, as they are called, exist because some people want to start their own business, but don't want to go through the agony of starting from scratch. They want to *buy in* on an already established business, and they have some money in their savings with which to do that. Fortunately for them, there are a lot of such franchises.

Franchises used to be much more popular than they are today. Blame it on the Internet. It is *so easy* to start your own business today, compared to, say, the 1980s.

So, I will mention briefly the existing business opportunities there are, which you may want to look at to see if there is a fit. But I also want to sound warning notes about each of them, so that you will go in with your eyes wide open, if you decide it might be a fit. We live in a world of spams and scams these days, and consequently the pathway to creating your own job has its perils, as well as its rewards.

To find the range of possibilities, to decide if any one of them might be a fit for you, start with the following sites:

www.franchiseopportunities.com

www.franchisedirect.com

www.franchisegenius.com

Now, here's the rub. Franchises require you, generally speaking, to have a bundle of cash, if you wish to buy in. And you may not be able to take much money out, the first year. And they are very risky businesses. Their failure rate is high, particularly in these difficult economic times. You have to guess what kind of services or products the public wants. And the public is tremendously fickle.

So, if you start out thinking that maybe, just maybe, a franchise might fit you—not only creating a job for you, but also for others— you owe it to yourself to investigate the whole idea, and that particular franchise, thoroughly. That's: thoroughly. *Thoroughly.*

Start that homework with these sites:

http://tinyurl.com/64gda2: Interesting checklist from *Entrepreneur Magazine* on "Are You Suited to Be a Franchisee?"

http://tinyurl.com/bv83cxu: The best franchises in 2013 according to their owners' ratings.

www.franchisematch.com: Helps you research franchises, based on your own interests and priorities. Uses 2013 data.

www.bbb.org/us/article/4580: A Better Business Bureau article (dated 2000) on the things to beware of, in purchasing a franchise.

http://tinyurl.com/3vv97lw: This site, Franchise Genius, tells you how to research a franchise thoroughly, before you buy it. It goes over all the things you need to know the answers to, if you're going to come up with a business plan.

http://tinyurl.com/3bzbrxw: This site, JasonTees.com, cleverly lists franchises whose owners have defaulted most frequently on their SBA (Small Business Administration) loans, as well as those franchises whose owners have defaulted the least frequently.

http://tinyurl.com/44yxdvh: Nolo Press has a good article here about *fit*, called "Starting the Right Business for You."

Please note that there isn't a franchising book, or site, that doesn't warn you eighteen times to go talk to people who have *already* bought that same franchise, before you ever decide to go with them. And I mean *several* people, not just one.

Most experts also warn you to go talk to *other* franchises in the same field, not just the kind you're thinking about signing up with. Maybe there's something better, which your research can uncover.

You want to keep in mind that some *types* of franchises have a failure rate *far* greater than others.

And you want to keep in mind also that some individual franchises are *economic horror stories*—and that includes well-known names. They charge too much for you to *get on board*, and often they don't do the advertising or other commitments that they promised they would.

If you are in a hurry, and you don't want to do this homework first, *'cause it's just too much trouble*, you will deserve what you get, believe me. You will rue the day.

How to Flourish in Your Own Business

Finding employees or vendors: With the Internet came globalization. And this changed everything for the self-employed. In this global age if you're operating on a shoestring, and you need, let us say, to have something printed or produced as inexpensively as possible, you can search for an inexpensive printer, vendor, or manufacturer anywhere in the world, and solicit bids. All you have to do is type in the name of the skill-set you need, plus the word "overseas," and the word "jobs"— and see what you can find.

Finding clients or customers: You now have a much larger market at your disposal where you can sell your skills, knowledge, services, and products, worldwide.

There are also some very successful strategies that the Internet offers you, to build up your business. There are a number of books to guide you in doing this. My personal favorite is a gem called *Marketing Shortcuts for the Self-Employed,* by Patrick Schwerdtfeger. Following Patrick's suggestions, here is how one man went about finding clients for his new business. *("Which business" is irrelevant, as these strategies apply to almost any self-employed person I can think of.)*

Patrick advised our friend that the basic strategy for building up your number of clients consists of the following:

1. Develop your own website.

2. Get people (*drive traffic*) to your website.

    a. Identify your ideal customers.

    b. Figure out where they're accessing the Internet: what *raging rivers,* as Patrick calls them (websites with tons of traffic) they visit.

    c. Throw *appetizing* bait into that river (give valuable demonstrations of your expertise) such that they will hunger for more. Always, always link back to your website, which will—incidentally—increase your Google PageRank score.

3. Impress them once they get to your website.

    a. Build trust first. Nobody is going to buy anything from you unless they first trust you.

    b. Provide value.

    c. Divide what you have to offer clients or customers into three categories: beginner, intermediate, advanced. Give beginner content away for free, ask for information in exchange for intermediate content (request an e-mail address, for example), and sell the advanced content.

With this basic strategy firmly in mind, our friend proceeded to do the following:

1. He set up a website of his own, using Wordpress (he Googled *how to set up a Wordpress website easy*).

2. He built up an initial mailing list by going to his local library and accessing the free lists at ReferenceUSA (www.referenceusa.com). He put these names on his computer.

    a. He set up an e-mail autoresponder, using aWeber (www.aweber .com). Alternatively he debated using Constant Contact (www.constantcontact.com) but went with aWeber in the end.

    b. He got people to subscribe to his mailing list·(subscription was free, and he guaranteed they would receive one e-mail tip every week for a year). He put a link back to his website, at the end of each e-mail.

    c. Before he began, he created an outline (only) of what he would cover, for the fifty-two weeks.

    d. What did he cover? Well, basically he pretended he was a teacher, and asked himself, what would I most like to teach my readers? What is my value to them? He identified not just what problems his potential clients were facing but from among those, which of them was causing them some kind of pain—physical, psychological, mental, or whatever.

    e. He wrote three articles before he started, then wrote another one of the fifty-two articles, weekly, just staying three weeks ahead of his first subscriber.

    f. He quickly learned that people needed to see his e-mails seven times before they remembered his ideas, and recognized him as an authority.

3. He set up an audio podcast course on iTunes.

   a. His basic maxim, learned from Patrick, is that people trust video most, audio next, photos next, and basic text the least.

   b. On Patrick's advice, he bought a $50 microphone, ignoring the built-in one on his Mac, because he wanted better sound quality. For this reason he also bought a stand for it, and a $10 buck "pop filter"—which looks like a large foam-rubber ball, that goes on the end of the microphone.

   c. He signed up for a RSS hosting account on a site called Libsyn.com.

   d. For basic recording software he used the GarageBand app, which comes installed on Macs—and he was working on a Mac. Had he had a PC, Patrick advised him to could use Audacity for PCs. He paid attention to audio effects such as compression and bass boost, to improve sound quality.

4. In addition to his website, weekly e-mails, and audio podcasts, he decided also to publish his own free educational articles and relevant photos online, using every outlet available, including Google+.

   a. He put posts on popular *online forums* related to his field and area of expertise. He tried to post on the most popular, trafficked ones, which he found by *Googling* his favorite keyword(s) plus the word "forum." He found that the most popular forums usually rise to the top of a search engine's list; that's where he wanted to enter his posts.

   b. He further searched for the most popular *blogs* by going to Technorati (http://technorati.com).

5. He tried to always ask interesting questions, or to offer a list of resources.

6. Finally, he set up a channel on YouTube, and regularly posted three-minute videos that he shot in his kitchen, using an inexpensive video camera he picked up on sale.

It's a whole new world with the Internet. As I have illustrated here, if you want to start your own business the Internet offers you an abundance of resources for finding customers and growing your business.

I wish you the best.

"YES, THE BUSINESS HAS BECOME BIGGER, BUT FRED STILL LIKES TO WORK AT HOME."

THE PINK PAGES

Appendix A

Finding Your Mission in Life

Introduction to Finding Your Mission in Life

There are those who think that belief in God is just some fairy tale that mankind (or humankind) invented, to fortify themselves against the darkness. Naturally, therefore, they think that anyone who says they believe in God these days is demonstrably feebleminded, or a pathetic child who has never grown up intellectually.

Given this view, they are horrified to find a section on faith or religion in a job-hunting book. They have written to me, and said so.

Well, here it is, anyway.

That's because the percentage of the world's population that says they don't believe there is a God averages less than 18% (it varies from country to country: here in the U.S. the figure is 11%, while in Canada that figure is 19%–30%).[1] Still, that leaves us with an overwhelming percentage of the U.S. population (89%) believing in God. And my more than ten million readers are a pretty typical cross section of this country.

So, leaving out a section that 89% of my readers might be interested in, and helped by, in order to please 11% of my readers, seems to me insane.

But you are welcome to skip this section, if you wish. It's not mandatory reading; that's why it is an Appendix to this book.

As I started writing this section, I toyed at first with the idea of following what might be described as an "all-paths approach" to religion:

---

1. See the *Atlantic* magazine poll, published 6/27/12, at http://tinyurl.com/aljh4ze.

trying to stay as general and nonspecific as I could. But, after much thought, I decided not to try that. This, because I have read many other writers who tried, and I felt the approach failed miserably. An "all-paths" approach to religion ends up being a "no-paths" approach, just as a woman or man who tries to please everyone ends up pleasing no one. It is the old story of the "universal" vs. the "particular."

Those of us who do career counseling could predict, ahead of time, that trying to stay universal is not likely to be helpful, in writing about faith. We know well from our own field that truly helpful career counseling depends upon defining the particularity or uniqueness of each person we try to help. No employer wants to know what you have in common with everyone else. He or she wants to know what makes you unique and individual. As I have argued throughout this book, the inventory of your uniqueness or *particularity* is crucial if you are ever to find meaningful work.

This particularity invades *everything* a person does; it is not suddenly "jettisonable" when he or she turns to matters of faith. Therefore, when I or anyone else writes about faith I believe we must write out of our own particularity—which *starts,* in my case, with the fact that I write, and think, and breathe as a Christian—as you might expect from the fact that I was an ordained Episcopalian minister for many years. Understandably, then, this chapter speaks from a Christian perspective. I want you to be aware of that, at the outset. Balanced against this is the fact that I have always been acutely sensitive to the fact that this is a pluralistic society in which we live, and that I in particular owe a great deal to my readers who have religious convictions quite different from my own. It has turned out that the people who work or have worked here in my office with me, over the years, have been predominantly of other faiths.

Furthermore, *Parachute's* more than ten million readers have included not only Christians of every variety and persuasion, Christian Scientists, Jews, Hindus, Buddhists, and adherents of Islam, but also believers in "new age" religions, secularists, humanists, agnostics, atheists, and many others. I have therefore tried to be very courteous toward the feelings of all my readers, *while at the same time* counting on them to translate my Christian thought-forms into their own. This ability to thus translate is the indispensable *sine qua non* of anyone who wants to communicate helpfully with others in this pluralistic society of ours.

In the Judeo-Christian tradition from which I come, one of the indignant biblical questions was, "Has God forgotten to be gracious?" The answer was a clear "No." I think it is important *for all of us* also to seek the same goal. I have therefore labored to make this chapter gracious as well as thought-provoking.

"WHAT DO YOU MEAN 'DON'T EXPECT MIRACLES'? WHY SHOULDN'T I EXPECT MIRACLES?"

ScienceCartoonsPlus.com

Turning Point

For many of us, the job-hunt offers a chance to make some fundamental changes in our whole life. It marks a turning point in how we live our life.

It gives us a chance to ponder and reflect, to extend our mental horizons, to go deeper into the subsoil of our soul.

It gives us a chance to wrestle with the question, "Why am I here on Earth?" We don't want to feel that we are just another grain of sand lying on the beach called humanity, unnumbered and lost in the billions of other human beings.

We want to do more than plod through life, going to work, coming home from work. We want to find that special joy, "that no one can take from us," which comes from having a sense of Mission in our life.

We want to feel we were put here on Earth for some special purpose, to do some unique work that only we can accomplish.

We want to know what our Mission is.

The Meaning of the Word "Mission"

When used with respect to our life and work, *Mission* has always been a religious concept, from beginning to end. It is defined by *Webster's* as "a continuing task or responsibility that one is destined or fitted to do or specially called upon to undertake," and historically has had two major synonyms: *Calling* and *Vocation*. These, of course, are the same word in two different languages, English and Latin. Both imply God. To be given a Vocation or Calling implies *Someone who* calls. To have a Destiny implies *Someone who determined the destination for us.* Thus, the concept of Mission lands us inevitably in the lap of God, before we have hardly begun.

I emphasize this, because there is an increasing trend in our culture to try to speak about religious subjects without reference to God. This is true of "spirituality," "soul," and "Mission," in particular. More and more books talk about Mission as though it were simply "a purpose you choose for your own life, by identifying your enthusiasms."

This attempt to obliterate all reference to God from the originally religious concept of Mission, is particularly ironic because the proposed substitute word—enthusiasms—is derived from two Greek words, "en theos," and means "God in us."

In the midst of this increasingly secular culture, we find an oasis that—along with athletics—is very hospitable toward belief in God. That oasis is *job-hunting.* Most of the leaders who have evolved creative job-hunting ideas were—from the beginning—people who believed firmly in God, and said so: Sidney Fine, Bernard Haldane, and John Crystal (all of whom have departed this life), plus Arthur and Marie Kirn, Arthur Miller, Tom and Ellie Jackson, Ralph Matson, and of course myself.

I mentioned at the beginning of this Appendix that 89% of us in the U.S. believe in God. According to the Gallup Organization, 90% of us pray, 88% of us believe God loves us, and 33% of us report that we have had a life-changing religious experience.

However, it is not clear that we have made much connection between our belief in God and our work. Often our spiritual beliefs and our attitude toward our work live in separate mental ghettos, within our mind.

A dialogue between these two *is* opened up inside our head, and heart, when we are out of work. Unemployment, particularly in this brutal economy, gives us a chance to contemplate why we are here on Earth, and what our Calling, Vocation, or Mission is, uniquely, for each of us.

Unemployment becomes *life transition*, when we can't find a job doing the same work we've always done. Since we have to rethink one thing, many of us elect to rethink *everything*.

Something awakens within us. Call it *yearning*. Call it *hope*. We come to realize the dream we dreamed has never died. And we go back to get it. We decide to resume our search . . . for the life we know within our heart that we were meant to live.

Now we have a chance to marry our work and our religious beliefs, to talk about Calling, and Vocation, and Mission in life—to think out why we are here, and what plans God has for us.

That's why a period of unemployment can absolutely change our life.

The Secret to Finding Your Mission in Life: Taking It in Stages

I will explain the steps toward finding your Mission in life that I have learned in all my years on Earth. Just remember two things. First, I speak from a lifelong Christian perspective, and trust you to translate this into your own thought-forms.

Second, I know that these steps are not the only Way. Many people have discovered their Mission by taking other paths. And you may, too. But hopefully what I have to say may shed some light upon whatever path you take.

I have learned that if you want to figure out what your Mission in life is, it will likely take some time. It is not a *problem* to be solved in a day and a night. It is a *learning process* that has steps to it, much like the process by which we all learned to eat. As a baby, we did not tackle adult food right off. As we all recall, there were three stages: first there had to be the mother's milk or bottle, then strained baby foods, and finally—after teeth and time—the stuff that grown-ups chew. Three stages—and the two earlier stages were not to be disparaged. It was all Eating, just different forms of Eating—appropriate to our development at the time. But each stage had to be mastered, in turn, before the next could be approached.

There are usually three stages also to learning what your Mission in life is, and the two earlier stages are likewise not to be disparaged. It is all "Mission"—just different forms of Mission, appropriate to your development at the time. But each stage has to be mastered, in turn, before the next can be approached.

Of course, there is a sense in which you never master any of these stages, but are always growing in understanding and mastery of them, throughout your whole life here on Earth.

As it has been impressed on me by observing many people over the years (admittedly through *Christian spectacles*), it appears that the three parts to your Mission here on Earth can be defined generally as follows:

1. *Your first Mission here on Earth* is one that you share with the rest of the human race, but it is no less your individual Mission for the fact that it is shared: and it is, **to seek to stand hour by hour in the conscious presence of God, the One from whom your Mission is derived.** *The Missioner before the Mission*, is the rule. In religious language, your Mission here is: *to know God, and enjoy Him forever, and to see His hand in all His works.*

2. Second, once you have begun doing that in an earnest way, *your second Mission here on Earth* is also one that you share with the rest of the human race, but it is no less your individual Mission for the fact that it is shared: and that is, **to do what you can, moment by moment, day by day, step by step, to make this world a better place, following the leading and guidance of God's Spirit within you and around you.**

3. Third, once you have begun doing that in a serious way, *your third Mission here on Earth* is one that is uniquely yours, and that is:

   a) **to exercise the Talent that you particularly came to Earth to use—your greatest gift, which you most delight to use,**

   b) **in the place(s) or setting(s) that God has caused to appeal to you the most,**

   c) **and for those purposes that God most needs to have done in the world.**

When fleshed out, and spelled out, I think you will find that there you have the definition of your Mission in life. Or, to put it another way, these are the three Missions that you have in life.

The Two Rhythms of the Dance of Mission: Unlearning, Learning, Unlearning, Learning

The distinctive characteristic of these three stages is that in each we are forced to *let go* of some fundamental assumptions that our culture has taught us, about the nature of Mission. In other words, throughout this quest and at each stage we find ourselves engaged not merely in a process of *Learning*. We are also engaged in a process of *Un*learning. Thus, we can restate the three Learnings, in terms of what we also need to *un*learn at each stage:

- We need in the first stage to *un*learn the idea that our Mission is primarily to keep busy *doing* something (here on Earth), and learn instead that our Mission is first of all to keep busy *being* something (here on Earth). In Christian language (and others as well), we might say that we were sent here to learn how *to be* sons of God, and daughters of God, before anything else. *"Our Father, who art in heaven. . . ."*

- In the second stage, "Being" issues into "Doing." At this stage, we need to *un*learn the idea that everything about our Mission must be *unique* to us, and learn instead that some parts of our

Mission here on Earth are *shared* by all human beings: e.g., we were all sent here to bring more gratitude, more kindness, more forgiveness, and more love, into the world. We share this Mission because the task is too large to be accomplished by just one individual.

- We need in the third stage to *un*learn the idea that the part of our Mission that is truly unique, and most truly ours, is something Our Creator just *orders* us to do, without any agreement from our spirit, mind, and heart. (On the other hand, neither is it something that each of us chooses and then merely asks God to bless.) We need to learn that God so honors our free will, that He has ordained that our unique Mission be something that we have some part in choosing.

  In this third stage we need also to *un*learn the idea that our unique Mission must consist of some achievement for all the world to see—and learn instead that as the stone does not always know what ripples it has caused in the pond whose surface it impacts, so neither we nor those who watch our life will always know *what we have achieved* by our life and by our Mission. *It may be* that by the grace of God we helped bring about a profound change for the better in the lives of other souls around us, but it also may be that this takes place beyond our sight, or after we have gone on. And we may never know what we have accomplished, until we see Him face to face after this life is past.

  Most finally, we need to *un*learn the idea that what we have accomplished is our doing, and ours alone. It is God's Spirit breathing in us and through us that helps us do whatever we do, and so the singular first-person pronoun is never appropriate, but only the plural. Not "*I* accomplished this" but "*We* accomplished this, God and I, working together. . . ."

That should give you a general overview. But I would like to add some random comments on my part about each of these three Missions of ours here on Earth.

Some Random Comments About . Your First Mission in Life

Your first Mission here on Earth is one that you share with the rest of the human race, but it is no less your individual Mission for the fact that it is shared: and that is, **to seek to stand hour by hour in the conscious presence of God, the One from whom your Mission is derived.** The Missioner before the Mission, is the rule. In religious language, your Mission is: to know God, and enjoy Him forever, and to see His hand in all His works.

Comment 1:
How We Might Think of God

Each of us has to go about this primary Mission according to the tenets of our own particular religion. But I will speak what I know out of the context of my own particular faith, and you may perhaps translate and apply it to yours. I will speak as a Christian, who believes (passionately) that Christ is the Way and the Truth and the Life. But I also believe, with St. Peter, "that God shows no partiality, but in every nation anyone who fears Him and does what is right is acceptable to Him" (Acts 10:34–35).

Now, Jesus claimed many unique things about Himself and His Mission; but He also spoke of Himself as the great prototype for us all. He called Himself "the Son of Man," and He said, "I assure you that the man who believes in me will do the same things that I have done, yes, and he will do even greater things than these . . ." (John 14:12).

Emboldened by His identification of us with His Life and His Mission, we might want to remember how He spoke about His Life here on Earth. He put it in this context: **"I came from the Father and have come into the world; again, I am leaving the world and going to the Father"** (John 16:28).

If there is a sense in which this is, in even the faintest way, true also of our lives (and I shall say in a moment in what sense I think it is true), then instead of calling our great Creator "God" or "Father" right off, we might begin our approach to the subject of religion by referring to the One Who gave us our Mission and sent us to this planet not as "God" or "Father" but—*just to help our thinking*—as: **"The One From Whom We Came and The One To Whom We Shall Return,"** when this life is done.

If our life here on Earth is to be at all like Christ's, then this is a true way to think about the One Who gave us our Mission. We are not some kind of eternal, preexistent *being*. We are creatures, who once did not exist, and then came into Being, and continue to have our Being, only at the will of our great Creator. But as creatures we are both body and soul; although we know our body was created in our mother's womb, our soul's origin is a great mystery. Where it came from, at what moment the Lord created it, is something we cannot know. It is not unreasonable to suppose, however, that the great God created our *soul* before it entered our body, and in that sense we did indeed stand before God before we were born; and He is indeed **"The One From Whom We Came and The One To Whom We Shall Return."**

Therefore, before we go searching for "what work was I sent here to do?" we need to establish—or in a truer sense *reestablish*—contact with **"The One From Whom We Came and The One To Whom We Shall Return."** Without this reaching out of the creature to the great Creator, without this reaching out of *the creature with a Mission* to *the One Who Gave Us That Mission*, the question *what is my Mission in life?* is void and null. The *what* is rooted in the *Who*; absent the Personal, one cannot meaningfully discuss The Thing. It is like the adult who cries, "I want to get married," without giving any consideration to *who* it is they want to marry.

Comment 2:
How We Might Think of Religion or Faith

In light of this larger view of our creatureliness, we can see that *religion* or *faith* is not a question of whether or not we choose to (*as it is so commonly put*) "have a relationship with God." Looking at our life in a larger context than just our life here on Earth, it becomes apparent that some sort of relationship with God is a given for us, about which we have absolutely no choice. God and we **were** and **are** related, during the time of our soul's existence before our birth and in the time of our soul's continued existence after our death. The only choice we have is what to do about **The Time in Between**, i.e., what we want the nature of our relationship with God to be during our time here on Earth and how that will affect the *nature* of the relationship, then, after death.

One of the corollaries of all this is that by the very act of being born into a human body, it is inevitable that we undergo a kind of *amnesia*— an amnesia that typically embraces not only our nine months in the womb, our baby years, and almost one-third of each day (sleeping), but more important any memory of our origin or our destiny. We wander on Earth as an amnesia victim. To seek after Faith, therefore, is to seek to climb back out of that amnesia. Religion or Faith is **the hard reclaiming of knowledge we once knew as a certainty.**

Comment 3:
The First Obstacle to Executing This Mission

This first Mission of ours here on Earth is not the easiest of Missions, simply because it is the first. Indeed, in many ways, it is the most difficult. All we can see is that our life here on Earth is a very physical life. We eat, we drink, we sleep, we long to be held, and to hold. We inherit a physical body, with very physical appetites, we walk on the physical earth, and we acquire physical possessions. It is the most alluring of temptations, *in our amnesia*, to come up with just a *Physical* interpretation of this life: to think that the Universe is merely interested in the survival of species. Given this interpretation, the story of our individual life could be simply told: we are born, grow up, procreate, and die.

But we are ever recalled to do what we came here to do: that without rejecting the joy of the Physicalness of this life, such as the love of the blue sky and the green grass, we are to reach out beyond all this to recall and recover a *Spiritual* interpretation of our life. *Beyond* the physical and *within* the physicalness of this life, to detect a Spirit and a Person from beyond this Earth who is with us and in us—the very real and loving and awesome Presence of the great Creator from whom we came—and the One to whom we once again shall go.

Comment 4:
The Second Obstacle to Executing This Mission

It is one of the conditions of our earthly amnesia and our creature-liness that, sadly enough, some very *human* and very *rebellious* part of us *likes* the idea of living in a world where we can be our own god—and therefore loves the purely Physical interpretation of life, and finds it *anguish* to relinquish it. Traditional Christian vocabulary calls this "sin" and has a lot to say about the difficulty it poses for this first part of our Mission. All who live a thoughtful life know that it is true: our greatest enemy in carrying out this first Mission of ours is indeed *our own* heart and our own rebellion.

Comment 5:
Further Thoughts About What Makes Us Special and Unique

As I said earlier, many of us come to this issue of our Mission in life, because we want to feel that we are unique. And what we mean by that, is that we hope to discover some "specialness" intrinsic to us, which is our birthright, and which no one can take from us. What we, however, discover from a thorough exploration of this topic, is that we are indeed special—but only because God thinks us so. Our specialness and uniqueness reside in Him, and His love, rather than in anything intrinsic to our own *being*. The proper appreciation of this distinction causes our feet to carry us in the end not to the City called Pride, but to the Temple called Gratitude.

> What is religion? Religion is the service of God out of grateful love for what God has done for us. The Christian religion, more particularly, is the service of God out of grateful love for what God has done for us in Christ.
> —PHILLIPS BROOKS, author of *O Little Town of Bethlehem*

Comment 6: The Unconscious Doing of the Work We Came to Do

You may have *already* wrestled with this first part of your Mission here on Earth. You may not have called it that. You may have called it simply "learning to believe in God." But if you ask what your Mission is in life, this one was and is the precondition of all else that you came here to do. Absent this Mission, it is folly to talk about the rest. So, if you have been seeking faith, or seeking to strengthen your faith, you have— willy-nilly—already been about *the doing of the Mission you were given.* Born into **This Time in Between**, you have found His hand again, and reclasped it. You are therefore ready to go on with His Spirit to tackle together what you came here to do—the other parts of your Mission.

Some Random Comments About Your Second Mission in Life

Your second Mission here on Earth is also one that you share with the rest of the human race, but it is no less your individual Mission for the fact that it is shared: and that is, **to do what you can moment by moment, day by day, step by step, to make this world a better place— following the leading and guidance of God's Spirit within you and around you.**

Comment 1: The Uncomfortableness of One Step at a Time

Imagine yourself out walking in your neighborhood one night, and suddenly you find yourself surrounded by such a dense fog, that you have lost your bearings and cannot find your way. Suddenly, a friend appears out of the fog, and asks you to put your hand in theirs, and they will lead you home. And you, not being able to tell where you are going, trustingly follow them, even though you can only see one step at a time. Eventually you arrive safely home, filled with gratitude. But as you reflect upon the experience the next day, you realize how unsettling it was to have to keep walking when you could see only one step at a time, even though you had guidance you knew you could trust.

Now I have asked you to imagine all of this, because this is the essence of the second Mission to which *you* are called—and *I* am called—in this life. It is all very different than we had imagined. When the question, *"What is your Mission in life?"* is first broached, and we have put our hand in God's, as it were, we imagine that we will be taken up to *some mountaintop*, from which we can see far into the distance. And that we will hear a voice in our ear, saying, "Look, look, see that distant city? That is the goal of your Mission; that is where everything is leading, every step of your way."

But instead of the mountaintop, we find ourselves in *the valley*— wandering often in a fog. And the voice in our ear says something quite different from what we thought we would hear. It says, "Your Mission is to take one step at a time, even when you don't yet see where it all is leading, or what the Grand Plan is, or what your overall Mission in life is. Trust Me; I will lead you."

Comment 2:
The Nature of This Step-by-Step Mission

As I said, in every situation you find yourself, you have been sent here to do whatever you can—moment by moment—that will bring more gratitude, more kindness, more forgiveness, more honesty, and more love into this world.

There are dozens of such moments every day. Moments when you stand—as it were—at a spiritual crossroads, with two ways lying before you. Such moments are typically called **"moments of decision."** It does not matter what the frame or content of each particular decision is. It all devolves, in the end, into just two roads before you, *every time*. **The one** will lead to *less* gratitude, *less* kindness, *less* forgiveness, *less* honesty, or *less* love in the world. **The other** will lead to *more* gratitude, *more* kindness, *more* forgiveness, *more* honesty, or *more* love in the world. Your Mission, each moment, is to seek to choose the latter spiritual road, rather than the former, *every time*.

Comment 3:
Some Examples of This Step-by-Step Mission

I will give a few examples, so that the nature of this part of your Mission may be unmistakably clear.

You are out on the freeway, in your car. Someone has gotten into the wrong lane, to the right of *your* lane, and needs to move over into the lane you are in. You *see* their need to cut in, ahead of you. **Decision time.** In your mind's eye you see two spiritual roads lying before you: the one leading to less kindness in the world (you speed up, to shut this driver out, and don't let them move over), the other leading to more kindness in the world (you let the driver cut in). **Since you know this is part of your Mission, part of the reason why you came to Earth, your calling is clear. You know which road to take, which decision to make.**

You are hard at work at your desk, when suddenly an interruption comes. The phone rings, or someone is at the door. They need something from you, a question of some of your time and attention. **Decision time.** In your mind's eye you see two spiritual roads lying before you: the one leading to less love in the world (you tell them you're just too busy to be bothered), the other leading to more love in the world (you put aside your work, decide that God may have sent this person to you, and say, "Yes, what can I do to help you?"). **Since you know this is part of your Mission, part of the reason why you came to Earth, your calling is clear. You know which road to take, which decision to make.**

Your mate does something that hurts your feelings. **Decision time.** In your mind's eye you see two spiritual roads lying before you: the one leading to less forgiveness in the world (you institute an icy silence between the two of you, and think of how you can punish them or otherwise get even), the other leading to more forgiveness in the world (you go over and take them in your arms, speak the truth about your hurt feelings, and assure them of your love). **Since you know this is part of your Mission, part of the reason why you came to Earth, your calling is clear. You know which road to take, which decision to make.**

You have not behaved at your most noble, recently. And now you are face to face with someone who asks you a question about what happened. **Decision time.** In your mind's eye you see two spiritual roads lying before you: the one leading to less honesty in the world (you lie about what happened, or what you were feeling, because you fear losing their respect or their love), the other leading to more honesty in the world (you tell the truth, together with how you feel about it, in retrospect). **Since you know this is part of your Mission, part of the reason why you came to Earth, your calling is clear. You know which road to take, which decision to make.**

Comment 4:
The Spectacle That Makes the Angels Laugh

It is necessary to explain this part of our Mission in some detail, because so many times you will see people wringing their hands, and saying, "*I want to know what my Mission in life is,*" all the while they are cutting people off on the highway, refusing to give time to people, punishing their mate for having hurt their feelings, and lying about what they did. And it will seem to you that the angels must laugh to see this spectacle. *For these people wringing their hands*, their Mission was right there, on the freeway, in the interruption, in the hurt, and at the confrontation.

Comment 5:
The Valley Versus the Mountaintop

At some point in your life your Mission may involve some grand *mountaintop experience*, where you say to yourself, "This, this, is why I came into the world. I know it. I know it." *But until then*, your Mission is here in *the valley*, and the fog, and the little callings moment by moment, day by day. More to the point, it is likely you cannot ever get to your mountaintop Mission unless you have first exercised your stewardship faithfully in the valley.

It is an ancient principle, to which Jesus alluded often, that if you don't use the information the Universe has already given you, you cannot expect it will give you any more. If you aren't being faithful in small things, how can you expect to be given charge over larger things? (Luke 16:10–12, 19:11–24). If you aren't trying to bring more gratitude, kindness, forgiveness, honesty, and love into the world each day, you can hardly expect that you will be entrusted with the Mission to help bring peace into the world or anything else large and important. If we do not live out our day-by-day Mission in the valley, we cannot expect we are yet ready for a larger *mountaintop* Mission.

Comment 6:
The Importance of Not Thinking of
This Mission as "Just a Training Camp"

The valley is not just a kind of "training camp." There is in your imagination even now an invisible *spiritual* mountaintop to which you may go, if you wish to see where all this is leading. And what will you see there, in the imagination of your heart, but the goal toward which all this is pointed: **that Earth might be more like heaven. That human life might be more like God's.** That is the large achievement toward which all our day-by-day Missions *in the valley* are moving. This is a *large* order, but it is accomplished by faithful attention to the doing of our great Creator's will in little things as well as in large. It is much like the building of the pyramids in Egypt, which was accomplished by the dragging of a lot of individual pieces of stone by a lot of individual men.

The valley, the fog, the going step by step, is no mere training camp. The goal is real, however large. **"Thy Kingdom come, Thy will be done, on Earth, as it is in heaven."**

Some Random Comments About
Your Third Mission in Life

Your third Mission here on Earth is one that is uniquely yours, and that is:

   a) **to exercise the Talent that you particularly came to Earth to use—your greatest gift that you most delight to use,**

   b) **in those place(s) or setting(s) that God has caused to appeal to you the most,**

   c) **and for those purposes that God most needs to have done in the world.**

Comment 1:
Our Mission Is Already Written,
"in Our Members"

It is customary in trying to identify this part of our Mission, to advise that we should ask God, in prayer, to speak to us—and tell us plainly what our Mission is. We look for a voice in the air, a thought in our head, a dream in the night, a sign in the events of the day, to reveal this thing that is otherwise (*it is said*) completely hidden. Sometimes, from just such answered prayer, people do indeed discover what their Mission is, beyond all doubt and uncertainty.

But having to wait for the voice of God to reveal what our Mission is, is not the truest picture of our situation. St. Paul, in Romans, speaks of a law "written in our members"—and this phrase has a telling application to the question of how God reveals to each of us our unique Mission in life. Read again the definition of our third Mission (on the previous page) and you will see: the clear implication of the definition is that God has **already** revealed His will to us concerning our vocation and Mission, by causing it to be **"written in our members."** We are to begin deciphering our unique Mission by studying our Talents and skills, and more particularly which ones (or one) we most rejoice to use.

God actually has written His will *twice* in our members: *first in the Talents* that He lodged there, and second *in His guidance of our heart*, as to which Talent gives us the greatest pleasure from its exercise (**it is usually the one that, when we use it, causes us to lose all sense of time**).

Even as the anthropologist can examine ancient inscriptions, and divine from them the daily life of a long-lost people, so we by examining **our Talents** and **our heart** can *more often than we dream* divine the Will of the Living God. For true it is, our Mission is not something He will reveal; it is something He **has already** revealed. It is not to be found written in the sky; it is to be found written in our members.

Comment 2:
Career Counseling—We Need You

Arguably, our first two Missions in life could be learned from religion alone—without any reference whatsoever to career counseling, the subject of this book. Why, then, should career counseling claim that this question about our Mission in life is its proper concern, *in any way?*

It is when we come to this third Mission, which hinges so crucially on the question of our Talents, skills, and gifts, that we see the answer. If you've read the body of this book, before turning to this section, then you know without my even saying it, how much the identification of Talents, gifts, or skills is the province of career counseling. Its expertise, indeed its *raison d'être*, lies precisely in the identification, classification, and (forgive me) "prioritization" of Talents, skills, and gifts. To put the matter quite simply, career counseling knows how to do this better than any other discipline—**including** traditional religion. This is not a defect of religion, but the fulfillment of something Jesus promised: "When the Spirit of truth comes, He will guide you into all truth" (John 16:12). Career counseling is part (we may hope) of that promised late-coming truth. It can therefore be of inestimable help to the pilgrim who is trying to figure out what their greatest, and most enjoyable, Talent is, as a step toward identifying their unique Mission in life.

If career counseling needs religion as its helpmate in the first two stages of identifying our Mission in life, then religion repays the compliment by clearly needing career counseling as its helpmate here in the third stage.

And this place where you are in your life right now—facing the job-hunt and all its anxiety—is the perfect time to seek the union within your own mind and heart of both career counseling (as in the pages of this book) and your faith in God.

Comment 3:
How Our Mission Got Chosen—
A Scenario for the Romantic

It is a mystery that we cannot fathom, in this life at least, as to why one of us has this Talent, and the other one has that; why God chose to give one gift—and Mission—to one person, and a different gift— and Mission—to another. Since we do not know, and in some degree cannot know, we are certainly left free to speculate, and imagine.

We may imagine that before we came to Earth, our souls, *our Breath*, *our Light*, stood before the great Creator and volunteered for this Mission. And God and we, together, chose what that Mission would be and what particular gifts would be needed, which He then agreed to give us, after our birth. Thus, our Mission was not a command given pre-emptorily by an unloving Creator to a reluctant slave without a vote, but was a task jointly designed by us both, in which as fast as the great Creator said, "I wish" our hearts responded, **"Oh, yes."** As mentioned in an earlier comment, it may be helpful to think of the condition of our becoming human as that we became amnesiac about any conscious-ness our soul had before birth—and therefore amnesiac about the nature or manner in which our Mission was designed.

Our searching for our Mission now is therefore a searching to recover the memory of something we ourselves had a part in designing.

I am admittedly a hopeless romantic, so of course I like this picture. If you also are a hopeless romantic, you may like it, too. There's also the chance that it just may be true. We will not know until we see Him face to face.

Comment 4:
Mission as Intersection

There are all different kinds of voices calling you to all different kinds of work, and the problem is to find out which is the voice of God rather than that of society, say, or the superego, or self-interest. By and large a good rule for finding out is this: the kind of work God usually calls you to is the kind of work a) that you need most to do and b) the world most needs to have done. If you really get a kick out of your work, you've presumably met requirement a), but if your work is writing TV deodorant commercials, the chances are you've missed requirement b). On the other hand, if your work is being a doctor in a leper colony, you have probably met b), but if most of the time you're bored and depressed by it, the chances are you haven't only bypassed a) but probably aren't helping your patients much either. Neither the hair shirt nor the soft birth will do. **The place God calls you to is the place where your deep gladness and the world's deep hunger meet.**

—FRED BUECHNER, *Wishful Thinking—A Theological ABC*

Excerpted from *Wishful Thinking—A Theological ABC* by Frederick Buechner, revised edition published by HarperOne. Copyright © 1973, 1993 by Frederick Buechner.

Comment 5:
Examples of Mission as Intersection

Your unique and individual Mission will most likely turn out to be a mission of Love, acted out in one or all of three arenas: either in the Kingdom of the Mind, whose goal is to bring more Truth into the world; or in the Kingdom of the Heart, whose goal is to bring more Beauty into the world; or in the Kingdom of the Will, whose goal is to bring more Perfection into the world, through Service.

Here are some examples:

"My mission is, out of the rich reservoir of love that God seems to have given me, to nurture and show love to others—most particularly to those who are suffering from incurable diseases."

"My mission is to draw maps for people to show them how to get to God."

"My mission is to create the purest foods I can, to help people's bodies not get in the way of their spiritual growth."

"My mission is to make the finest harps I can so that people can hear the voice of God in the wind."

"My mission is to make people laugh, so that the travail of this earthly life doesn't seem quite so hard to them."

"My mission is to help people know the truth, in love, about what is happening out in the world, so that there will be more honesty in the world."

"My mission is to weep with those who weep, so that in my arms they may feel themselves in the arms of that Eternal Love that sent me and that created them."

"My mission is to create beautiful gardens, so that in the lilies of the field people may behold the Beauty of God and be reminded of the Beauty of Holiness."

Comment 6:
Life as Long as Your Mission Requires

Knowing that you came to Earth for a reason, and knowing what that Mission is, throws an entirely different light upon your life from now on. You are, generally speaking, delivered from any further fear about how long you have to live. You may settle it in your heart that you are here until God chooses to think that you have accomplished your Mission, or until God has a greater Mission for you in another Realm. You need to be a good steward of what He has given you, while you are here; but you do not need to be an anxious steward or stewardess.

You need to attend to your health, *but you do not need to constantly worry about it*. You need to meditate on your death, *but you do not need to be constantly preoccupied with it*. To paraphrase the glorious words of G. K. Chesterton: **"We now have a strong desire for living combined with a strange carelessness about dying. We desire life like water and yet are ready to drink death like wine."** We know that we are here to do what we came to do, and we need not worry about anything else.

Comment 7:
Using Internet Resources

There is a website that deals with news, etc., about all faiths, which you may want to look at: www.beliefnet.com.

Then there is a Jesuit site that leads you in a daily meditation for ten or more minutes (in more than twenty languages with a visual, but otherwise no sound or distraction): http://sacredspace.ie.

There is also a site that gives you a daily podcast of church bells, music, Scripture reading, and meditations or homily, with no visuals, but with sound, and an audio MP3 file that can be sent to your phone, computer, PDA, etc.: www.pray-as-you-go.org.

There is a site dedicated to helping you keep a divine consciousness 24/7, by helping you link up to other people of faith, through prayer circles, sharing of personal stories of faith, etc., aimed especially, but not exclusively, toward young adults. Its ultimate message: you are not alone: www.24-7prayer.com/communities.

Lastly, there is a site dedicated to helping you find a spiritual counselor (or "spiritual director"), as well as retreat centers, in the Christian, Islamic, Buddhist, Jewish, or Interfaith faiths: www.sdiworld.org.

Final Comment:
A Job-Hunt Done Well

If you approach your job-hunt as an opportunity to work on this issue as well as the issue of how you will keep body and soul together, then hopefully your job-hunt will end with your being able to say: "Life has deep meaning to me, now. I have discovered more than my ideal job; I have found my Mission, and the reason why I am here on Earth."

A Guide to Dealing with Your Feelings While Out of Work

Introduction

Unemployment can take a terrible toll upon the human spirit. In a recent study of over 6,000 job-hunters, interviewed every week for up to twenty-four weeks, it was discovered

> *that many workers become discouraged the longer they are unemployed. In particular, the unemployed express feeling more sad the longer they are unemployed, and sadness rises more quickly with unemployment duration during episodes of job search. In addition, reported life satisfaction is lower for the same individual following days in which comparatively more time was devoted to job search. . . . These findings suggest that the psychological cost of job search rises the longer someone is unemployed. . . . One reason why job search assistance may have been found to consistently speed individuals' return to work in past studies is that it may help the unemployed to overcome feelings of anxiety and sadness that are associated with job search.*[1]

---

1. Alan B. Krueger and Andreas Mueller, "Job Search, Emotional Well-Being and Job Finding in a Period of Mass Unemployment: Evidence from High-Frequency Longitudinal Data," *Brookings Papers on Economic Activity*, March 8, 2011. Found on the Web at http://tinyurl.com/4olmpj9.

I know the truth of this from my own experience. I have been fired twice in my life. I remember how it felt each time I got the lousy news. I walked out of the building dazed, as though I had just emerged from a really bad train wreck. The sun was shining brightly, not a cloud in the sky; and, since it was lunch hour, as it happened, the streets were filled with laughing happy people, who apparently had not a care in the world.

I remember thinking, "The world has just caved—my world at least. How can all these people act as though nothing has happened?"

And I remember the feelings. The overwhelming feelings, that only intensified in the weeks after that. Describe my state however you want—feeling sad, being in a funk, feeling despair, feeling hopeless, feeling like things "will always be this way," or feeling depressed—it doesn't matter. I was terribly unhappy. Unemployment was rocking my soul to its foundations. I needed to know what to do about my feelings.

I have since learned that my experience was not the least unusual. Many of us, if not most of us, when we are out of work for a long time feel weary and depressed.[2] Our greatest desire is to get rid of these depressed feelings. After talking to thousands of job-hunters, I think there are:

Ten Things We Can Do to Deal with Our Feelings, When We Are Unemployed

1. We can catch up on our sleep, even if it means we have to take naps during the day because our attempt to sleep at nighttime is, at the moment, a disaster. We tend to feel depressed if we are short on our sleep, or our body is otherwise run-down.

---

2. Serious clinical depression often has a lifelong history, and requires treatment, particularly when a person is feeling endangering impulses, such as suicide. In such a case, you should seek competent psychological or psychiatric help. (For immediate help, this minute, call 1-800-273-8255 or go online to www.suicidepreventionlifeline.org. There are counselors 24/7 at both places who deal with anyone, including the military or veterans, in trouble.)

There are two states that can be easily confused:

First of all, the world never looks bright or happy to us when we are very short on sleep.

Secondly, the world never looks bright or happy to us when we are feeling depressed.

It is therefore easy to confuse the two feeling-states. Over the years, I have seen many job-hunters who first thought they were really depressed over their situation, later discover they were really depressed just because they were so tired. Or a bit of both. Anyway, sleep or nap, we often turn into happier, more upbeat people, just by catching up on our sleep. This can make us feel better—sometimes much better.

2. There are other things that we can do to keep ourselves more physically fit while unemployed. Job-hunters have told me they found it important to:

- get regular exercise, involving a daily walk;

- drink plenty of water each day (this seems silly, but I found out we tend to skip the water, and get dehydrated, when we're out of work);

- eliminate sugar as much as possible from the diet;

- take supplementary vitamins daily (no matter how many doctors and nutritionists try to tell us that we already get enough from our daily food);

- eat balanced meals (not just pig out on junk food in front of the telly);

- and all that other stuff that our mothers always told us to do.

3. We can do something about the physical space around us. Our surroundings often mirror how we feel about ourselves. If our physical environment looks like a disaster area, that in itself can make us depressed. When we are unemployed, we can vow we will live simpler—something that maybe we've wanted to do, for a long time. We can begin by taking care that each time we handle a thing, we take it all the way to its new destination; we don't just drop it on the counter, thinking that we will deal with it later. We can take care that when we take our clothes off at

night, we don't just drop them on the floor, but hang them up or put them in a laundry-hamper. And that, when we finish eating, we put the dishes where they are going to be washed, and put our food back in the refrigerator. And we can determine that when we do such things as get a screwdriver out, to fix a screw that's dropped out of something, that we take the screwdriver all the way back to the tool box or wherever its final destination is. And so on.

When we determine to always put our things away in a timely fashion, neatness will start to appear in our physical environment; this can help lift our spirits immensely, as our physical space mirrors an upbeat life.

4. **We can get outdoors daily and take a good walk.** Hiding in our cave (figuratively speaking) will only make us feel more *down*. Seeing green trees (in season), sunlight, mountains, flowers, people, will do our heart good, each day.

5. **We can focus on other people** and their problems—not just our own. If our unemployment is dragging on and on, and we're starting to have a lot of time on our hands, we can find someplace in town that is dealing with people worse off than we are, and go volunteer there. I'm talking food banks, hospitals, housing aid, anything dealing with kids—especially deprived kids, or kids with tremendous handicaps—that sort of thing. We can do a search on Google, put in the name of our town or city plus the name of the problem we want to help with, and see what turns up. If we determine to help someone else in need, while we're unemployed, we won't feel so discarded by society.

And speaking of other people, we can renew our acquaintance with old friends. We can explore the friendships we already have, not because they are useful in our job-hunt, but just because they are valuable human beings. A wise man named Phillips Brooks used to say there are two kinds of exploration: one involves going out to explore new country; the other involves digging down more deeply into the country we already occupy. Do both, when you're feeling *down*.

6. **We can go on fun mini-adventures.** Often there are portions of our surroundings that we have never explored, but a tourist would "hit" on, the very first day they were there. I lived in New York City for a long time; never once went up in the Empire State Building. I lived in San Francisco for years; never once went out to the Zoo. You get the point. If I lived in either of these cities today, and was unemployed for any length of time, I would set out to visit places I'd never seen. We can stop obsessing about how much we lost from our past, and turn our face toward the future. There are new worlds to conquer, after all.

7. **We can deal with our feelings by expanding our mental horizons, and learning something new.** We can go read up on subjects that have always interested us, but we've never had enough time to explore. While we're unemployed, we have the time. If we can't think of any subject, there's always the human mind. The mind, after all, is what is trying hard to figure out what we should do next. The more we understand it, the better we can heal. If you're looking for suggestions, I'd read anything by Martin Seligman. There's *Learned Optimism: How to Change Your Mind and Your Life*, which, as one reviewer commented, "vaulted me out of my funk." It has excellent chapters on dealing with depression. Or there's Seligman's most recent book, *Flourish: A Visionary New Understanding of Happiness and Well-being*. If you want to delve into improving your memory, there's Joshua Foer's *Moonwalking with Einstein: The Art and Science of Remembering Everything*. And, last but not least, if you want to learn more about how one mind influences another mind, there is Robert B. Cialdini's *Influence: The Psychology of Persuasion*. All these authors have extensive videos on YouTube.

   Speaking of videos, there are a million *free* videos online, where you can learn just about anything. In addition to videos, there are videocasts, webcasts, podcasts, and every other kind of *-cast*. You can type the word "webcast," plus the subject in which you are interested, into your favorite browser like Google, and then pick through whatever turns up. There are also, of course, books. For our Kindle Fire or Nook or iPad, or from online

bookstores like Amazon or Barnes & Noble, there are tons of
eBooks available, running around ten bucks, or a little more.

Another subject to explore is the world around us. I love *The
Unofficial U.S. Census: Things the Official U.S. Census Doesn't Tell
You About America*, by Les Krantz and Chris Smith. My favorite
factoid there, because it's related to what I was talking about in
our first suggestion: "More than one-third of Americans take
naps." *Yes!*

8. We can talk, talk, talk with our loved ones, or a close friend,
   about all the feelings we have. It's amazing how giving voice
   to thoughts and feelings, particularly when we don't much care
   for those thoughts and those feelings, causes them to lose their
   power over us. So we should do it, because otherwise stuff
   bottled up inside us tends to fester and grow. We don't want
   that. We must just take care that we don't pick *the town gossip* to
   confide in, nor a friend or loved one who just can't keep their
   mouth shut. You know who they are.

9. We can pound a punching bag or even some pillows, to get
   some of the angry energy out of us. I don't know why, but it's
   astonishing how many of the unemployed have told me this
   actually helps them get rid of some of their anger. And this
   helps lift our depression as well. Sometimes feeling *down*, and
   feeling *angry* seem almost to be two different sides of the same
   coin. If we don't have a gym in our life we can build one at home,
   simply by putting a pile of pillows on top of our bed, and then
   pounding the pillows repeatedly, as hard as we can—without
   breaking anything in our hands, wrists, or arms. This often
   really helps. We are strange creatures.

10. We can make a list each day of the things that make us grate-
    ful, glad, or even happy, day by day. There is a habit of mind
    that is deadly while we're out of work, and that is spending too
    much of our day, every day, brooding about what is wrong in
    our lives: what is wrong with people, what is wrong with our
    situation, what is wrong with anything and everything. By list-
    ing the things we are thankful for, we teach ourselves to focus

on what precious gifts we still have, whether they be intelligence, health, or love.

If we want to get over being depressed, it is crucial that we give up endless complaint, it is crucial that we come to forgiveness for any past wrongs done to us, it is crucial that we, as Baltasar Gracián put it, "Get used to the failings of our friends, family, and acquaintances. . . ." We are all human. We are all capable of turning our face toward the future, rather than toward the past.

Postscript

Millions of people in this country have no religious beliefs. But untold millions do. And it is not uncommon that for them, unemployment turns out to be a major spiritual crisis in their life. They cry out, "How could God have let this happen to me—if He truly loved me?" Their faith, far from helping them out of depression, often plunges them into it. They write me and ask for some help and advice. Here is what I tell them.

We can revisit our picture of God and how He works in this world. In the Christian church, for example, the Creed does not begin with "I believe *there is a* God. . . ." It begins with "I believe *in* God. . . ." I think we all understand this distinction, between believing something about a friend of ours, say that she is tall, or smart, versus *believing in* that friend. To believe in someone is to trust them, and to trust that they feel toward us as they say they feel.

We can, instead of abandoning our faith, put some energy into rethinking our faith on a higher level. Some 89% of us in the U.S. say we believe in God, but the question is, What kind of God do we believe in? Half a century ago, a man wrote a book titled, *Your God Is Too Small*. Unemployment or any crisis often reveals how poor and small our concept of God is. It is small because it holds God responsible for everything that happens in the world.

Each of us has to figure this out for ourselves. But since people have asked me what I think, after eighty-five years on this Earth, my thoughts ramble along in this fashion: In the Christian faith, Jesus said the most important thing in the world, to God, was that we love Him. Robots can't love. He has to give us freedom so we can choose to love, or not. With that freedom, however, comes the possibility that we will make wrong choices, and thus introduce tragedy into the world. Look at the mess the world is in right now. Look at Congress. God didn't do that!

Well, then, what does God do? To what larger conception of God might we press? Let's try this: imagine that you have, in your dining room, a fine wooden chair, which one day has its back broken off completely—I mean, into smithereens—by a guest in your home. You run down the street, to summon a carpenter who lives nearby. He comes and examines the chair. He pronounces the back unrepairable. "But," he says, "I think I could make a fine wooden stool out of the remainder of the chair, for you." And so he spends much time, shaping, polishing and sanding it, and fashioning out of the former chair a fine stool, more resplendent than anything you have ever dreamed. He inlays it with precious metals, and soon it is the treasure of your house.

This is, of course, a parable. And I know you understand it. But let me underline a couple of key points in it. First of all, the carpenter did not break the chair. Your houseguest did that. But the carpenter came quickly, and with all his art and powers he tried, first of all, to see if he could repair it. Finding it was too late for that, he determined to make of it something even finer than it had been before. And, he labored mightily, to that end. A beautiful stool was the result.

A faith that thinks God is responsible for our unemployment, and He could have and should have prevented it, needs to grow up. It is too small a faith. It has too small a God.

While we are out of work, we can reach toward a larger conception of our God and of ourselves. For, "to believe in God" has the power to lift us out of depression, unless our God is too small.

We can, realize that religion isn't necessarily a blessing. Much depends on whether it is *healthy* religion, or *unhealthy* religion. Your choice. Here is the distinction between them:

Healthy Religion	Unhealthy Religion
Is obsessed with gratitude	Is obsessed with guilt
Focuses on the presence of God in the world; sees holiness everywhere	Focuses on the presence of evil in the world; sees contamination everywhere
Sees all the world as "us"	Sees all the world as "us vs. them"
Is closely related to mental health with its emphasis on repentance (metanoia) or "Most of my ills are self-inflicted."	Is distantly related to mental illness (paranoia) or "Most of my ills stem from what others are doing 'out there.'"
Unconsciously exhibits humility	Unconsciously exhibits arrogance
Treasures the differences in others	Wants everyone to be like them
Has a high sense of "all the saints" worshipping God together	Has a high sense of "the individual alone with his or her God"
Believes in learning from others	Believes in confronting others
Renounces manipulation of others, and lets them have their own beliefs	Desires to manipulate others into accepting their every belief
Wants God's forgiveness toward those who have harmed them or follow other gods; forgives readily	Wants God's vengeance toward those who have harmed them or follow other gods; often has low, long-simmering anger, masked beneath a smile
Focuses on what one can give, out of faith; anxious to give others benefits	Focuses on what one gets out of faith; anxious to get for themselves the benefits
Faith is primarily a matter of actions; words are used only to interpret one's actions	Faith is primarily a matter of words used as tests or orthodoxy. Shibboleth and sibboleth.
Is well aware that their faith may have some unhealthiness to it	Doesn't even dream their faith may be unhealthy

Feelings are often a messenger bringing gifts, if only we open our eyes to see them. If our feelings while we are out of work push us to get more sleep, drink more water, get more physically fit, get outdoors more, look harder at other people who are worse off than we are, renew old neglected friendships, embark on mini-adventures, expand the horizons of our mind, and get us to rethink our faith, then that is a gift indeed. A great gift.

A Guide to Choosing a Career Coach or Counselor

If You Decide You Need One

All readers of this book divide into two families, or groups. The first group are those who find the book is all they need, particularly if they do the exercises in chapter 7 successfully, on their own.

The second group are those who find they need a little bit of extra help. Either they bog down in their effort to complete the whole book, or they start the exercises in chapter 7 and then get stuck, at some point. So they want some additional help.

Fortunately, there are a lot of people out there, anxious to help you with your job-hunt or career-change, in case this book isn't sufficient by itself. They go by various names: career coach, career counselor, career development specialist, you name it. They're willing to help you for a fee—because this is how they make their living. That fee will usually equal the fee charged by other types of counselors in town, say a good psychologist. That will range from about $40 an hour in rural areas, on up to . . . *you don't want to know*. The fee may be charged by the hour (recommended) or as one large lump sum up front (definitely not recommended). And most towns or cities of any size have free or almost-free help, too, even though it's likely to be in a group and not face-to-face with an individual counselor. For "free," or "almost free," see Susan Joyce's marvelous website (job-hunt.org, or as she likes to say, "job dash hunt dot org") for the section called *Networking and Job Search Support by State*, at http://tinyurl.com/7a9xbb.

Now, about those coaches or counselors who charge to help you. There are some simply excellent ones, out there. In fact, I wish I could say that *everyone* who hangs out a sign in this business could be completely recommended. But—alas! and alack!—they can't all be. This career-coaching or career-counseling field is largely unregulated. And even where there is some kind of certification, resulting in their being able to put a lot of degree-soundin' initials after their name, that doesn't really tell you much. It means a lot *to them* of course; in many cases, they purchased those initials with their blood, sweat, and tears. (*Although a few, sad to say, got the initials after their name by mail-order or after one long weekend of training. Tsk, tsk. But, oh well, no different I suppose from a lot of other professions. Some people are always looking for shortcuts.*)

I used to try to explain what all those initials meant. There is a veritable alphabet-soup of them, with new ones born every year. But no more; I've learned, from more than forty years of experience in this field, that 99.4% of all job-hunters and career-changers don't care a fig about these initials. All they want to know is: *do you know how to help me find a job?* Or, more specifically, *do you know how to help me find my dream job—one that matches the gifts, skills, and experience that I have, one that makes me excited to get up in the morning, and excited to go to bed at night, knowing I helped make this Earth a little better place to be in?* If so, I'll hire you. If not, I'll fire you.

How to Lose Your Shirt (or Skirt)

So, *bye-bye initials!* Let us start, instead, with this basic truth: *All coaches and counselors divide basically into three groups:*
   a) those who are honest, compassionate, and caring, and know what they're doing;
   b) those who are honest but don't know what they're doing; and
   c) those who are dishonest, and merely want your money—large amounts, in a lump sum, and up front. These are often so-called executive counseling firms—*some* executive counseling firms—rather than individual counselors.

In other words, you've got compassionate, caring people in the same field with bums and crooks. Your job, if you want help and don't want to waste your money, is to learn how to distinguish the one from the other.

It would help, of course, if someone could just give you a list of those who are firmly in the first category—honest and know what they're doing. But unfortunately, no one (including me) has such a list, or ever has had. You've got to do your own homework or research here, and your own interviewing, in your chosen geographical area. *And if you're too lazy to take the time and trouble to do this research, you will deserve what you get.*

Why is it that *you* and only *you* can do this particular research? Well, let's say a friend tells you to go see so-and-so. He's a wonderful coach or counselor, but unhappily when you meet him he reminds you of your Uncle Harry, whom you detest. Bummer! But, no one except you knows that you've always disliked your Uncle Harry.

That's why no one else can do this research for you—because the real question is not "Who is best?" but "Who is best for you?" Those last two words demand that it be you who "makes the call."

A special word, here, to those considering paying any firm that focuses on executives or people who make or would like to make a high salary. (This warning is regarding *firms*, not *individual* counselors.) If you are an executive you are considered a fair target for any scam the mind can imagine. New ones appear every year. I have consulted with the Federal Trade Commission in Washington, and States Attorneys General over the years, where they have described the scams to me in detail. I have collected news items, done individual interviews with those who got "taken," and I wish I could tell you about individual firms, but that's not my job. Do your own research. If you are considering signing up with any such firm, Google them first: you will come across timely research about *any* firm. Example: http://corcodilos.com/blog/3219/theladders-how-the-scam-works-2. If you are too lazy to do this research, and subsequently get "taken,"

let me share the words a Scotsman once said to me, when I got "taken"·
"I'm sorry ya lost yer money, but ya dinna do your homework."

Now, for all my other readers: your dilemma is between categories
a and *b* on page 299. How do you find an honest counselor *who knows
what they're doing,* and can give you a little bit of help, if you bog down
in using this book, most especially chapter 7?

The first bright idea that will occur to you might be something
along the lines of "Well, I'll just see who Bolles recommends." Sorry,
no such luck. I rarely if ever recommend anyone. Some of the coaches
or counselors listed in the *Sampler* at the end of this Appendix, try to
claim that their very listing here constitutes a recommendation from
me. Oh, come on! They're there because they asked to be. I ask a few
questions, but I don't have time to do any thorough research on them.
This *Sampler* is more akin to the Yellow Pages, than it is to *Consumer
Reports.* Let me repeat this—as I have for forty years now—and repeat
it very loudly:

> The listing of a career counselor or coach in this book does NOT con-
> stitute an endorsement or recommendation by me. Never has meant
> that. Never will. (Any counselor or coach listed here who claims that it
> does—either in their ads, or brochures, or publicity—gets permanently
> removed from this Sampler the following year after I find out about it,
> and without warning.) This is not "a hall of fame"; it is just a *Sampler*
> of names of those *who have* asked *to be listed, and have answered some
> reasonable questions.*

Consider the listings as just a starting point for your search. You
must check them out. You must do your own homework. You must do
your own research.

A Guide to Choosing a Good
Career Coach

So, how do you go about this research toward the goal of finding a good career coach or counselor, if you decide you need more help than this book can give you? Well, you start by collecting three names of career coaches or counselors in your geographical area.

How do you find those names? Several ways:

First, you can get names from your friends: ask if any of them have ever used a career coach or counselor. And if so, did they like 'em? And if so, what is that coach's or counselor's name? And how do you get in touch with them, so you can ask them some questions before deciding whether you want to sign up with them, or not?

Second, you can get some names from the aforementioned Sampler in Appendix D (which begins on page 315). See if there are any career coaches or counselors who are near you. They may know how you can find still other names in your community.

Need more names? Try your telephone book's Yellow Pages, under such headings as: *Aptitude and Employment Testing, Career and Vocational Counseling, Personnel Consultants,* and (if you are a woman) *Women's Organizations and Services.*

Once you have three names, it's time to go do some comparison shopping. You want to talk with all three of them and decide which of the three (if any) you want to hook up with.

What will this initial interview cost you, with each coach or counselor? The answer to that is easy: when first setting up an appointment, *ask.* You do have the right to inquire ahead of time how much they are going to have to charge you for the exploratory interview.

Some—a few—will charge you nothing for the initial interview. One of the brightest counselors I know says this: *I don't like to charge for the first interview because I want to be free to tell them I can't help them, if for some reason we just don't hit it off.*

However, do not expect that most coaches or counselors can afford to give you this exploratory interview for nothing! If they did that, and got a lot of requests like yours, they would never make a living.

If this is not an individual counselor, but *a firm* trying to sell you a "pay-me-first" package *up front*, I guarantee they will give you the initial interview for free. They plan to use that "intake" interview (as they call it) to sell you a much more expensive program. They will even ask you to bring your spouse or partner along. (If they can't persuade one of you, maybe they can persuade the other.)

The Questions to Ask

When you are face to face with the coach or counselor, you ask each of them the same questions, listed on the form below. (Keep a little pad, notebook, or smartphone with you, so you can write down their answers.)

After visiting the three places you chose for your comparison shopping, you can go home, sit down, put your feet up, look over your notes that evening, and compare those places. A chart like this, drawn in your notebook, may help:

MY SEARCH FOR A GOOD CAREER COUNSELOR

Questions I Will Ask Them	Answer from Counselor #1	Answer from Counselor #2	Answer from Counselor #3
1. What is your program?			
2. Who will be counseling? And how long has this person been counseling?			
3. What is your success rate?			
4. What is the cost of your services?			
5. Is there a contract up front? If so, may I see it please, and take it home with me?			

You need to decide a) whether you want **none** of the three, or b) **one** of the three (and if so, which one).

Remember, you don't have to choose *any* of the three coaches, if you didn't really care for any of them. If that is the case, go choose three new names out of the Yellow Pages or wherever, dust off the notebook, and go out again. It may take a few more hours to find what you want. But **the wallet, the purse, the job-hunt, and the life, you save will be your own.**

As you look over your notes, you will soon realize there is no definitive way for you to determine a career coach's intentions. It's something you'll have to *smell out*, as you go along. But here are some clues.

Bad Vibes, on Up to Real Bad Vibes

If they give you the feeling that everything will be done for you, by them (*including interpretation of tests, and decision making about what this means you should do, or where you should do it*)—rather than asserting that you are going to have to do almost all the work, with their basically being your coach,

(Give them 15 bad points)

You want to learn how to do this for yourself; you're going to be job-hunting again, you know. That's the nature of our world today. Job-hunting is a repetitive activity in human life.

If you don't like the counselor, period!

(Give them 150 bad points)

I don't care what their expertise is, if you don't like them, you're going to have a rough time getting what you want. I guarantee it. Rapport is everything.

If you ask how long this particular counselor has been doing this, and they get huffy or give a double-barreled answer, such as: "I've had eighteen years' experience in the business and career counseling world,"

(Give them 20 bad points)

What that may mean is: seventeen and a half years as a fertilizer salesman, and one half year doing career counseling. Persist: "How long have you been with this firm, and how long have you been doing formal career coaching or counseling, as you are here?" You don't want someone who's brand new to advising job-hunters. They may call this "their practice," but what they mean is that they are practicing . . . on you.

If they try to answer the question of their experience by pointing to their degrees or credentials,

(Give them 3 bad points)

Degrees or credentials tell you they've passed certain tests of their qualifications, but often these tests bear more on their expertise at career assessment, than on their knowledge of creative job-hunting.

If, when you ask about that firm's success rate, they say they have never had a client who failed to find a job, no matter what,

(Give them 500 bad points)

They're lying. I have studied career counseling programs for more than forty years, have attended many, have studied records at state and federal offices, and have hardly ever seen a program that placed more than 86% of their clients, tops, in their best years. And it goes downhill from there. A prominent executive counseling firm was reported by the Attorney General's Office of New York State to have placed only 38 out of 550 clients (a 93% failure rate). On the other hand, if they make it clear that they have had a good success rate, but if you fail to work hard at the whole process, then there is no guarantee you are going to find a job, give them three stars.

If any counselor shows you letters from ecstatically happy former clients, but when you ask to talk to some of those clients, you get stonewalled,

(Give them 200 bad points)

Here is a job-hunter's letter about his experience with an executive counseling firm he was considering:

> *I asked to speak to a former client or clients. You would have thought I asked to speak to Elvis. The counselor stammered and stuttered and gave me a million excuses why I couldn't talk to some of these "satisfied" former clients. None of the excuses sounded legitimate to me. We went back and forth for about thirty minutes. Finally, he excused himself and went to speak to his boss, the owner. The next thing I knew I was called into the owner's office for a more "personal" sales pitch. We spoke for about forty-five minutes as he tried to convince me to use his service. When I told him I was not ready to sign up, he became angry and asked my counselor why I had been put before "the committee" if I wasn't ready to commit?*

The counselor claimed I had given a verbal commitment at our last meeting. The owner then turned to me and said I seemed to have a problem making a decision and that he did not want to do business with me. I was shocked. They had turned the whole story around to make it look like it was my fault. I felt humiliated. In retrospect, the whole process felt like dealing with a used car salesman. They used pressure tactics and intimidation to try to get what they wanted. As you have probably gathered, more than anything else this experience made me angry.

If you are dealing with a career counseling firm, and you ask what is the cost of their services, and they reply that it is a lump sum that must all be paid "up front" before you start or shortly after you start, all at once or in rapid installments,

(Give them 300 bad points)

We're talking about firms here, not the average individual counselor or coach. The basic problem with firms is that both "the good guys" and "the crooks" do this. The good guys operate on the theory that if you give them a large sum up front, you will then be really committed to the program. The crooks operate on the theory that if you give them a large sum up front, they don't have to give you anything back, except endless excuses and subterfuge, after a certain date (quickly reached).

And the trouble is that there is absolutely no way for you to distinguish crook from good guy, at first impression; they only reveal their true nature after they've got all your money. And by that time, you have no legal way to get it back, no matter what they verbally promised.[1]

---

1. Sometimes the written contract—there is *always* a written contract, when you are dealing with the bad guys, and they will probably ask your partner to sign it, too—will claim to provide for an almost complete refund, at any time, until you reach a cutoff date in the program, which the contract specifies. Unfortunately, fraudulent firms bend over backward to be extra nice, extra available, and extra helpful to you, from the time you first walk in, until that cutoff point is reached. Therefore, when the cutoff point for getting a refund has passed, you let it pass because you are very satisfied with their past services, and believe there will be many more weeks of the same. Only, there aren't. At fraudulent firms, once the cutoff point is passed, the career counselor suddenly becomes virtually impossible for you to get ahold of. Call after call will not be returned. You will say to yourself, "What happened?" Well, what happened, my friend, is that you paid up in full, they have all the money they're ever going to get out of you, and now, they want to move on.

Let me repeat: with firms that make you sign a contract and pay basically up front, there is no way to distinguish the good guys from the crooks. The only safe counseling is one with no contract, and you just pay for each hour, as you use it.

I have tried for years to think of some way around this dilemma, to be fair to the good guys, but there just is none. So if you decide to pay up front, be sure it is money you can afford to lose.

If Money Is a Problem for You: Hourly Coaching

Most career coaches or counselors charge by the hour. You pay only for each hour as you use it, according to their set rate. Each time you keep an appointment, you pay them at the end of that hour for their help, according to that rate. Period. Finis. You never owe them any money (unless you made an appointment, and failed to keep it). You can stop seeing them at any time, if you feel you are not getting the help you wish. The fee will probably range from $40 an hour on up to $200 an hour or more. It varies *greatly*. Counselors in cities tend to charge more than counselors out in the country.

That fee is for *individual time* with the career coach or counselor. If you can't afford that fee, ask whether they also run groups. If they do, the fee will be much less. And, in one of those delightful ironies of life, since you get a chance to listen to problems that other job-hunters in your group are having, the group will often give you more help than an individual session with a counselor would have. Not always; but often. It's always ironic when *cheaper* and *more helpful* go hand in hand.

If the career counselor in question does offer groups, there should (again) never be a contract. The charge should be payable at the end of each session, and you should be able to drop out at any time, without further cost, if you decide you are not getting the help you want.

There are some career counselors who run free (or almost free) job-hunting workshops through local churches, synagogues, chambers of commerce, community colleges, adult education programs, and the like, as their community service or *pro bono* work (as it is technically called). I have had reports of workshops from a number of places in the U.S. and Canada. They exist in other parts of the world as well. If money is a problem for you, in getting help with your job-hunt, ask around to see if workshops exist in your community. Your chamber of commerce will know, or your church or synagogue.

As I mentioned earlier, you can find an incredibly useful list of all the job support groups in the U.S. compiled by Susan Joyce, on her site job-hunt.org: http://tinyurl.com/7a9xbb.

If Your Location Is a Problem for You: Distance-Coaching or Telephone-Counseling

The assumption, from the beginning, was that career counseling would always take place face to face. Both of you, counselor and job-hunter, together in the same room. Just like career counseling's close relatives: marriage counseling, or even AA.

Of course, a job-hunter might—on occasion—phone his or her counselor the day before an interview, to get some last-minute tips or to answer some questions that a prospective interviewer might ask, *tomorrow.*

What is different, today, is that in some cases, career counseling is being conducted exclusively over the phone from start to finish. Some counselors now report that they haven't laid eyes on over 90% of their clients, and wouldn't know them if they bumped into them on a street corner. I call this "distance-coaching" or "telephone-counseling."

With the invention of the Internet, with the invention of Internet *telephoning*, we are witnessing "the death of distance"—that is to say, the death of distance as an obstacle. The world, as the wonderful *New York Times* columnist Thomas Friedman has famously written, is in effect *flat.*

An increasing number of counselors or executive coaches are doing this *distance-counseling.*[2] This increasing availability of "distance-counseling" is good news, and bad news.

---

2. Two famous "distance coaches" are Joel Garfinkle in Oakland, California, www.dreamjobcoaching
.com; and Marshall Goldsmith of www.marshallgoldsmithlibrary.com, international coach to
the executive elite, and author (with Mark Reiter) of the popular book, *What Got You Here Won't
Get You There.*

Why good news? Well, in the old days you might be a job-hunter in some remote village, with a population of only eighty-five, back in the hills somewhere, or you might be living somewhere in France or in China, miles from any career counselor or coach, and so, be totally out of luck. Now, these days you can be anywhere in the world, but as long as you have the Internet on your desk, you can still connect with the best distance-counseling there is.

And the bad news?

Well, just because a counselor or coach does distance-counseling or phone-counseling, doesn't mean they are really good at doing it. Some are superb; but some are not. So, you're still going to have to research any *distance-counselor* very carefully.

It is altogether too easy for a counselor to get sloppy doing distance-counseling—for example, browsing the newspapers while you are telling some long personal story, etc., to which they are giving only the briefest attention. (Of course, the increasingly wider use of video calling programs such as Skype may cure that!) To avoid any kind of sloppiness, *you* and the counselor need discipline. Experienced distance-counselors, such as Joel Garfinkle,[3] insist on forms being used, both before and after each phone session. With his permission, I have adapted his forms, and print them here. *And, P.S., they are equally useful for normal, face-to-face counseling, as well.*

Client Coaching Forms

1. Before You Start

Prior to beginning the counseling, it helps if your coach or counselor asks you to fill out the following kind of form, for you to give to him or her. They are written by the counselor, addressed to you, the potential counselee. (And if they don't ask for a form like this to be filled out, you might volunteer to give them such a form on your own.)

---

3. www.dreamjobcoaching.com/about.

Questions to Understand You Better

(Copy this onto another sheet of paper, and leave lots of space on the form for your answer, after each question below.)

1. Why have you decided to work with me?

2. How can I have the most impact on your life in the next ninety days (three months)?

3. List three key goals you want to accomplish through our work together.

4. What stops you from achieving what you want in question #2 or #3 above?

5. Project ahead one year: As you look back, and things went well, how did you benefit from our coaching relationship?

6. What are your expectations from our work together? How can we exceed these expectations?

7. What else is helpful for me to know about you?

8. Explain your background (use the same format as the examples below).

Examples:

1. After thirty years as a commercial insurance broker, I hit a wall last May, and decided to change careers . . .

2. After twelve successful years in the high-tech industry, I found myself unfulfilled in finding a satisfying career. Over the years, I read countless books on the topic of finding one's true purpose in career pursuits, but was still missing a sense of purpose and clarity on what I wanted to do . . .

3. After working for twenty years in the investment industry I decided to start my own company . . .

4. Etc.

2. Before Each Session, Preparation Form

Please fill out this form #2 for each coaching session. It should be filled out and e-mailed to me twenty-four hours before the next coaching session to assist me in preparing for that session.

(Copy this onto another sheet of paper, and leave lots of space on the form for your answer, after each question below.)

1. **Commitments that I made to myself on the last coaching session and what I accomplished since we had the coaching session:**

2. **The challenges and opportunities I am facing now:**

3. **The one action I can take that will most affect my current goals and provide the highest payoff:**

4. **My agenda for the coaching session is:**

3. After Each Session: Reflection Form

Immediately after each coaching session e-mail me form #3.

(Copy this onto another sheet of paper, and leave lots of space on the form for your answer, after each question below.)

1. **This week's commitment:**

2. **My greatest insights during this session were:**

3. **What you, my coach, said or asked during the session that impacted me most:**

4. **What I'd like you, as my coach, to do differently/more of/less of:**

5. **How I feel I am evolving from our work together:**

What happens in a counseling session is our responsibility, not just the counselor's or coach's.

The forms, above, are one way of our taking responsibility. Another, is that when you first contact prospective coaches for distance-counseling in particular, you have a right to ask them: (1) "What training have you completed, relevant to distance-counseling, such as telephone skills, and supervised counseling?" (2) "How will our distance-counseling be organized and scheduled?" and (3) "What will the two of us do if and when interruptions occur during a session, at either end?"

You must always remember: distance-counseling, attractive as it will be for many, as necessary as it will be for some, definitely has its limits.

To the caveman, the technology that enables all this to happen in this twenty-first century, would be jaw-droppingly awesome. But, good career counseling or coaching *is not just about technology*. What is really truly awesome, in the end, is simply our power to help each other on this Earth. And how much that power resides, not in techniques or technology—though these things are important—but in each of us just being a good human being. A *loving* human being.

A Sampler

The following Appendix is exactly what its name implies: a Sampler. Were I to list all the career coaches and counselors there are in the U.S. (never mind the world), we would end up with an encyclopedia. Some states, in fact, have encyclopedic lists of counselors and businesses, in various books or directories, and your local bookstore or library should have these, in their Job-Hunting Section, under such titles as "How to Get a Job in . . ." or "Job-Hunting in . . ." Now, let me repeat this:

I did not choose the places listed in this Sampler; rather, they are listed at their own request, and I offer their information to you simply as suggestions of where you can begin your investigation—when you're trying to find decent help.

Do keep in mind that many truly helpful places and coaches are not listed here. If you discover such a coach or place, which is very good at helping people with *Parachute* and creative job-hunting or career-change, do send us their pertinent information. We will ask them, as we do all the listings here, a few intelligent questions, and if they sound okay, we will add that place as a suggestion in next year's edition.[4]

What kind of questions? This directory appears nowhere but in this book, so we may presume you are interested in this book's approach, and if you need a little help it is help with the process in this book. We tried being broader in the past—there are obviously excellent counselors out there who have never heard of this book—but it turned out that our readers wanted counselors and places that have some expertise with *Parachute*, and can help job-hunters or career-changers finish the job-hunt in this book.

So, if they've never even heard of *Parachute*, we don't list them anymore. But even among those who have, we can't automatically assume they're good at what they do, no matter how many questions we asked them. So we list them and leave the research to you.

You must do your own sharp questioning before you decide to go with anyone. If you don't take time to research two or three places, before choosing a counselor, you will deserve whatever you get (or, more to the point, don't get). So, please, do some research.

---

4. Yearly readers of this book will notice that we do remove people from this Sampler, without warning. First of all, there are accidents: we drop places we didn't mean to, but a typographical error was made, somehow (it happens). *Oops!* Counselor or coach: call this to our attention; we'll put you back in next year.

But accidents aside, we do deliberately remove the following: places that have moved, and don't bother to send us their new address. *Coaches and counselors: If you are listed here, we expect you to be a professional at communication. When you move, your first priority should be to let us know, immediately. As one exemplary counselor wrote: "You are the first person I am contacting on my updated letterhead . . . hot off the press just today!" So it should always be, if you want to continue to be listed here. A number of places get removed every year, precisely because of their sloppiness in keeping us up-to-date with their phone and other contact information.*

Other causes for removal: Places that have disconnected their telephone, or otherwise suggest that they have gone out of business. Places that our readers lodge complaints against with us, as being unhelpful or even obnoxious. The complaints may be falsified, but we can't take that chance. Places that change their personnel, and the new person has never even heard of *Parachute*, or "creative job-search techniques." College services that we discover (belatedly) serve only "Their Own." Counseling firms that employ salespeople as the initial "intake" person that a job-hunter meets. If you discover that any of the places listed in this Sampler fall into any of the above categories, you would be doing a great service to our other readers by dropping us a line and telling us so (10 Stirling Drive, Danville, CA 94526-2921).

The listings that follow are alphabetical within each state, with counselors listed by their name in alphabetical order, according to their last name.

Some offer group career counseling, some offer testing, some offer access to job-banks, etc. Ask.

One final note: places and counselors listed here have said they counsel anyone; 99% of them can absolutely be trusted, in this. A few, however, may turn out to have restrictions unknown to us ("we counsel only women," or "we only deal with alumni," etc.). If that turns out to be the case, your time isn't wasted. They may be able to help you with a referral. So, ask them, "Who else in the area can you tell me about, who helps with job-searches, and are there any (among them) that you think are particularly effective?" (Also, write us and let us know they only counsel *some* people, so we can remove them from this Sampler next year.)

Area Codes

If you call a phone number in the Sampler that is any distance geographically from you, and they tell you "this number cannot be completed as dialed," the most likely explanation is that the area code was changed—maybe some time ago. Throughout the U.S. now, area codes are subdividing constantly, sometimes more than once during a short time span. (We ask counselors listed here to notify us when the area code changes, but some do and some don't.) Anyway, call Information and check, or look up their phone number on the Web.

Of course, if you're calling a local counselor, you won't need the area code (unless you live in one of the metropolitan areas in the U.S. that requires ten-digit dialing).

Appendix D

Sampler List of Coaches

* *Throughout this Sampler, an asterisk before their name, in red, means they offer religious counseling as well as secular—"religious" means they're not afraid to have you talk about God, if you're looking for some help in finding your Mission in life through faith.*

UNITED STATES

Alabama

Chemsak, Maureen J., LPC, NCC, MCC
NorthStart Counseling and
Consulting, PC
P.O. Box 2065
Madison, AL 35758
Athens, AL 35611
Phone: 256-520-7650
E-mail: mjchemsak104@gmail.com

HRM Inc.
1950 Stonegate Dr., Ste. 300
Birmingham, AL 35243
Phone: 205-533-0429
Contact: Michael Tate
E-mail: mike@hrmasap.com
www.michaelalantate.com

Alaska

Career Transitions
4141 B St., Ste. 308
Anchorage, AK 99503
Phone: 907-274-4500
Fax: 907-274-4510
Contact: Deeta Lonergan, President
E-mail: deeta@alaska.net
www.careertransitions.biz

Arizona

Boninger, Faith, PhD
10965 E. Mary Katherine Dr.
Scottsdale, AZ 85259
Phone: 480-390-6736
E-mail: faithboninger@cox.net

Passport to Purpose
7735 East Bravo Ln.
Prescott Valley, AZ 86314
Phone: 928-775-4949
Contact: Cathy Severson, MS
E-mail: cathy@passporttopurpose.com
www.passporttopurpose.com
www.retirementlifematters.com

Renaissance Career Solutions
PO Box 30118
Phoenix, AZ 85046-0118
Phone: 602-867-4202
Contact: Betty Boza, MA, LCC
E-mail: bboza@att.net
http://bboza-ivil.tripod.com

California

Bauer, Lauralyn Larsen
Career Counselor & Coach
Napa, CA 94558
Phone: 707-363-7775
E-mail: lauralynbauer@hotmail.com

Berrett & Associates
533 E. Mariners Cir.
Fresno, CA 93730
Phone: 559-284-3549
Contact: Dwayne Berrett, MA, RPCC
E-mail: dberrett@me.com
www.berrett-associates.com

California Career Services
6024 Wilshire Blvd.
Los Angeles, CA 90036
Phone: 323-933-2900
Fax: 323-933-9929
Contact: Susan Wise Miller, MA
E-mail: susan@californiacareerservices
.com
www.californiacareerservices.com

Career Balance
215 Witham Rd.
Encinitas, CA 92024
Phone: 760-436-3994
Fax: 760-632-9871
Contact: Virginia Byrd, MEd
Career and Work-Life Consultant
E-mail: virginia@careerbalance.net
www.careerbalance.net

*Career Choices
Dublin, CA
Contact: Dana E. Ogden, MS Ed, CCDV
E-mail: dana@careerchoices.us
www.careerchoices.us

**Career Counseling and
Assessment Associates**
9229 W. Sunset Blvd., Ste. 502
Los Angeles, CA 90069
Phone: 310-274-3423
Contact: Dianne Y. Sundby, PhD
Director and Psychologist
E-mail: DYSD99@aol.com
www.dscounseling.com

**Career and Personal
Development Institute**
582 Market St., Ste. 410
San Francisco, CA 94104
Phone: 415-982-2636
Contact: Bob Chope
www.cpdicareercounseling.com

**Center for Career Growth
and Development**
453 Alberto Way, Ste. 257D
Los Gatos, CA 95032
Phone: 408-354-7150
Contact: Steven E. Beasley
E-mail: stevenbeasley@verizon.net

*Center for Creativity and Work
228 Carmel Ave.
El Cerrito, CA 94530
Phone: 510-526-1600
Contact: Allie Roth, Career Transitions
and Encore Career Coach
E-mail: allie@allieroth.com
www.allieroth.com

*Center for Life & Work Planning
1133 Second St.
Encinitas, CA 92024
Phone/Fax: 760-943-0747
Contact: Mary C. McIsaac,
Executive Director

*Cheney-Rice, Stephen, MS
2113 Westboro Ave.
Alhambra, CA 91803-3720
Phone: 626-824-5244
E-mail: sccheneyrice@earthlink.net

*Clear Change Group
223 San Anselmo Ave., Ste. 6
San Rafael, CA 94960
Phone: 415-488-4998
Contact: Audrey Seymour, MA,
PCC, CPCC
E-mail: inquiry@clearchangegroup.com
www.clearchangegroup.com

**Coaches Certification in Job
and Career Transition**
Contact: Richard (Dick) Knowdell
www.CareerNetwork.Org
(Dick offers three-day workshops,
limited to twenty-four participants;
over forty years, he has trained and
certified six thousand career counselors.)

Collaborative Solutions
3130 W. Fox Run Way
San Diego, CA 92111
Phone: 858-268-9340
Contact: Nancy Helgeson, MA, LMFT
E-mail: nhelgeson@san.rr.com

Dream Job Coaching
6918 Thornhill Dr.
Oakland, CA 94611
Phone: 510-339-3201
Contact: Joel Garfinkle
E-mail: joel@dreamjobcoaching.com
www.dreamjobcoaching.com
www.garfinkleexecutivecoaching.com

Experience Unlimited Job Clubs
There are many Experience Unlim-
ited clubs in California, found at the
Employment Development Department
(EDD) in the following locations:
Anaheim, Canoga Park, Contra Costa,
Fremont, Fresno, Irvine, Lancaster,
Manteca, Murrieta, Pasadena, San Fran-
cisco, San Rafael, Santa Barbara, Santa
Cruz/Capitola, Santa Maria, Simi Val-
ley, Sunnyvale, Torrance, West Covina.
Contact the chapter nearest you
through your local EDD office. Details
about office hours and such are on their
website, http://tinyurl.com/lww4ux.

*Frangquist, Deborah Gavrin, MS
Chosen Futures
1801 Bush St., Ste. 121
San Francisco, CA 94109
Phone: 415-346-6121
E-mail: Deborah@ChosenFutures.com
www.ChosenFutures.com

Fritsen, Jan, MS, MFT
Career Counseling and Coaching
23181 La Cadena Dr., Ste. 103
Laguna Hills, CA 92653
Phone: 949-497-4869
E-mail: janfritsen@cox.net
www.janfritsen.com

Geary & Associates, Inc.
1100 Coddingtown Ctr., Ste. A
PO Box 3774
Santa Rosa, CA 95402
Phone: 707-525-8085
Fax: 707-528-8088
Contact: Jack Geary, MA
Edelweiss Geary, MEd, CRC
E-mail: esgeary@sbcglobal.net
www.gearyassociates.com

Hilliard, Larkin, MA
Counseling Psychology
250 Curtner Avenue, Apt. 3
Palo Alto, CA 94306
Phone: 805-680-3496
E-mail: larkinhilliard@yahoo.com
(English, French, German, and Russian)

HRS
4421 Alla Rd., #2
Marina del Rey, CA 90292
Phone: 310-577-0972
Contact: Nancy Mann, MBA
Career Coach
E-mail: nanmanhrs@aol.com

*Miller, Lizbeth, MS
Nationally Certified Career Counselor
3425 S. Bascom Ave., Ste. 250
Campbell, CA 95008
and 306 Esmeralda Dr.
Santa Cruz, CA 95060
Phone: 408-486-6763
Fax: 408-369-4990
E-mail: lizmillercareers@yahoo.com
www.lizmillercareers.com

Nemko, Marty, PhD
Career and Education Strategist
5936 Chabolyn Terr.
Oakland, CA 94618
Phone: 510-655-2777
E-mail: mnemko@comcast.net
www.martynemko.com

Piazzale, Steve, PhD
Career/Life Coach
Mountain View, CA
Phone: 650-964-4366
E-mail: Steve@BayAreaCareer
Coach.com
www.BayAreaCareerCoach.com

Saraf, Dilip G.
Career and Worklife Strategist
Career Transitions Unlimited
39159 Paseo Padre Pkwy., #221
Fremont, CA 94538
Phone: 510-791-7005
E-mail: dilip@7keys.org
www.7keys.org

*Schoenbeck, Mary Lynne, MA,
NCCC, MCC
Career/Retirement Counselor,
Coach, Consultant
Schoenbeck & Associates
Los Altos, CA
Phone: 650-964-8370
E-mail: schoenbeck@mindspring.com

Struntz and Associates
Career & Job Search Consulting
Saint Helena, CA 94574
Phone: 707-963-0843
Contact: Wolfgang Struntz, MA
E-mail: Struntz@netwiz.net

Transitions Counseling Center
171 N. Van Ness Ave.
Fresno, CA 93701
Phone: 559-233-7250
Contact: Margot E. Tepperman, MA,
LCSW, ACC
E-mail: mtepperman@aol.com
www.transitionscoaching.com

Wilson, Patti
Career Company
PO Box 35633
Los Gatos, CA 95030
Phone: 408-354-1964
E-mail: patti@careercompany.com
www.pattiwilson.com

Zenoff, Victoria
El Cerrito, CA
Phone: 510-526-5210
E-mail: vickiezenoff@earthlink.net
www.victoriazenoff.com
(Vicki taught with me for many years
and is co-author of *The Beginning
Job-Hunting Map* with me.)

**Zitron Parham Career Counseling
& Life Coaching**
4724 25th St., Ste. A
San Francisco, CA 94114
Phone: 415-648-7377
Contact: Nick Parham,
Career & Life Coach
E-mail: npcoach@gmail.com
www.zitronparhamcareerservices.com

Colorado

Arapahoe Community College
Career Center
Career Planning Seminars
Job Postings
5900 S. Santa Fe Dr.
PO Box 9002
Littleton, CO 80160-9002
Phone: 303-797-5805
E-mail: careers@arapahoe.edu

Gary Ringler & Associates
1747 Washington St., #203
Denver, CO 80203
Phone: 303-863-0234
E-mail: garyringler@msn.com

Helmstaedter, Sherry, MS
Englewood, CO 80111-1122
Phone: 720-560-9601
E-mail: changegrow@aol.com

Pivotal Choices, Inc.
PO Box 1098
Durango, CO 81302
Phone: 970-385-9597
Contact: Mary Jane Ward, MEd,
NCC, NCCC
E-mail: mjw@pivotalchoices.com
www.pivotalchoices.com

Women's Resource Agency
750 Citadel Dr. E., Ste. 312B
Colorado Springs, CO 80909
Phone: 719-471-3170
www.wrainc.org

Connecticut

Accord Career Services, LLC
Salmon Brook Corporate Park
500 Winding Brook Dr
Glastonbury, CT 06033
Phone: 860-674-9654 or 860-508-1026
Contact: Tod Gerardo, MS, Director
E-mail: tod@accordcareerservices.com
www.accordcareerservices.com

Center for Professional Development
University of Hartford
50 Elizabeth St.
Hartford, CT 06105
Phone: 860-768-5619
Contact: Eleta Jones, PhD, LPC
E-mail: ejones@hartford.edu
www.hartford.edu/cpd

The Offerjost-Westcott Group
263 Main St., Ste. 100
Old Saybrook, CT 06475
Phone: 860-388-6094
Contact: Russ Westcott
E-mail: russwest@snet.net

Pannone, Bob, MA
Career Specialist
62 Lane St.
Huntington, CT 06484
Phone: 203-513-2290
E-mail: upstartinc@yahoo.com

Preis, Roger J.
RPE Career Dynamics
Stamford, CT
E-mail: rjpreis@rpecareers.com
www.rpecareers.com

Delaware

Bronson, Kris, PhD
1409 Foulk Rd., Ste. 204
Foulkstone Plaza
Wilmington, DE 19803
Phone: 302-477-0708, ext. 4
www.krisbronsonphd.com

District of Columbia

Roggenkamp, Robin
Certified Career and Leadership Coach
Washington, DC area (NoVa)
Phone: 703-298-2964
E-mail: robin@myauthenticcareer.com
www.myauthenticcareer.com

The Women's Center
1025 Vermont Ave. NW, Ste. 310
Washington, DC 20005
Phone: 202-293-4580
www.thewomenscenter.org

Florida

Career Choices Unlimited
4465 Baymeadows Rd., Ste. 7
Jacksonville, FL 32217
Phone: 904-443-0059 or 904-262-9470
Contact: Marilyn A. Feldstein, MPA,
JCTC, MBTI, PHR,
Career Coach and Professional Speaker
www.careerchoicesunlimited.com

**Chabon-Berger, Toby, MEd,
NCC, NCCC**
Career and Professional
Development Coach
4900 Boxwood Circle
Boynton Beach, FL 33436
Phone: 561-596-3656
E-mail: tberger@chabongroup.com
www.tobycareer.com

The Clarity Group
PO Box 110084
Lakewood Ranch, FL 34211
Phone: 941-388-8108
Contact: George H. Schofield, PhD
E-mail: george.schofield@clarity-group
.com
or george@georgeschofield.com
or george@newbrightlife.com
www.clarity-group.com
www.georgeschofield.com
www.newbrightlife.com

Cohen, James, PhD
7177 Granville Ave.
Boynton Beach, FL 33437
Fax/Phone: 561-509-9150
E-mail: vocdoc56@yahoo.com

**Focus on the Future:
Displaced Homemaker Program**
Santa Fe College
3000 NW 83rd St., I-40
Gainesville, FL 32606
Phone: 352-395-5047
Contacts: Nancy Griffin
or JoAnn Wilkes
E-mail: focusonthefuture@sfcollege.edu
www.sfcollege.edu/Displaced
Homemakers (Classes are free.)

Life Designs, Inc.
19526 E. Lake Dr.
Miami, FL 33015
Phone: 305-829-9008
Contact: Dulce Muccio Weisenborn
E-mail: dmw@lifedesigns-inc.com
www.lifedesigns-inc.com

TransitionWorks
Delray Beach, FL
Phone: 301-233-4287
Contact: Nancy K. Schlossberg, EdD,
Principal
E-mail: nancyks4@gmail.com
Contact: Stephanie Kay, MA, LCPC,
Principal
E-mail: stephaniekay4@gmail.com
(They also have offices in Rockville,
Maryland, and Sarasota, Florida.)

Georgia

Ashkin, Janis, MEd, MCC, NCC, NCCC
2365 Winthrope Way Dr.
Alpharetta, GA 30009
Phone: 678-319-0297
E-mail: jashkin@bellsouth.net

Career Indulgence
Specialist for High School and
College Students
Atlanta, GA
Phone: 404-642-8189
Contact: Crystal Kadakia,
Certified Career Coach
E-mail: Crystal@CareerIndulgence.com
www.CareerIndulgence.com
Twitter: @CareerNdulgence

Career Quest/Job Search Workshop
St. Ann's Catholic Church
4905 Roswell Rd. NE
Marietta, GA 30062-6240
Phone: 770-552-6400 ext. 6104
Contact: John Marotto
E-mail: careerquest-sa@comcast.net
www.st-ann.org/career_quest.php
LinkedIn Group: Career Quest at
St. Ann's Church

D & B Consulting, Inc.
3355 Lenox Rd., Ste. 750
Atlanta, GA 30326
Phone: 404-504-7079
Contact: Deborah R. Brown, SPHR,
MBA, MSW, Career Consultant
E-mail: Debbie@DandBconsulting.com
www.dandbconsulting.com

Satterfield, Mark
720 Rio Grand Dr.
Alpharetta, GA 30022
Phone: 770-643-8566
E-mail: msatt@mindspring.com

Waldorf, William H., MBA, LPC
Path Unfolding Career Development
5755 North Point Parkway., Ste. 39
Alpharetta, GA 30022
Phone: 678-822-5505
E-mail: wwaldorf@earthlink.net

Idaho

*Career Coaching 4U**
9882 W. View Dr.
Boise, ID 83704
Phone: 208-323-2462
Contact: Michael W. Reed, MEd, MS
Counseling, LPC
E-mail: michael@careercoaching4u.com
www.careercoaching4u.com

Illinois

Alumni Career Center
University of Illinois Alumni Association
200 S. Wacker Dr., First Floor
Chicago, IL 60606
Phone: 312-575-7830
Contact: Julie Hays Bartimus,
Vice President
Bernice Allegretti, Assistant Director
E-mail: careers@uillinois.edu
www.uiaa.org/careers

Career Vision/The Ball Foundation
526 N. Main St.
Glen Ellyn, IL 60137
Phone: 800-469-8378
Contact: Peg Hendershot, Director;
Paula Kosin, MS, LCPC;
Mary Hanney, MSEd, MBA, LCPC;
Nancy Ryan Krane, PhD
E-mail: info@careervision.org
www.careervision.org

Davis, Jean, MA
Counseling Psychology, specializing
in adult career transitions
1405 Elmwood Ave.
Evanston, IL 60201
Phone: 847-492-1002
E-mail: jdavis@careertransitions.net
www.careertransitions.net

**Dolan Career & Rehabilitation
Consulting, Ltd.**
307 Henry St., Ste. 411
Alton, IL 62002
Phone: 618-474-5328
Fax: 618-462-3359
Contact: J. Stephen Dolan, MA, CRC,
Career & Rehabilitation Consultant
E-mail: dolanrehab@att.net

Grimard Wilson Consulting, Inc.
333 W. Wacker Dr., Ste. 500
Chicago, IL 60606
and
1140 W. Lake St., Ste. 302
Oak Park, IL 60301
Phone: 312-925-5176
Contact: Diane Wilson, LCPC, BCN
E-mail: diane.g.wilson@gmail.com
www.grimardwilson.com

**Harper College Community
Career Services**
1200 W. Algonquin Rd., Rm. A-347
Palatine, IL 60067
Phone: 847-925-6220
Contact: Kathleen Canfield, Director
E-mail: careercenter@harpercollege.edu
www.harpercollege.edu

Inspired Career Options
PO Box 7174
Buffalo Grove, IL 60089
Phone: 847-808-9982
Contact: Deb Morton, Certified Executive
Career & Entrepreneur Coach
E-mail: deb@inspiredcareeroptions.com
www.inspiredcareeroptions.com

*Lansky Career Consultants
500 N. Michigan Ave. #820
Chicago, IL 60611
Phone: 312-494-0022
Contact: Judi Lansky, MA, MBA
E-mail: lanskycareers@yahoo.com

LeBrun, Peter
Career/Leadership Coach
Executive Career Management
4333 N. Hazel St., Ste. 100
Chicago, IL 60613
Phone: 773-281-7274
E-mail: peterlebrun@aol.com

Moraine Valley Community College
Job Resource Center
9000 College Pkwy.
Palos Hills, IL 60465
Phone: 708-974-5737
www.morainevalley.edu/jrc

Iowa

**Sucher, Billie, MS, CTMS, CTSB,
JCTC, CCM**
Private Practice Career Transition
Consultant
7177 Hickman Rd., Ste. 10
Des Moines, IA 50322
Phone: 515-276-0061
E-mail: billie@billiesucher.com
www.billiesucher.com

Zilber, Suzanne, PhD
Licensed Psychologist
Catalyst Counseling
600 5th St., Ste. 302
Ames, IA 50010-6072
Phone: 515-232-5340
Fax: 515-232-2070
www.catalystcounseling.com

Kansas

Keeping the People, Inc.
12213 Westgate St.
Overland Park, KS 66213
Phone: 913-620-4645
Contact: Leigh Branham
E-mail: LB@keepingthepeople.com
www.keepingthepeople.com

Kentucky

Career Span, Inc.
620 Euclid Ave., Ste. 210
Lexington, KY 40502
Phone: 859-233-7726 (233-SPAN)
Contact: Carla Ockerman-Hunter, MA,
MCC, NCC
E-mail: careerspan@aol.com
www.careerspanUSA.com

Louisiana

Career Center
River Center Branch, EBR Parish Library
120 St. Louis St.
Baton Rouge, LA 70802
Phone: 225-381-8434
Fax: 225-389-8910
Contact: Anne Nowak, Program Director
E-mail: anowak@careercenterbr.com
www.careercenterbr.com

Maine

Heart at Work Associates
Career Counseling, Outplacement
Services, Second Half of Life Career
Transitions
22 Free St., Ste. 201
Portland, ME 04101
Phone: 207-775-6400
Contact: Barbara Babkirk, Master
Career Counselor
E-mail: barb@barbarababkirk.com
www.heartatworkassociates.com

Women's Worth Career Counseling
9 Village Ln.
Westbrook, ME 04092
Phone: 207-856-6666
Contact: Jacqueline Murphy,
Career Counselor
E-mail: wethepeople@maine.rr.com

Maryland

**The Career Evaluation and
Coaching Center**
21 West Rd., Ste. 150
Baltimore, MD 21204
Phone: 410-825-0042
Fax: 410-825-0310
Contact: Ralph D. Raphael, PhD
E-mail: drraphael@ralphraphael.com
www.ralphraphael.com

CTS Consulting, Inc.
3126 Berkshire Rd.
Baltimore, MD 21214-3404
Phone: 410-444-5857
Contact: Michael Bryant
E-mail: mb3126@gmail.com
www.go2ctsonline.com

Friedman, Lynn, PhD
Psychologist, Psychoanalyst,
Work-Life Consultant
Johns Hopkins University
5480 Wisconsin Ave.
Chevy Chase, MD 20815
Phone: 301-656-9050
E-mail: drlynnfriedman@verizon.net
www.washington-dc-psychologist.com
www.drlynnfriedman.com

Headley, Anne S., MA
6510 41st Ave.
University Park, MD 20782
Phone: 301-779-1917
E-mail: asheadley@verizon.net
www.anneheadley.com

Horizons Unlimited, Inc.
17501 McDade Ct.
Rockville, MD 20855
Phone: 301-258-9338
Contact: Marilyn Goldman,
LPC, NCCC, MCC
E-mail: horizons@career-counseling.com
www.career-counseling.com

**Positive Passages Life/Career
Transition Counseling and Coaching**
4702 Falstone Ave.
Chevy Chase, MD 20815
Phone: 301-580-5162
Contact: Jeanette Kreiser, EdD
E-mail: jskreiser@yahoo.com

Prince George's Community College
Career Services
301 Largo Rd.
Largo, MD 20774
Phone: 301-322-0109
Contact: H. Randall Poole,
Manager of Career Services;
Stephanie Pair, Senior Career Advisor
E-mail: Career_Job@pgcc.edu
www.pgcc.edu

TransitionWorks
Rockville, MD
Phone: 301-233-4287
Contact: Nancy K. Schlossberg, EdD,
Principal
E-mail: nancyks4@gmail.com
Stephanie Kay, MA, LCPC, Principal
E-mail: stephaniekay4@gmail.com
(With offices in Delray and Sarasota, FL.)

Massachusetts

Berke & Price Associates
Newtown Way #6
Chelmsford, MA 01824
Phone: 978-256-0482
Contact: Judit E. Price, MS, CDFI, IJCTC,
CCM, CPRW,
Career Consultant, Certified Resume
Writer, and Brand Specialist
E-mail: jprice@careercampaign.com
www.careercampaign.com
www.careercampaign.com/blog
www.linkedin.com/in/juditprice

The Boston Career Coach
26 Shanley St.
Brighton, MA 02135
Phone: 617-254-0791
Contact: Tom Jackson
www.thebostoncareercoach.com

Career in Progress
2 Marie Ann Dr.
Westford, MA 01886
Phone: 617-925-5289
Fax: 781-407-0955
Contact: Heather Maietta, EdD, GCDF,
JCDC, CPRW,
Career and Professional
Development Coach
E-mail: info@careerinprogress.com
www.careerinprogress.com

*Career Management Consultants**
108 Grove St., Ste. 204
Worcester, MA 01605
Phone: 508-756-9998
Contact: Patricia Stepanski Plouffe,
Founder/Consultant
E-mail: info@careermc.com

Career Source
186 Alewife Brook Pkwy., Ste. 310
Cambridge, MA 02138
Phone: 617-661-7867
www.yourcareersource.com

*Center for Career Development
& Ministry**
30 Milton St., Ste. 107
Dedham, MA 02026
Phone: 781-329-2100
Fax: 781-407-0955
E-mail: info@ccdmin.org
www.ccdmin.org

Hadlock, Joanne, EdD, NCCC
Career/Life Transitions
223 Sandy Pond Rd.
Lincoln, MA 01773
Phone: 781-259-3752
E-mail: joannehadlock@comcast.net
www.joannehadlock.us

**Jewish Vocational Service,
Career Moves**
29 Winter St., 5th Floor
Boston, MA 02108
Phone: 617-399-3131
Contact: Judy Sacks, Director
www.career-moves.org

**Jewish Vocational Service,
Career Moves**
Career Counseling and Testing
333 Nahanton St.
Newton, MA 02159
Phone: 617-965-7940
Contact: Amy Mazur, Career Counselor
E-mail: amazur@jvs-boston.org;
www.career-moves.org

*Liebhaber, Gail, MEd
40 Cottage St.
Lexington, MA 02420
Phone: 781-861-9949
Contact: Gail Liebhaber, MEd
E-mail: gail@yourcareerdirection.com
www.yourcareerdirection.com

Miller, Wynne W.
Leadership Coaching
Brookline, MA 02446-4707
Phone: 617-232-4848
E-mail: wynne@win-coaching.com
www.win-coaching.com

New Beginnings Beyond Cancer
10 Beach Ct.
Gloucester, MA 01930-5021
Phone: 978-821-3713
Contact: Sidney Falthzik, MEd,
Transition and Life Work Coach

Szekely, Bill
10 Doral Dr.
N. Chelmsford, MA 01863
Phone: 978-423-3196
E-mail: TheParachute@me.com

Michigan

*Careers Through Faith
3025 Boardwalk St.
Ann Arbor, MI 48108
Phone: 734-332-8800, ext. 228
Contact: Cathy Synko
E-mail: Cathy@CareersThroughFaith.org
www.CareersThroughFaith.org

Feeney, Cindy J., LMSW
Grand Rapids, MI
Phone: 616-443-9549
E-mail: CindyJFreeney@gmail.com
(Forty years empowering others
through the *Parachute* process.)

*Keystone Coaching & Consulting, LLC
22 Cherry St.
Holland, MI 49423
Phone: 616-396-1517
Contact: Mark de Roo
E-mail: mderoo@keystonecoach.com
www.keystonecoach.com

*LifeSteward/EaRN Employment
& Resource Network
PO Box 888187
Grand Rapids, MI 49588-8187
Phone: 616-813-4998
Contact: Ken Soper, MDiv, MA,
MCC, NCCC
E-mail: kensoper@yahoo.com
www.kensoper.com
www.earn-network.org

**New Options Town & Country
Counseling**
Specializing in Careers, Education,
and Lifestyle Choices
Ann Arbor, MI
Phone: 734-973-0003 or 734-973-8699
Contact: Phyllis Perry, MSW, MFA
E-mail: pepstar27@yahoo.com

Synko Associates, LLC
3025 Boardwalk, Ste. 120
Ann Arbor, MI 48108
Phone: 734-332-8800, ext. 212
E-mail: csynko@SynkoAssociates.com
www.SynkoAssociates.com

Minnesota

*North Central Ministry
Development Center
(an Interdenominational Church
Career Development Center)
516 Mission House Ln.
New Brighton, MN 55112
Phone: 651-636-5120
Contact: Mark Sundby, MDiv, PhD, LP,
Executive Director
E-mail: ncmdc@comcast.net
www.ncmdc.org

Prototype Career Service
626 Armstrong Ave.
St. Paul, MN 55102
Phone: 800-368-3197
Contact: Amy Lindgren,
Job Search Strategist
E-mail: getajob@prototypecareerservice
.com
www.prototypecareerservice.com

Missouri

Eigles, Lorrie, PCC, MSED, LPC
Authentic Communication
Life and Career Coach
432 W. 62nd Terr.
Kansas City, MO 64113
E-mail: Lorrie@myauthenticlifecoaching
.com
http://myauthenticlifecoaching.com

The Job Doctor
505 S. Ewing Ave.
St. Louis, MO 63103
Phone: 314-863-1166
Contact: M. Rose Jonas, PhD
E-mail: Rose@RoseJonas.com
www.rosejonas.com

MU Career Center
201 Student Success Center
909 Lowry Mall
University of Missouri
Columbia, MO 65211
Phone: 573-882-6801
Fax: 573-882-5440
Contact: Craig Benson
E-mail: career@missouri.edu
http://career.missouri.edu

Patricia Katzfey Counseling LLC
222 South Merimec, Ste. 303
St. Louis, MO 63105
Phone: 314-925-5961
Contact: Patricia Katzfey,
"Master Career Counselor"

Werner Associates, LLC
2200A Yale Avenue
St. Louis, MO 63143
Phone: 314-644-2221
Contact: Wendy L. Werner
E-mail: wendy@wendywerner.com
www.wendywerner.com/associates

Women's Center
University of Missouri-Kansas City
5100 Rockhill Rd., 105 Haag Hall
Kansas City, MO 64110
Phone: 816-235-1638
Contact: Brenda Bethman, Director
E-mail: umkc-womens-center@unkc.edu
www.umkc.edu/womenc

Montana

Career Transitions
189 Arden Dr.
Belgrade, MT 59714
Phone: 406-388-6701
Contact: Darla Joyner,
Executive Director
E-mail: ct@careertransitions.com
www.careertransitions.com

Christen, Carol
Consultant, Career & Job Search Strategy
Butte, MT
Phone: 406-491-6160
E-mail: carol@carolchristen.com
www.parachute4teens.com
(Co-author, *What Color Is Your
Parachute? For Teens*)

New Hampshire

Individual Employment Services (I.E.S)
1 New Hampshire Ave., Ste. 125
Portsmouth, NH 03801
Phone: 603-570-4850
or 800-734-JOBS (5627)
Fax: 603-766-1901
Contact: James Otis, Principal,
Career Counselor/Recruiter
Anita Labell, Principal, Certified
Professional Resume Writer/
Career Coach
E-mail: ies@iosnh.com

Tucker, Janet, MEd
Career Counselor
10 String Bridge
Exeter, NH 03833
Phone: 603-772-8693
E-mail: jbtucker@comcast.net

New Jersey

***CareerQuest**
2165 Morris Ave., Ste. 15
Union, NJ 07083
Phone: 908-686-8400
Contact: Don Sutaria, MS, IE (Prof.)
Founder, President, and Life-Work Coach
E-mail: don@careerquestcentral.com
www.careerquestcentral.com

Creating Life Options
Mendham, NJ 07945
Phone: 201-874-3264 or 973-543-3458
Contact: Katie McGinty
E-mail: katie@creatinglifeoptions.com
www.creatinglifeoptions.com
www.linkedin.com/in/katiemcginty

Grundfest, Sandra, EdD
Certified Career Counselor, Licensed
Psychologist
601 Ewing St., C-1
Princeton, NJ 08540
Phone: 609-921-8401
and
35 Clyde Rd., Ste. 101
Somerset, NJ 08873
Phone: 732-873-1212

Job Seekers of Montclair
St. Luke's Episcopal Church
73 S. Fullerton Ave.
Montclair, NJ 07042
Phone: 973-783-3442
www.jobseekersofmontclair.org
(Meets Wednesdays, 7:30–9:15 p.m.,
free of charge)

JobSeekers in Princeton
Trinity Church
33 Mercer St.
Princeton, NJ 08540
Phone: 609-921-9427
www.trinityprinceton.org
(Meets Tuesdays, 7:30–9:30 p.m.)

Mercer County Community College
Career Services
Student Center Room 229
1200 Old Trenton Rd.
West Windsor, NJ 08550
Phone: 609-570-3399
Fax: 609-570-3880
Contact: Gail C. La France,
Career Counselor
www.mccc.edu/careerservices

New York

Bernstein, Alan B., LCSW, PC
122 E 82nd St.
New York, NY 10028
Phone: 212-288-4881
www.loveworkbalance.com
www.yourretirementyourway.com

*CareerQuest
c/o TRS, Inc., Professional Ste.
44 E. 32nd St.
New York, NY 10016
Phone: 908-686-8400
Contact: Don Sutaria, MS, IE (Prof.),
Founder, President, and Life-Work
Coach
E-mail: don@careerquestcentral.com
www.careerquestcentral.com
www.careerquestcentral.blogspot.com

Careers in Transition, LLC
Professional Career Services
and Counseling
11 Computer Dr. W., #112
Albany, NY 12205
Phone: 518-366-8451
Contact: Dr. Thomas J. Denham, MCDP,
Founder and Career Counselor
E-mail: careersintransition@yahoo.com
www.careersintransitionllc.com

*Center for Creativity and Work
19 W. 34th St., Penthouse Floor
New York, NY 10001
Phone: 212-490-9158
Contact: Allie Roth, Career Transitions
and Encore Career Coach
E-mail: allie@allieroth.com
www.allieroth.com

*Greene, Kera, MEd, DTM
Board Member of the
Career Counselors Consortium,
Adjunct Lecturer, New York University
(NYU)
Career Counselor/Workshop Leader/
Lecturer
200 E. 24th St., #1008
New York, NY 10001
Cell: 917-496-1804
E-mail: KeraGr@gmail.com
www.keragreenecareers.com

*Judith Gerberg Associates
250 W. 57th St., Ste. 2315
New York, NY 10107
Phone: 212-315-2322
E-mail: judith@gerberg.com
www.gerberg.com

Optima Careers
575 Madison Ave., between 56th and
57th Streets, Tenth Floor
New York, NY 10019
Phone: 212-876-3488
Contact: Marianne Ruggiero, President
and Founder
E-mail: mcruggiero@optimacareers.com
www.optimacareers.com

Orange County Community College
Office of Career and Internship Services
115 South St.
Middletown, NY 10940
Phone: 845-341-4444
Contact: Petra Wege-Beers, Director
E-mail: pwtra.wegegeers@sunyorange
.edu
www.sunyorange.edu/careers

Personnel Sciences Center
140 Briarcliff Rd.
Westbury, NY 11590
Phone: 516-338-5340
Fax: 516-338-5341
Contact: Jeffrey A. Goldberg, PhD,
President, Licensed Psychologist
E-mail: jag_psc@juno.com
(Services also provided in Manhattan)

North Carolina

Career Focus Workshops
8301 Brittains Field Rd.
Oak Ridge, NC 27310
Phone: 336-643-1419
Contact: Glenn Wise, President
E-mail: gwise001@triad.rr.com
http://careerfocusworkshops.com

*Crossroads Career Network
PO Box 49664
Charlotte, NC 28277
Phone: 800-941-3566
www.CrossroadsCareer.org
(Nonprofit Christian network of member
churches equipped to help people find
jobs, careers, calling)

Joyce Richman & Associates, Ltd.
2911 Shady Lawn Dr.
Greensboro, NC 27408
Phone: 336-288-1799
E-mail: jerichman@aol.com
www.joycerichman.com
www.richmanresources.com

Kochendofer, Sally, PhD
2218 Lilac Ln.
Indian Land, SC 29707
Phone: 803-396-0979
E-mail: westiefriend@comporium.net

*The Life/Career Institute
131 Chimney Rise Dr.
Cary, NC 27511
Phone: 919-469-5775
Contact: Mike Thomas, PhD
E-mail: mikethomas@nc.rr.com
www.LifeCareerInstitute.com

Ohio

Cuyahoga County Public Library
The Career Center
5225 Library Ln.
Maple Heights, OH 44137-1291
Phone: 216-475-2225
E-mail: beaston@cuyahogalibrary.org
www.cuyahogalibrary.org

*Flood, Kay Reynolds, MA
3600 Parkhill Cir. NW
Canton, OH 44718
Phone: 330-493-1448
E-mail: nana1725@aol.com

New Career
328 Race St.
Dover, OH 44622
Phone: 330-364-5557
Contact: Marshall J. Karp, MA, NCC,
LPC, Career Counselor
E-mail: marshallkarp@hotmail.com

Oklahoma

Career Development Partners, Inc.
4137 S. Harvard Ave., Ste. A
Tulsa, OK 74135
Phone: 918-293-0500
Toll-free: 866-466-1162
Fax: 918-293-0503
E-mail: Nancy@cdpartnersinc.com
www.cdpartnersinc.com

Oregon

Careerful Counseling Services
12555 SW First St.
Beaverton, OR 97005
Phone: 503-997-9506
Contact: Andrea King, MS, NCC, MCC,
Career Counselor
E-mail: aking@careerful.com
www.careerful.com

*Exceptional Living Coach, LLC
1230 Arthur St.
Eugene, OR 97402
Phone: 541-484-6785
Contact: Lisa R. Anderson, MA, NCC,
GCDF
E-mail: lisa@ExceptionalLivingCoach
.com
www.ExceptionalLivingCoach.com
(English and Spanish)

Pennsylvania

*Bartholomew, Uda
Vocational Transformations/
Vocational Liberation Workshops
PO Box 2112
Center City Philadelphia, PA 19103
Phone: 215-618-1572
Contact: Uda Bartholomew,
Lead Facilitator
E-mail: VocTransVocLib@gmail.com

**Delaware Valley Family
Business Center**
340 N. Main St.
Telford, PA 18969
Phone: 215-723-8413, ext. 204
Contact: Henry D. Landes, Consultant
E-mail: henry@dvfbc.com
www.dvfbc.com

*Hannafin, Christine, PhD
Personal and Career Counseling
Bala Farm
380 Jenissa Dr.
West Chester, PA 19382
Phone: 610-431-0588
E-mail: chrishannafin@aol.com
www.christinehannafin.com

Haynes, Lathe, PhD
401 Shady Ave., Ste. C107
Pittsburgh, PA 15206
Phone: 412-361-6336

Kessler, Jane E., MA
Licensed Psychologist
252 W. Swamp Rd., Ste. 56
Doylestown, PA 18901
Phone: 215-348-8212, ext. 1
Fax: 215-348-0329
E-mail: jane@kesslerandclark.com

William D. Morgan and Associates
Career Counseling & Coaching Services
63 Chestnut Road, Ste. 3
Paoli, PA 19301
Phone: 610-644-8182
E-mail: info@Counseling4Careers.com
www.Counseling4Careers.com

South Carolina

Crystal-Barkley Corp.
(formerly the John C. Crystal Center)
293 E. Bay St.
Charleston, SC 29401
Phone: 800-333-9003
Fax: 800-560-5333
Contact: Nella G. Barkley, President
E-mail: crystalbarkley@careerlife.com
www.careerlife.com
(John Crystal, the founder of the John C.
Crystal Center, died in 1988; Nella, his
business partner for many years, now
continues his work throughout the U.S.
and in the UK and the Netherlands.)

White Ridgely Associates,
Success Management
26 River Bend Dr.
Okatie, SC 29909
Phone: 443-829-9014
Contact: Daisy Nelson White, PhD
E-mail: Daisy@whiteridgely.com
www.WhiteRidgely.com

Tennessee

*Career Resources, Inc.
208 Elmington Ave.
Nashville, TN 37205
Phone: 615-957-0404
Contact: Jane C. Hardy, Founder and
Strategic Career Counselor
E-mail: JHardy@CareerResources.net
www.CareerResources.net

Texas

*Civitelli, Janet, PhD, MCC
16107 Kensington Dr., #115
Sugar Land, TX 77479
Phone: 281-912-1198
E-mail: janet@vocationvillage.com
www.vocationvillage.com

NB Careers
New Braunfels, TX 78130
Phone: 830-237-2735
Contact: Shell Mendelson, MS
E-mail: shell@passiontocareer.com
www.passiontocareer.com

Quereau, Jeanne, MA, LPC, CPC
Life/Career Coach & Psycotherapist
9500 Jollyville Rd., #121
Austin, TX 78759
Phone: 512-342-9552
E-mail: jeanneq19@gmail.com
www.therapysites.com/sites/
counselingforachange.com
www.linkedin.com/in/
jeannequeraeaucareerlifecoach

Utah

Lue, Keith
PO Box 971482
Orem, UT 84097-1482
Phone: 801-885-1389
E-mail: keithlue@keydiscovery.com
www.keydiscovery.com

Vermont

Career Networks, Inc.
1372 Old Stage Rd.
Williston, VT 05495
Phone: 802-872-1533
Contact: Markey Read
E-mail: markey@careernetworksvt.com
www.careernetworksvt.com

Preis, Roger J.
RPE Career Dynamics
PO Box 115
Shelburne, VT 05482
Phone: 802-985-3775
E-mail: rjpreis@rpecareers.com
www.rpecareers.com

Virginia

The BrownMiller Group
312 Granite Ave.
Richmond, VA 23226
Phone: 804-288-2157
Contact: Bonnie Miller
E-mail: brownmillergroup@gmail.com
www.BrownMiller.com

McCarthy & Company
Executive Coaching,
Career Transition Management
4201 S. 32nd Rd.
Arlington, VA 22206
Phone: 703-671-4300
Contact: Peter McCarthy, President
E-mail: mccarthy@careertran.com
www.careertran.com

The Women's Center
127 Park St. NE
Vienna, VA 22180
Phone: 703-281-2657
E-mail: twc@thewomenscenter.org
(Subject line should read,
"Attention: Lauren Kellar")
www.thewomenscenter.org

Bridgeway Career Development
1611 116th Avenue NE, Ste. 219
Bellevue, WA 98004
Phone: 877-250-2103
Contact: Carolyn Kessler, Maria
Escobar-Bordyn, Partners
E-mail: services@bridgewaycareer.com
www.bridgewaycareer.com

Career Management Institute
8404 27th St. W.
University Place, WA 98466
Phone: 253-565-8818
Contact: Ruthann Reim McCaffree, MA,
NCC, LMHC, CPC
E-mail: careermi@nwrain.com
www.CareerMI.com

**Centerpoint Institute for Life and
Career Renewal**
4000 NE 41st St., Bldg. D West, Ste. 2
Seattle, WA 98105-5428
Phone: 206-686-LIFE (5433)
Contact: Leah Krieger
www.centerpointseattle.org

Ticich, Frank E., MS, CRC, CVE
Career Consultant
153 Tartan Dr.
Follansbee, WV 26037
Phone: 304-748-1772
E-mail: frankticich@comcast.net

*Career Momentum, Inc.
49 Kessel Court, Ste. 103,
Madison, WI 53711
Phone: 608-274-2430
Contact: Clara Hurd Nydam,
MDiv, MCC, SPHR
E-mail: Clara.Nydam@
CareerMomentum.com
www.CareerMomentum.com

Guarneri Associates
6670 Crystal Lake Rd.
Three Lakes, WI 54562
Phone: 715-546-4449
Contact: Susan Guarneri, NCCC, MCC,
CERW, CPBS, COIMS, MRW
E-mail: Susan@AssessmentGoddess.com

University of Wyoming
The Center for Advising and
Career
Services
1000 E. University Ave., Dept. 3195
Laramie, WY 82071-3195
Phone: 307-766-2398
E-mail: uwcacs@uwyo.edu
www.uwyo.edu/cacs

Curtis, Susan, MEd, RCC, CEAP
Vancouver, BC
Phone: 604-228-9618
E-mail: susancurtis@telus.net

*Careers by Design
Coaching and Counseling
80 Harrison Garden Blvd.
Toronto, ON, M2N 7E3
Phone: 416-519-8408
Contact: (Ms.) Shirin Khamisa, BA
Hons., BEd, ICF-Certified Coach and
Career Counselor, Licenced
HeartMath Coach
E-mail: shirin@careersbydesign.ca
www.careersbydesign.ca

*CareersPlus Inc.
55 Village Pl., Ste. 203
Mississaugua, ON L4Z 1V9
Phone: 905-272-8258
Contact: Douglas H. Schmidt,
BA, MEd, EdD
E-mail: info@careersplusinc.com
www.careersplusinc.com

Career Strategy Counselling
2 Briarhill Pl.
London, ON N5Y 1P7
Phone: 519-455-4609
Contact: Ruth Clarke, BA
E-mail: rclarke4609@rogers.com
www.careerstrategycounselling.com

donnerwheeler
1 Belvedere Ct., Ste. 1207
Brampton, ON L6V 4M6
Phone: 905-450-1086
Contact: Mary M. Wheeler, RN,
MEd, PCC
E-mail: info@donnerwheeler.com
www.donnerwheeler.com

Human Achievement Associates
22 Cottonwood Crescent
London, ON N6G 2Y8
Phone: 519-657-3000 or 226-926-5932
Contact: Mr. Kerry A. Hill
E-mail: kerryahill@rogers.com

Puttock, Judith, BBA, CHRP
Career Management Consultant
The Puttock Group
913 Southwind Ct.
Newmarket, ON L3Y 6J1
Phone: 905-717-1738
E-mail: j.puttock@rogers.com

**YMCA Career Planning &
Development**
2200 Yonge St.
Toronto, ON M4S 2B8
Phone: 416-928-3362
Contact: Mr. Franz Schmidt
E-mail: franz.schmidt@ymcagta.org
www.ymcagta.org

Quebec

Agence Ometz
Employment, Family, and
Immigration Services
1 Cummings Square
Montreal, QC H3W 1M6
Phone: 514-342-0000
Fax: 514-342-2371
Contact: Howard Berger or Gail Small,
Co-Executive Directors
E-mail: info@ometz.ca
www.ometz.ca
(Uses both French and English versions
of *Parachute*. Utilise des versions Fran-
caises et Anglaises de *Parachute*.)

**La Passerelle Employment
& Career Transition Centre**
1255 Phillips Square, Ste. 903
Montreal, QC H3B 3G1
Phone: 514-866-5982
Contact: Leslie (Laszlo) Acs,
Executive Director
E-mail: info@lapasserelle.ca
www.lapasserelle.ca

New Career Options
80 Coolbreeze (Pointe Claire)
Montreal, QC H9R 3S7
Contact: Don Smith
Phone: 514-816-2803
E-mail: DonSmithnco@bell.net
www.NewCareerOptions.ca

OVERSEAS

Australia

Career Action Centre
5 Bronte Ave.
Burwood, Victoria 3125
Phone: 03 9808 5500
Cell: 0403 136 260
Contact: Jackie Rothberg
E-mail: jackie@careeractioncentre.com.au
www.careeractioncentre.com.au

The Growth Connection
32 Grove St.
Earlwood, NSW 2206
Phone: 61 2 9787 2748
Fax: 612 9787 3185
Cell: 0407 477 225
Contact: Imogen Wareing, Director
E-mail: iwareing@growconnect.com.au
www.linkedin.com/in/imogenwareing
www.growconnect.com.au

Life by Design
PO Box 50
Newport Beach, NSW 2106
Phone: 61 2 9979 4949
Contact: Ian Hutchinson,
Lifestyle Strategist
E-mail: info@lifebydesign.com.au
www.lifebydesign.com.au

Milligan, Narelle
Career Consultant (regional NSW)
Phone: 2 6584 3271
Cell: 0411 236 124
E-mail: nmilligan2000@yahoo.com.au

Taccori, John, EdD
Career Counsellor
Blue Mountains, NSW 2777
Phone: 04 0093 8574
www.careersdoctor.net

France

Chavigny, Catherine
11 bis, rue Huyghens
75014 Paris
Phone: (33) 6 30 51 40 56
E-mail: catherine.chavigny@me.com

Germany

Buddensieg, Marc
Niemeyerstrasse 17a
30449 Hannover
Phone: 49 0 163 624 2639
Fax: 49 0 12120 277 627
E-mail: buddensieg@gmx.de
www.www.lwp-institut-hannover.de

Leitner, Madeleine, Dipl. Psych.
Ohmstrasse 8
80802 Munchen
Phone: 089 33079444
Fax: 089 33079445
E-mail: ML@Karriere-Management.de
www.Karriere-Management.de
(Madeleine is one of the best *Parachute*
counselors in Europe. She translated
Parachute into German.)

Webb, John Carl
Meinenkampstr 83a
48165 Munster-Hiltrup
Phone: +49 0 2501 92 16 96
E-mail: john@muenster.de
www.lifeworkplanning.de
(Universities offering Life/Work
Planning courses designed by John,
and based on *Parachute*, are located in
Berlin, Bochum, Bremen, Freiburg,
Hannover, Konstanz, Leipzig, and
Potsdam. John was on staff at my
international Two-Week Workshops;
he is a master of the *Parachute* process
and one of the best *Parachute* counselors
in Europe.)

Ireland

Brian McIvor & Associates
Newgrange Mall, Unit 4B
Slane, County Meath
Phone: 353 41 988 4035
E-mail: brianmcivor@gmail.com
www.brianmcivor.com
(Brian was on staff at my international
Two-Week Workshop for five years.)

Israel

Mendel, Lori
PO Box 148
Caesarea, Israel 38900
Phone: 972 3 524 1068
Cell: 972 54 814 4442
E-mail: bizcom@bezeqint.net

Transitions & Resources, Ltd.
Tzipornit, 6/3
Modiin, 71808 Israel
Phone: 08 926 6102
U.S. phone line in Israel until 4 p.m.
EST: 516-216-4457
Fax: 08 926 6103
Contact: Judy Feierstein, CEO
E-mail: info@maavarim.biz
www.maavarim.biz

The Netherlands

Crystal-Barkley Corp.
Service in The Netherlands
Phone: 800-333-9003
E-mail: crystalbarkley@careerlife.com
www.careerlife.com

Pluym Career Consultants
Career Executive & Expats
Coaching Services
Boshoekerweg 16
NL/8167 LS EPE/OENE
Contact: Johan Veeninga,
Senior Consultant
E-mail: johan.veeninga@gmail.com
or
info@careerconsultants.nl
www.careerconsultants.nl

New Zealand

Career Lifestyle
Auckland CBD
Contact: Paula Stenberg
www.cvstyle.co.nz

*CV.CO.NZ (NZ) Ltd.
373 Masters Rd.
Auckland 2682
Toll-Free: 0800 282 669
Phone: 09 235 8484
Contact: Tom O'Neil
E-mail: tom@cv.co.nz
www.cv.co.nz

Strategic Career Services
PO Box 27072
Hamilton 3257
Phone: 64 7 849 0909
Contact: Tui Needham
E-mail: tui@tuineedham.co.nz
www.tuineedham.co.nz

Poland

JC Coaching Justyna Ciecwierz
Tarniny 5a
05-515 Nowa Iwiczna
Cell: 48 600 327 163
Contact: Justyna Ciecwierz, ACCC,
Career Coaching, Work/Life Planning
E-mail: justyna.ciecwierz@jc-coaching.pl
www.jc-coaching.pl

Singapore

Transformation Technologies
122 Thomson Green
574986 Singapore
Phone: 65 98197858
Contact: Anthony Tan, Director
E-mail: anthonyt@singnet.com.sg

South Africa

Andrew Bramley Career Consultants
12 Ridge Way
PO Box 1311
Proteaville, Durbanville 7550
Phone: 27 0 21 9755573
Fax: 27 0 88 0 21 9755573
Contact: Andrew Bramley
E-mail: info@andrewbramley.co.za
www.andrewbramley.co.za

South Korea

Byung Ju Cho, PhD
Professor Emeritus of Business and
Career, Emeritus
Ajou University
Suwon
Phone: 82 31 219 2709
Fax: 82 2 594 6236
Cell: 82 10 9084 6236
E-mail: chobju@ajou.ac.kr
(Byung Ju Cho is the translator of the
2013 Korean version of *Parachute*.)

Analisi-Nic
Via Augusta, 120
Principal 1
08006 Barcelona
Phone: 34 932119503
Fax: 34 932172128
Contact: José Arnó
E-mail: analisi@arrakis.es

Baumgartner, Peter
Hummelwaldstrasse 18a
8645 Rapperswil-Jona
Phone: +41 0 55 534 14 47
E-mail: lebensunternehmer@bluewin.ch

KLB LifeDesigning
Alpenblickstrasse 33
8645 Jona-Kempraten
Phone: +41 0 55 211 09 77
Fax: +41 0 55 211 09 79
Contact: Peter Kessler,
LifeDesigning Coach
E-mail: p.kessler@bluewin.ch
www.LifeDesigning.ch

Porot & Partenaire
Rue de la Terrassière 8
1207 Genève-Suisse
Phone: +41 0 22 700 82 10
Fax: +41 0 22 700 82 14
Contact: Daniel Porot, Founder
E-mail: daniel@porot.com
www.porot.com
(Daniel is the premiere career expert in
Europe; for the twenty years that I did
two-week workshops each August,
Daniel was always co-leader with me
each summer.)

Sauser, Hans-U.
Beratung und Ausbildung
Im Bungert 2
5430 Wettingen
Phone: 056 426 64 09
E-mail: husauser@gmx.ch

Vollenweider, Peter A.
Career and Transition Coaching,
Work/Life Planning, Consulting
Kaepfnerweg 20
8810 Horgen/Zurich
Phone: +41 0 44 715 15 63
Cell: +41 0 78 626 11 58
Contact: Dr. Peter A. Vollenweider
E-mail: peter.vollenweider@gmail.com

Can Do It Now
Contact: Janie Wilson
UK: London, Surrey, and Sussex;
France:
Languedoc
Phone: +44 (0)7968 027344
E-mail: janie@candoitnow.co.uk
or
Contact: Alix Nadelman
London, Cambridge, and East Counties
Phone: +44 (0)7977 930223
E-mail: alix@candoitnow.co.uk
www.candoitnow.co.uk
www.lepuget.com

Career Dovetail
4 E. Hill Court
Oxted, Surrey RH8 9AD
and
Hub Working Centre
5 Wormwood St.
London EC2M 1RW
Contact: Duncan Bolam, Dip. CG,
Director, Career Coach, and Founder
E-mail: duncanbolam@careerdovetail.
co.uk or enquiries@careerdovetail.co.uk
www.careerdovetail.co.uk

Crystal-Barkley Corp.
Service in the United Kingdom
Phone: 800-333-9003
E-mail: crystalbarkley@careerlife.com
www.careerlife.com

Hawkins, Dr. Peter
Mt. Pleasant
Liverpool, L3 5TF
Phone: 0044 0 151 709-1760
Fax: 0044 0 151 709-1576
E-mail: p.Hawkins@gieu.co.uk

John Lees Associates
37 Tatton St.
Knutsford, Cheshire WA16 6AE
Phone: 01565 631625
Contact: John Lees
E-mail: johnlees@johnleescareers.com
www.johnleescareers.com

Sherridan Hughes
Career Management Expert
110 Pretoria Rd.
London SW16 6RN
Phone: 020 8769 5737
E-mail: sherridan@sherridanhughes.com
www.sherridan-hughes.co.uk

Notes from the Author for This Edition

May 6, 2013

Thoughts from the Fisherman

First of all, this isn't really a book. The way I think about it, it's more of a yearly journal. A journal rewritten every year for the past forty-two years.

I rethink the whole book, I rewrite, and drastically change it, every single year—taking into careful consideration an author's dilemma.

An author's dilemma is easily stated: How much is too much information? How much is too little? I think there is too much information floating around out there—particularly on the Internet—and if I tried to include it all, this book would turn into a ten-volume encyclopedia. So it is my responsibility to sift it down, and talk only about the most essential truths. But (a big "but") I must first gather as much of the information as possible here on my desk, before I sift it down to what seem to me to be the essentials.

So, year by year, I have come to think of an author's task as that of a fisherman: I must cast a wide net, haul in a large catch, but then pick out only the best fish from all those taken in the net, in order to keep this book as brief as can be.

That said, this book demands a lot of you. Mostly in the way of thinking, and rethinking, what you thought were essential truths about job-hunting, what you thought were essential truths about

337

yourself. But the rewards for this bit of thinking are considerable. Use it, and good health!

I am a grateful man, and I will close this Final Word this year, by noting the things I'm grateful for.

First of all, I am enchanted by every moment of my life with such a wondrous woman as my wife, Marci. I am so grateful for her brains, wit, and love. Then I am grateful for the family that brought me into this world, who loved me and played with me. I had a wonderful Mother and Dad. I had great siblings: one brother (the famous reporter/martyr Don Bolles), and one sister (Ann). They're all gone now; I'm the only survivor from those generations.

I had four children; I lost one this year to a sudden massive cerebral hemorrhage, at age fifty-eight. That was Mark. I have wept over that, a lot, and miss him greatly. He lived with me for six out of the last twelve years of his life. He was the author of our book on online job-hunting. He was a treasure.

So, I'm grateful for my three remaining grown children and their families: Stephen, Gary, and Sharon, plus their most-loving mother, my former wife, Jan, who shares in all our family gatherings; and my former stepdaughter, Dr. Serena Brewer, whom I helped raise for twenty years, and is now a physician in the city of Butte, Montana. I'm grateful for Marci's grown children, Janice and Adlai, with their families, and Marci's first grandchild, Logan, now four years old. (I have ten of my own. They are all as dear as can be, to me.)

We lost two giants in our profession this year. I prized them both as friends: Bill Bridges and Nathan Azrin. They both had a tremendous influence on a lot of people's lives. Bill for his work on *Transitions*, and Nathan for his creation of job-clubs.

As for the living, I want to express my gratitude to my dearest friend (besides Marci), Daniel Porot of Geneva, Switzerland—we taught together for two weeks every summer, for nineteen years; then there is Dave Swanson, ditto; plus my international friends, Brian McIvor of Ireland; John Webb and Madeleine Leitner of Germany; Yves Lermusi, of Checkster fame, who came from Belgium; Pete Hawkins of Liverpool, England; Debra Angel MacDougall of Scotland; Byung Ju Cho of South Korea; Tom O'Neil of New Zealand; and, in this country, Howard Figler, beloved friend and co-author of our manual for career counselors; Marty Nemko; Joel Garfinkle; Dick Knowdell; Rich Feller; Dick Gaither; Warren Farrell; Chuck Young; Susan Joyce; and the folks over at Ten Speed Press in Berkeley, California, now an imprint of the Crown Publishing Group of Random House, plus Crown's head, Maya Mavjee, who has been very kind to me.

My original publisher, Phil Wood, is gone now. He was my publisher for almost forty years; he was a dear man, and I owe him more than I can say for helping *Parachute* find its audience, and for letting me have great control over the annual editions. *Parachute* would never have sold ten million copies, if it were not for him.

I much appreciate my current friends over at Ten Speed: Aaron Wehner (publisher), George Young, Lisa Westmoreland, Kara Van de Water, Chris Barnes, Betsy Stromberg, Katy Brown, and Colleen Cain. My especial thanks to my readers—more than ten million of you—for buying my books, trusting my counsel, and following your dream. I have never met so many wonderful souls. I am so thankful for you all.

It is not fashionable these days to talk about one's faith, but I'm going to do it anyway. I am very quiet about my faith; it's just . . . there. But I want to quietly acknowledge that it is the source of whatever grace, wisdom, or compassion I have ever found, or shared with others. I have all my life been a committed Christian, a devoted follower of Jesus Christ, and an Episcopalian (I was an ordained priest in that Church for fifty years). I thank my Creator every night for such a life, such a wonderful mission, as He has given me: to help millions of people make their lives really count for something, as we all go spinning through space, here on Spaceship Earth.

Dick Bolles
dickbolles40@gmail.com
www.eParachute.com
www.jobhuntersbible.com

A Grammar and Language Note

I want to explain four points of grammar, in this book of mine: pronouns, commas, italics, and spelling. My unorthodox use of them invariably offends unemployed English teachers so much that instead of finishing the exercises, they immediately write to apply for a job as my editor.

To save us unnecessary correspondence, let me explain. Throughout this book, I often use the apparently plural pronouns "they," "them," and "their" after singular antecedents—such as, "You must approach someone for a job and tell them what you can do." This sounds strange and even wrong to those who know English well. To be sure, we all know there is another pronoun—"you"—that may be either singular or plural, but few of us realize that the pronouns "they," "them," and "their" were also once treated as both plural and singular in the English language. This changed, at a time in English history when agreement in number became more important than agreement as to sexual gender. Today, however, our priorities have shifted once again. Now, the distinguishing of sexual gender is considered by many to be more important than agreement in number.

The common artifices used for this new priority, such as "s/he," or "he and she," are—to my mind—tortured and inelegant. Casey Miller and Kate Swift, in their classic, *The Handbook of Nonsexist Writing*, agree, and argue that it is time to bring back the earlier usage of "they," "them," and "their" as both singular and plural—just as "you" is/are. They further argue that this return to the earlier historical usage has already become quite common out on the street—witness a typical sign by the ocean that reads, "Anyone using this beach after 5 p.m. does so at their own risk." I have followed Casey and Kate's wise recommendations in all of this.

As for my commas, they are deliberately used according to my own rules—rather than according to the rules of historic grammar (which I did learn—I hastily add, to reassure my old Harvard professors, who despaired of me weekly, during English class). In spite of those rules, I follow my own, which are: to write conversationally, and put in a comma wherever I would normally stop for a breath, were I speaking the same line.

The same conversational rule applies to my use of italics. This book is a conversation: I'm sitting down with you to tell you what I know. Conversations have rhythms. You emphasize a word here, you speak a word softly, there. There are pauses. The speed of one sentence sometimes changes from the previous. All of this is difficult to reproduce in print, if all the text looks equal. So I use italics, I use dashes, I use parentheses, I use color, etc. to reproduce in print—as much as I can—the rhythms of natural speech.

Finally, I guess some of my spelling (and capitalization) is weird. (You say "weird"; I say "playful.") I sometimes like writing it as "e-mail," for example, but other times I feel like writing it as "email." Fortunately, since this is my own book, I get to play by my own peculiar inclinations and playfulness; I'm just grateful that ten million readers have gone along. Nothing delights a child (at heart) more, than being found at play.

—Dick Bolles

P.S. Over the last forty years a few critics have complained that this book is too complicated in its vocabulary and grammar for anyone except a college graduate. Two readers, however, have written me with a different view.

The first one, from England, said there is an index that analyzes a book to tell you what grade in school you must have finished, in order to be able to understand it. My book's index, he said, turned out to be 6.1, which means you need only have finished sixth grade in a U.S. school in order to understand it.

Here in the U.S., a college instructor came up with a similar finding. He phoned me to tell me that my book was rejected by the authorities as a proposed text for the college course he was teaching, because (they said) the book's language/grammar was not up to college level. "What level was it?" I asked. "Well," he replied, "when they analyzed it, it turned out to be written on an eighth grade level."

Sixth or eighth grade—that seems just about right to me. Why make job-hunting complicated, when it can be expressed so simply even a child could understand it? (D.B.)

ABOUT THE AUTHOR

DICK BOLLES—more formally known as Richard Nelson Bolles—has been featured in *Time*, the *New York Times*, *BusinessWeek*, *Fortune*, *Money*, *Fast Company*, the *Economist*, and *Publishers Weekly*. He has appeared on the *Today* show, CNN, CBS, ABC, PBS, and other popular media. Bolles has keynoted hundreds of conferences, including the American Society for Training & Development and the National Career Development Association. He is a member of Mensa and the Society for Human Resource Management. "He is the most recognized job-hunting authority on the planet" (*San Francisco Chronicle*) and "America's top career expert" (*AARP*).

Bolles is the author of *What Color Is Your Parachute?*, the most popular job-hunting book in the world. *Time* magazine chose it as one of the hundred best nonfiction books written since 1923. The Library of Congress chose it as one of twenty-five books down through history that have shaped people's lives. It is a *New York Times* best seller, appearing on its list for more than five years. The book has sold 10 million copies, to date, and is revised every year. It has been translated into twenty languages and is used in twenty-six countries.

Bolles was trained in chemical engineering at Massachusetts Institute of Technology, and holds a bachelor's degree cum laude in physics from Harvard University, a master's in sacred theology from General Theological (Episcopal) Seminary in New York City, and three honorary doctorates. He lives in the San Francisco Bay Area with his wife, Marci.

E-mail address: dickbolles40@gmail.com

Websites: www.jobhuntersbible.com; www.eparachute.com

Blog: http://jobhuntersbible.typepad.com

Facebook: http://tinyurl.com/4zwxws6

LinkedIn: http://tinyurl.com/24mtryz

Twitter: http://twitter.com/@ParachuteGuy

INDEX

UPDATE 2015

To: PARACHUTE
10 Stirling Drive
Danville, CA 94526-2921

I think that the information in the 2014 edition needs to be changed, in your next revision, regarding (or, the following resource should be added):

_____

_____

_____

_____

_____

_____

I cannot find the following resource, listed on page _____:

_____

_____

_____

_____

_____

_____

Name _____

Address _____

_____

Please make a copy.
Submit this so as to reach us by February 1, 2014 .
Thank you.

352

RECENT FOREIGN EDITIONS OF
WHAT COLOR IS YOUR PARACHUTE?

Chinese, Complex (Faces Publications, 2006)

Chinese, Simplified (China CITIC Press, 2010)

Dutch (Nieuwezijds Publishers, 2013)

French (Editions Reynald Goulet, 2013)

German (Campus Verlag, 2011)

Hungarian (HVG Kiado, 2012)

Indonesian (PT Gramedia Pustaka Utama, 2010)

Italian (Edizioni Sonda, 2008)

Japanese (Tatsumi Publishing, 2012)

Korean (KED, 2013)

Polish (Studio Emka, 2010)

Portuguese (Actual Editora, 2010)

Romanian (SC Publica, 2012)

Russian (Mann, Ivanov & Ferber Publishers, 2010)

Serbian (Carobna Knjiga, 2012)

Spanish (Gestion 2000, 2013)

Spanish in the U.S. (Santillana USA Publishing Company, 2012)

Turkish (Optimist/BZD Yayin ve Iletisim Hizmetleri, 2011)

Vietnamese (TGM Books, 2012)

ADDITIONAL HELPFUL RESOURCES
FROM THE AUTHOR

What Color Is Your Parachute? Job-Hunter's Workbook, Fourth Edition
A fill-in edition of the famous Flower Exercise by Richard N. Bolles

What Color Is Your Parachute? Job-Hunter's Workbook, Tablet Edition
An interactive edition for your iPad and Nook by Richard N. Bolles

The Job-Hunter's Survival Guide
A quick guide for when time is of the essence by Richard N. Bolles

What Color Is Your Parachute? Guide to Job-Hunting Online, Sixth Edition
Internet job-search tips from Mark Emery Bolles and Richard N. Bolles

What Color Is Your Parachute? for Teens, Second Edition
Advice tailored for high schoolers by Carol Christen and Richard N. Bolles

What Color Is Your Parachute? for Retirement, Second Edition
Retirement advice from John E. Nelson and Richard N. Bolles

The Career Counselor's Handbook, Second Edition
A complete guide for practicing or aspiring career counselors by Howard Figler and Richard N. Bolles

Available from
TEN SPEED PRESS
wherever
books are sold.
www.tenspeed.com